Essentials of
Public Speaking
Second Edition

ESSENTIALS OF PUBLIC SPEAKING

Second Edition

Charles R. Gruner

COLLEGIATE PRESS

San Diego

Collegiate Press
San Diego, California

Executive editor: Christopher Stanford
Senior editor: Steven Barta
Senior developmental editor: Arlyne
Lazerson
Production editor: Jackie Estrada
Copyeditor: Julie Olfe
Designer: John Odam
Illustrator: Paul Slick
Cover design: Paul Slick

*Library of Congress Catalog Card Number:
92-071058*

ISBN 0-939693-27-5

Printed in the United States of America

10 9 8 7 6 5 4 3 2 1

Contents

1 WHY STUDY PUBLIC SPEAKING? 1

WHY SO MANY SPEECHES ARE DULL 2
APPROACHING SPEAKING WITH A POSITIVE ATTITUDE 4

2 THE BASIC PLAN FOR SPEAKING 7

PLANNING YOUR SPEECH: SEVEN STEPS 8
Choosing Your Topic 9
Deciding on Your Specific Purpose 10
Deciding on Your Main Points 11
Assembling the Supporting Material You Have 12
Gathering Additional Supporting Material 12
Outlining 13
Rehearsing 14
CONSIDERING THE LISTENER 16

3 CONQUERING STAGE FRIGHT 19

THE SYMPTOMS OF STAGE FRIGHT 20
THE ORIGINS OF STAGE FRIGHT 21
SELF-IMAGE AND STAGE FRIGHT 24
SOME REMEDIES FOR STAGE FRIGHT 27
Reducing the Size of the Threat 28
Countering Physiological Reactions 30
Replacing Emotion with Intellectual Activity 31
Countering Emotion with Emotion 33

4 SECURING MATERIAL FOR YOUR SPEECH 35

A GUIDE TO THE LIBRARY 37
SUPPORTING MATERIAL 42
Facts and Figures 42
Examples 44
Comparison and Contrast 48
Testimony 49
Repetition and Restatement 51
Definition 52
Description 53
Wit and Humor 54
Visual Aids 55

CONTENTS

5 ORGANIZING YOUR SPEECH 61

THE INTRODUCTION 62
THE BODY 64
THE CONCLUSION 65
ARRANGING MAIN IDEAS 67
THE OUTLINE 68

6 USING EFFECTIVE LANGUAGE 73

DIFFERENTIATING BETWEEN WRITTEN AND SPOKEN LANGUAGE 74
CHOOSING THE APPROPRIATE WORD 77
EXPANDING YOUR VOCABULARY 78
ACHIEVING VIVIDNESS 81
   Allegory 82
   Alliteration 83
   Analogy 83
   Antithesis 83
   Epigrams 84
   Epithets 84
   Hyperbole 84
   Metaphor and Simile 85
   Metonymy 86
   Oxymorons 87
   Understatement 87
   Rhetorical Questions 87
   Personification 88
   Onomatopoeia 88
   Irony 88
E-PRIME 88

7 DELIVERING YOUR SPEECH 91

VOCAL DELIVERY 93
   Rate 93
   Volume 93
   Quality 94
   Pitch 95
   Variety 95
VISUAL DELIVERY 96
   Eye Contact 97
   Posture 97
   Facial Expression 98
   Gesture 98
   Dress and Appearance 98
LEADERSHIP 99

8 SPEAKING TO INFORM 103

WHY SPEECHES FAIL TO INFORM   104
   Language Too Specialized   104
   Content Too Broad   104
   Content Too Obvious   104
   Content Too Hard to Remember   105
   Content Not Interesting   107
CREATING AND MAINTAINING INTEREST   108
   Audience Analysis   108
   Good Organization   109
   Attention-Getting Devices   109
TYPES OF INFORMATIVE SPEECHES   113
   Speeches That Explain Processes   113
   Speeches on Products or Discoveries   114
   Speeches That Introduce or Discuss Ideas   114
   Speeches about People or Places   115
   Oral Reports   115

9 SPEAKING TO PERSUADE 119

WHAT MOTIVATES PEOPLE?   120
THE PSA (PROBLEM/SOLUTION/AROUSAL) PLAN   124
   The Introduction   125
   Establish the Problem   126
   Provide the Solution   128
   Arouse Emotions   130
   The Conclusion   132
PERSUASION IN CAMPAIGNS   134
TYPES OF PERSUASIVE SPEECHES   136
   Speeches to Convince   136
   Speeches to Actuate   144
   Speeches to Stimulate   145
ON PROOF   146

10 SPEAKING TO ENTERTAIN 149

HOLDING AUDIENCE INTEREST   150
   Animation   151
   Vitalness   152
   Familiarity   154
   Novelty   154
   Conflict   155
NONHUMOROUS SPEECHES TO ENTERTAIN   156
   The True-Life Adventure   156
   Nonuseful Information   157
   The Travelogue   159
   The One-Point Anecdotal Speech   161

HUMOROUS SPEECHES TO ENTERTAIN 162
    The One-Point Speech 163
    Satire 165
    Exaggeration 168
    The Reversal of Values Speech 169
    Parody 170
THE HUMOROUS SPEAKER 173
RESOURCES FOR THE HUMOROUS SPEAKER 176

11 SOLVING PROBLEMS IN GROUPS 181

CHARACTERISTICS OF A DISCUSSION GROUP 182
    Planning 182
    Informality 183
    Participation 183
    Common Purpose 183
    Leadership 183
THE DISCUSSION PROCESS 185
    Recognize the Problem 185
    Word the Problem as a Question 185
    Explore the Problem 186
    Develop Criteria for Evaluating Solutions 186
    Consider Possible Solutions 187
    Choose the Best Solution 187
    Implement the Solution 188
SELECTED RESEARCH FINDINGS 188

APPENDIX SAMPLE SPEECHES AND OUTLINES 191

SPEECH 1: A SPEECH TO INFORM 192
SPEECH 2: A SPEECH TO INFORM 195
    Outline for "How to Remember What's-Her-Name" 195
SPEECH 3: A SPEECH TO INFORM 200
SPEECH 4: A SPEECH TO CONVINCE 202
SPEECH 5: A SPEECH TO CONVINCE 205

uring my freshman year of college I found myself in a beginning pubic speaking course. For the assignment "Speech to Convince," I chose from a list the professor had given to us the topic "Capital Punishment." It held some interest for me since I had seen several prison movies in which convicts faced execution in the electric chair. My interest in the topic included a vague belief that the state *should* execute criminals who murder other human beings.

My research uncovered a wealth of information on the subject. I read dozens of articles, book chapters, and speeches. I especially profited from volume 284 of *The Annals of the American Academy of Political and Social Scientists*, a full volume devoted exclusively to capital punishment.

That research changed my mind; it thoroughly convinced me (for a time, anyway) that "Governments should make capital punishment illegal." I made that statement my thesis and set myself the task of doing the best possible job of convincing my classmates to accept that position.

Following the directions of my textbook and my instructor, I prepared diligently for the speech. The day I took the podium to deliver it, I felt a burning urgency to brand my message onto the very consciences of my fellow students.

About halfway through my speech I came to a sudden realization. Every pair of eyes in the audience seemed welded to mine; each attentive face told me, "This makes sense; I *agree* with you!" I felt a startling surge of power and accomplishment, equal to the way I had felt two years before when the team I played with had won the Illinois state high school basketball championship.

I received many congratulatory postspeech comments. I also, incidentally, received an A on the speech.

I did not realize it at the time, but this experience had hooked me on public speaking. I sincerely believe that my successful speech on capital punishment proved instrumental in steering me into a field where I can introduce other young people to the promise, the satisfaction, and the thrilling sense of accomplishment that successful public speaking can bring. This book represents my latest effort in attempting to achieve that goal.

A great football coach once said something like, "Great football teams stick to the basics. The team that does the best blocking and tackling usually wins the game." This book emphasizes the basic "blocking and tackling" of speechmaking. If you will follow these basics—and put in the requisite amount of time and effort—you will win over more audience members than you will lose.

Over the years I have found that beginning speakers who deliberately, systematically follow the seven-step formula presented in Chapter 2 (the basic "blocking and tackling" chapter) for their every speechmaking effort usually achieve the audience response they seek. I have also found that beginners who attempt to shortcut or circumvent those seven steps fail, in varying degrees, to inform or persuade their audiences.

To help you create effective speeches with this seven-step formula, this book provides information to calm your fears and to reveal how you can find and use good content, organization, style of language, and vocal and visual delivery. The book also addresses the special problems of preparing speeches to inform, persuade, and entertain your audiences.

I *assume* that you hold this book in your hands because you wish to become a better public speaker. If you will let this book help, you *will*.

1
WHY STUDY PUBLIC SPEAKING?

ill speechmaking become part of your future? If so, will you do a really good job of it? You may harbor some doubts. After all, when did you last hear or see a really *good* speech? Since when has a speaker lifted your heart, inspired you to action, dazzled you with an original thought, or taught you a new slant on an old idea? When did a speech so hold your attention that you felt disappointment when it ended?

Given the quality of most public speaking today, you may have difficulty remembering when you last heard a really stirring speech. Most speeches seem pretty drab and dreary; seldom do we experience the pulse-quickening, blood-pressure-raising, mentally invigorating event that a really effective speaker/audience "happening" produces.

Why? Several reasons come to mind.

Why So Many Speeches Are Dull

In the first place, most people who make public speeches have received little or no special training in speechmaking. Groups often invite as speakers such experts as doctors, lawyers, college deans, businesspeople, athletic coaches, and others with particular areas of knowledge. Sometimes we want to hear from the neighbor who grows the finest roses or the biggest tomatoes, from an adventurer who hiked the Appalachian Trail or scaled Mt. Everest, or from an author who wrote a best-seller. In short, we choose speakers for their positions or areas of expertise, not for their speech training.

Second, some speakers either refuse or fail to think to expend the time and energy required to produce a first-rate speech. And doing a good job at speechmaking does require time and energy—in short, work. Many people behave as if they believe they can crank out an effective speech with a bare minimum of effort. Would these same folks think that one can create a beautiful painting, an insightful essay, a haunting musical performance, a professional-looking wood-carving, or a successful advertising campaign without some hard work?

The third culprit behind poor public speaking: egocentricity, both positive and negative. *Positive egocentricity* manifests itself in the speaker's complete oblivion to the discomfort or boredom suffered by the poor audience. Such a speaker parades self-satisfaction, personal virtues, and abstract, foggy ideas (that only he or she understands) before an audience about whom the speaker cares not a whit. We call such a speaker "self-centered," as opposed to "audience-centered."

I once had the misfortune to have a student who had taken a commercial course in "speaking." Academic speech teachers usually consider such courses more of an ego-building exercise than a sound, rigorous educational experience. This student, for his "self-introduction" speech, bored the class into a stupor for over twenty minutes reciting personal trivia of interest to no one but himself. (The assigned speech length: two minutes.) The experience became quite embarrassing for everyone but the speaker. He might have gone on forever had I not finally interrupted. I consequently spent the rest of the quarter in a futile attempt to convince this confirmed narcissist that he really could not claim the greatest oratorical skill since the passing of Sir Winston Churchill.

Negative egocentricity takes the form of what we call *stage fright* (what modern scholars have obscured with the label *communication apprehension*). The novice speaker, obviously scared witless, shivers and stammers through a pitiful monologue. An empathic audience picks up on the speaker's misery, and everyone becomes more uncomfortable than a sinner in church. (Chapter 3 provides a number of suggestions for dealing with stage fright.)

*M*ost speakers lack the talent and training to read (or recite) words in such a way that the words sound as if they came from the speaker's heart and mind, rather than from a sheet of paper.

A fourth reason why much public speaking resembles anesthesiology: too many speakers read words from a piece of paper instead of "speaking the speech." Speakers read words from a lifeless manuscript (perhaps even written by someone else) as their listeners either nod off or wonder, "If the *speaker* can't remember the words, why expect *us* to remember them!" Most speakers lack the talent and training to read (or recite) words in such a way that the words sound as if they came from the speaker's heart and mind, rather than from a sheet of paper. Instead, the speaker monotonously reads off the words without, perhaps, even thinking about what they mean. Such mindless delivery can result in some interesting mistakes. It leads to most of the radio and TV "bloopers," such as "General Marshall arrived at the conference tall, dignified, and uninformed."

So there you have it. We find most public speaking really deplorable because speakers (1) lack training in speaking, (2) do not prepare adequately, (3) suffer from self-centeredness or fear of failure, or (4) read bloodlessly from prepared scripts.

Although widespread, these problems can be overcome. If you will follow the training tips in this book; if you will work at speechmaking; if you can take to heart the advice on stage fright in Chapter 3; and if you will dare to learn to speak without the crutch of a manuscript, you can become a good mind-appeal speaker.

I use the term *mind-appeal* deliberately to distinguish between the kind of speaker one can become through training from the kind who has inherited the genes to produce what Jenkin Lloyd Jones calls the haranguer; you cannot become a haranguer through training. Jones cites three great haranguers: Cuba's Fidel Castro, the late Huey Long of Louisiana, and the former president of Egypt, Gamal Abdel Nasser. These hypnotic speakers, according to Jones, could rant and rave for hours, making little sense, yet could sway their hordes of followers as the wind blows the grass. Even though you probably cannot become a great haranguer, with the right attitude you can train yourself to speak with eminent good sense (with help from your teacher and this book, of course).

Approaching Speaking with a Positive Attitude

Do you have to give a speech? Or do you have a speech to give? These questions represent a profound difference in a speaker's attitude toward the speaking situation.

If you find yourself taking a course in speech, you have to make speeches. But if you can resist seeing each speech as "just an assignment," as something you *have* to do, you can approach it more positively. If you believe that you have a worthwhile message for your audience, you can accept each assignment as an opportunity to communicate information and ideas. You can approach the job with energy and industry, looking forward to the moment when you step to the podium. You will present your speech with natural earnestness and enthusiasm, and the audience will pick up on your enthusiasm through the process of empathy. Both you and your audience will enjoy the experience and get a lot out of it. And you will probably get a good grade!

In short, you will w*ant* to give each speech. And when people do what they *want* to do, they usually do it *well*.

> *Learning to speak well represents the kind of education we hear referred to as learning by doing, long recognized as the kind of learning that lasts.*

Learning to speak well represents the kind of education we hear referred to as learning by *doing*, long recognized as the kind of learning that lasts. Do we know of any good reasons why learning to speak well *needs* to last? Yes, we do.

In the first place, the odds that you will speak in public after graduation prove higher than you might think. In a house-to-house survey of blue-collar (working class) neighborhoods in Albany, New York, 46 percent of those polled responded that they had "spoken in public" at least once in the past two years. They had "made speeches" at work, PTA meetings, church, Sunday school, and other public gatherings. Another poll, taken by telephone in the village of Auburn, Alabama (home of Auburn University), found that nearly three-quarters of this more-educated audience admitted to having participated in "public speaking" during the past two years. This study also found a correlation between education and incidence of public speaking: the more education a person had, the more likely that person was to have spoken in public.

Second, skill in public speaking can further one's career. At one professional meeting I attended, three representatives from private industry discussed the qualities they look for when hiring new college graduates. All three—one from R. J. Reynolds, one from IBM, and another from TRW—agreed that skill in spoken and written communication headed their lists of important criteria for hiring and advancement. For instance, the young executive from IBM cautioned that an employee should never ask his or her boss for twenty minutes to explain a new idea; he or she should ask for no more than *five* minutes. The idea here: If you can't briefly explain a new idea clearly and in an organized way, you need to work on your presentation. The representative from TRW confided that a man in her organization—currently supervising two thousand employees—expected an imminent promotion but that she doubted he would get it. The reason? Although he considered himself an able public speaker, the employees that he supervised only politely tolerated his feeble attempts to communicate to them en masse. And the poor man's superiors knew about his failure in this regard.

To summarize, I hope you will use this book and your course wisely. Learn the craft. Speak always as if you "have a speech to give." The skill will become a part of you, and your effective use of that skill may boost your career. Good luck!

2

THE BASIC PLAN FOR SPEAKING

I n his nightclub act, comedian Mort Sahl used to remark that, just before being hanged as an American spy in the Revolution, Nathan Hale said, "I only regret that I have but one life to lose for my country." A lot has changed in two centuries, Sahl noted: American pilot Francis Gary Powers, when shot down in his U-2 spy plane and captured by the Russians during the Cold War, muttered, "This destroys all my plans."

No one doubts the importance of plans, of planning. Probably no significant human endeavor has succeeded without careful and systematic planning. Builders do not randomly throw up skyscrapers overnight. Instead, they determine a future building's purpose, select a site, draw up detailed blueprints, solicit bids, order building materials, and so on. To develop a speech, you should follow a similar orderly process.

Planning Your Speech: Seven Steps

This chapter presents seven systematic steps that can lead to successful speaking. For each speech you prepare, you should follow these steps carefully. Eventually, when you become an experienced speaker, you will incorporate these seven steps into your speech preparation without conscious awareness, slipping from one to another, back and forth, as the need arises—much as you do when driving your car (open the door, get in, close the door, insert key in ignition, fasten seat belt, turn key, engage gears, check mirror, etc.). But for now, take them chronologically and deliberately, as presented here:

1. Choose a topic.

2. Decide on and write down your specific purpose, or goal, in terms of desired audience response.

3. Decide which main points, or ideas, you must get across to your audience in order to achieve your goal.

4. Assemble all the material you already have at hand to prove, explain, or illustrate each of your main points.

5. Gather further materials to support your main points.

6. Cast the assembled materials into a logical outline.

7. Rehearse from the outline, in a realistic manner, until satisfied that you can deliver your speech well.

Now let's take up each step in more detail.

Choosing Your Topic

The expert finds the first step, selecting a topic, easy; the beginner has a tougher job.

The expert, by definition, already has a topic. A lawyer can speak about new tax laws; a physician might speak on cardiac arrest or recent research on AIDS; an ardent hiker might speak about experiences along the Bartram Trail; a first-aid instructor can speak on CPR or the Heimlich maneuver. In fact, experts usually speak about their specialties because those who engage them to speak request speeches on those topics.

But the young speech student asks, "What can I give a speech on?" By this question the student usually means, "I don't *have* a speech I can give right now." However, most students really *do* have topics on which they can speak. They just need to convert them from "topics" to "speeches."

If you sit down and take a careful mental inventory, you can probably come up with a number of topics on which you have some knowledge or opinion that you could turn into a speech.

First, think of a topic already familiar to you. Almost everyone has some special interest: a hobby; the subject of a successful paper; a skill or concept picked up in scouts, athletics, or club work; or an interest acquired from reading a book or series of books. If you sit down and take a careful mental inventory, you can probably come up with a number of topics on which you have some knowledge or opinion that you could turn into a speech. Take a pencil and paper and write down all the topics that at one time or another interested you enough to merit some time and effort to learn more about or do something about. Such a list might astound you by its length.

In narrowing down your choice of topic, choose something that suits your audience—a topic they will find useful, interesting, or entertaining. If you want to speak persuasively, you should pick a subject that you can argue convincingly to them about. Again, an invited expert has little problem here, since by their very invitation the audience has indicated that the speaker's topic suits them. But as a student in a speaking course, you need to analyze your audience to decide on a good topic for them (or how you can make a topic suitable for them). Because the audience—your fellow students— probably resemble you in many ways, begin by asking yourself, "What would *I* like to hear a speech on?" (or conversely, "What would I *not* like to hear a speech on?"). This questioning involves audience analysis, a topic we take up again in Chapters 8 and 9.

Deciding on Your Specific Purpose

All good speeches have a goal. A good speech seeks a specific audience response and focuses directly on obtaining that response. Most poor speeches lack this singleness of purpose. Choosing the specific response you want from your audience represents a critical step. It determines all else that follows in your preparation.

> *The speaker with a clear goal resembles the purposeful automobile traveler . . . the speaker with* no *specific goal resembles the Sunday driver . . .*

The speaker with a clear goal resembles the purposeful automobile traveler, who first settles on a destination. The traveler then consults maps, chooses routes, calculates driving times, considers possible stops for food and gasoline, figures costs, and packs the requisite clothing and other supplies.

Conversely, the speaker with *no* specific goal resembles the Sunday driver, who starts out with no specific goal and thus without knowing where he or she will end up, what route to take, or how long the trip will last.

The speaker with a clear goal, like the careful traveler, can make purposeful, systematic plans. Given your chosen goal, what main points must you make in order to achieve it? What information do you need to include, and what information can you safely leave out?

General speech goals include speaking to entertain, inform, and persuade. *Specific* speech goals indicate what you wish to achieve in the particular speech: "I intend to entertain my audience for twenty minutes with my slides of and experiences on the Appalachian Trail"; "I propose to teach my audience how the ionosphere affects radio transmission"; "I want to motivate my audience to donate blood to the Red Cross on March 15."

A speaker with any of these particular goals would see a clear path ahead for preparing a speech. A speaker without such a specific goal might ramble along like a Sunday driver. The "Sunday driver speaker" has no goal other than "to give a speech." Such a speaker may not know how the audience will respond to the speech, exactly what he or she will say (what material to include and what to leave out), or exactly how long the speech will last. Such a speaker will probably come across as a crashing bore. Or, even if the speaker holds the audience's interest, its members will walk away thinking: "Very interesting! But I wonder what he was driving at?"

Deciding on Your Main Points

If you have a clear goal in terms of audience response, and if you already know a lot about your speech topic, the next step should come easily to you. The main points you will need to make in your speech will appear obvious. For instance, if you wish to teach the Heimlich maneuver, you will need to explain the following points:

1. You must differentiate the victim of a clogged windpipe from the victim of a heart attack. The symptoms include . . .

2. You must act quickly to remove the obstruction. Do it in the following manner . . .

3. Please understand that this maneuver almost always works because . . .

If you wish to convince your audience to vote for a new school bond issue, you must convince them that:

1. Our school's current physical plant has become (outdated, obsolete, overcrowded, etc.).

2. A new bond issue, if passed, would bring the plant up to par.

3. A new bond issue will provide what we need in the most feasible manner.

Do you want to motivate your audience members to donate blood? Then you need to make the following points:

1. We currently have a severe shortage of whole blood.

2. Donating your blood can help remedy this shortage (and also satisfy your desire to contribute to your community).

3. Donating blood causes no real pain and even provides some fun; and it makes you feel proud of yourself.

Assembling the Supporting Material You Have

You now know your specific purpose and which main points you need to make in order to accomplish it. Now you need to assemble the material you already possess that will help you develop those main points.

Sit down with pen and paper. Write down every specific fact, figure, comparison, and example you can think of that will help flesh out your speech. You will find it a good idea to put each fact or example on a separate notecard. Later, you can shuffle and reshuffle as you organize your speech into final form. One item per card also makes it easier to add and remove items from later versions of the speech.

As you write down each supporting item, make it as specific as possible. In casual conversation you can get away with something like "Several years ago when I was out West . . ." or "Firemen around here make pretty good money, considering . . . ," but in a formal speech you must use precision and accuracy: "In 1976, while in Tucson, Arizona, I . . ." or "Firemen in our city start at $27,400 per year . . ." If you lack these precise details, you need to do some checking, to sharpen up your information. You can do so during the next step.

Gathering Additional Supporting Material

You will probably not have all the information you need for your speech and you will have to supplement what you can provide from your own mind by doing some research.

Research usually means library work. Access to a good library will help immensely. But you may not know how to find just the right kind of information you need. Your library personnel and the material in Chapter 4 can help you.

You can do research elsewhere than in the library, too. Can you find any experts on your topic whom you can visit or call? Do you know (or can you find) any business nearby that may have information to give you, since providing such data might promote their own best interests? (For instance, the power company can probably provide material on insulation or nuclear fission; a local beverage plant will have information about recycling aluminum and glass; your hospital will have brochures on CPR and blood donation.) Do you have any books in your home, such as a good encyclopedia, a copy of *The Guinness Book of World Records,* a good dictionary, or a paperback copy of *Statistical Abstracts* (available from most newsstands)?

An important point here: *Gather far more material than you will need just for your speech.* Cram yourself full of your subject; assure yourself, thereby, that you know the topic backward and forward. Remember that an expert preparing a speech has more trouble deciding what to leave out than in finding enough material to put in. You should try to duplicate this situation. The amount of material you actually use in your speech should relate to how much you know on the topic in the same way that the tip of an iceberg relates to how much of it remains underwater.

> *The amount of material you actually use in your speech should relate to how much you know on the topic in the same way that the tip of an iceberg relates to how much of it remains underwater.*

Outlining

After you have gathered far more than enough material for your speech, with one point per card, organize your cards according to the main points they support. Then create an outline of your speech; arrange it so that each main point has its subpoints and supports indented and recorded under it. You will find more details about outlining in Chapter 5. After you properly outline your main points and support, you can begin work on a good introduction and a conclusion to your speech. But you should use this outline for one particular purpose: to rehearse from.

During the outlining process you can also begin to pick and choose from the supporting materials on the piles of cards you have accumulated. Because each card contains only one point, you can easily narrow items down to the best of the lot, even though you may find it emotionally difficult to discard the fruits of your labor.

Rehearsing

So far we have considered mostly the spadework for your speech. Now we come to a more creative and less mechanical area, which different people approach in different ways.

Some people go over and over the outline orally, changing the specific wording each time, perhaps, but still learning the sequence of ideas nonetheless. Most who prepare this way generally stop rehearsing after they have gone through the outline several times and feel satisfied with their delivery. Learning the speech this way has merit. You master the sequence of ideas and then present the actual speech by choosing words to express the ideas as they come to mind in the proper order. Thus you will speak your thoughts in the conversational manner that you normally use. You will "converse with your audience," and they will thank you for that.

> *You master the sequence of ideas and then present the actual speech by choosing words to express the ideas as they come to mind in the proper order. Thus you will speak your thoughts in the conversational manner that you normally use.*

Others speak the outline into a tape recorder one or more times, transcribe the speech from the recorder, then edit and polish that "already-oral-style" language. Finally, they rehearse the manuscript until it becomes second nature. This technique assures a more oral than a "manuscript" style; the speaker spoke the speech first, then wrote it, instead of vice versa.

Some speakers skip the tape-recording step; they go right from an outline to a written manuscript, which someone then edits. The speaker then polishes the manuscript performance by rehearsing. This technique often results in what sounds like "an essay on its hind legs" because of the nature of the written style that results (see Chapter 6).

Most academic speech teachers prefer the first method, rehearsing only from the outline. This extemporaneous method usually produces the most effective (and enjoyable) communication between speaker and audience. If one absolutely *must* use a manuscript, teachers prefer the method of tape-recording before manuscript-writing.

No doubt your speech (whether assigned or invited) will entail some sort of time limit. For this and other reasons, you must make your rehearsals as *realistic* as possible. If the speech clocks out as too long, you will have to squeeze some of the material out; if it comes out short, you will have to add more material. By realistic rehearsal I mean several things:

1. Rehearse the speech out loud and standing up. We can't call sitting at your desk and reading over your notecards *rehearsal*—maybe "study" or "preparation," but not rehearsal. To familiarize yourself with the actual coming event you must stand up and give your speech out loud.

2. Rehearse with whatever materials you will use in your real presentation. Will you use 35mm slides? Have them at each rehearsal. Will you use charts? A chalkboard? A flannel board? An overhead projector? Charts or graphs? Rehearse with them, too. (See Chapter 4 for advice on using visual aids.) Eventually, have a dress rehearsal or two, wearing the actual clothes you will wear for the speech.

3. Rehearse in a room of the same size and type as the room in which you will speak. Can you get into the actual room in which you will speak, at least for a rehearsal or two? That would help. Then when you give the actual speech, it won't seem so strange.

4. Perhaps most important: rehearse before an audience as much as you can. Get your friends, your roommates, your secretary, your spouse to listen to your speech. Did they understand it? Did they become confused by anything you said? Did you look and sound OK to them? Did any of your mannerisms, gestures, or whatever bother them? Did your clothes look appropriate to them?

In my class I have seen speakers show up with borrowed projectors they had never before operated; speakers who had never rehearsed with their visual aids and who discovered that using the aids doubled the time for their speeches; and speakers who became upset after receiving audience feedback for the first time. Again, good preparation will please you, your audience, and your instructor.

Considering the Listener

If you follow the basic plan of speech-building presented in this chapter, your speeches will probably encourage effective listening. After all, it takes both a speaker and an attentive audience to make a speech event. So let's look at the process, for a moment, from the viewpoint of the listener.

Your commitment will generate enthusiasm and empathy in your audience, and your dynamic delivery, sharpened through realistic rehearsal, will help your listeners concentrate on hearing and understanding your message.

1. We know that people listen as individuals and because of self-motivation. No speaker without a voice like a cannon can *make* people listen. And research tells us that persons who deliberately and actively try to listen carefully tend to learn more than those who do not make such attempts. You can make this active listening easier for your audience by clearly stating your precise goal and by keeping the speech focused and marching steadily toward that goal. Your commitment will generate enthusiasm and empathy in your audience, and your dynamic delivery, sharpened through realistic rehearsal, will help your listeners concentrate on hearing and understanding your message.

2. Reinforcement helps listeners remember and learn. After you have clearly enunciated your purpose and main points early in the speech, you must refer to them throughout your speech in restatement and in transitions. (See Chapter 5 for more details about reinforcing your organizational pattern.)

3. Listeners who concentrate on ideas, or main points, as opposed to details, tend to learn more from oral discourse. This conclusion might seem difficult to believe, as it once did for me. But it makes sense. When you pay close attention to the main ideas, the details (supporting material) adhere to these ideas. While conferring with a student of mine, I asked him about how he had studied in order to get an A on my difficult first exam in a research methods course. I asked whether

he had found useful the numerous interesting (and often humorous) examples in the textbook. "No," he said, "I didn't study the examples. In fact, when I study for a test and come to an obvious 'example,' I skip over it. Such examples only detract from my concentrating on the important point." Although I consider that student's attitude pretty extreme, I also see his point. And as we shall see later, especially in Chapter 8, in public speaking we concern ourselves with getting across main ideas, and our seven steps of speech development tend to ensure that we do so.

4. Listening can suffer if audience members react emotionally to certain red-flag words. So texts advise potential listeners to avoid knee-jerk emotional reactions—to disregard "red-flag" words and listen for the more important content in the speech. In a more innocent period of our history such words as *syphilis, abortion,* and *cancer* could temporarily shock people enough to interfere with their attention. If you will systematically construct your speech according to the plan in this chapter, you can constantly scan your material for scare words. Your rehearsal sessions before audiences of one (parent, friend, roommate, etc.) should turn up any emotion-loaded words you might want to replace. For example, you may not want to refer to a "tax increase" when you can use "governmental revenue enhancement." Advising people to watch a "TV rerun" may have less effect than urging them to catch an "encore telecast."

I once asked a good friend, a high school biology teacher, whether she taught biology as evolution. Her reply: "You cannot teach real biology without teaching evolution." I then asked her if she did not encounter ideological resistance from her more religiously fundamental students when she even mentioned the word *evolution.* She responded, "I don't use the word; I call it *change.*"

5. Good listeners avoid, deliberately adapt to, or disregard any physical obstacle to attentive listening. Such obstacles as a static-prone sound system, noise from an open window, or an overheated room represent minor annoyances that good listeners ignore in order to get the message. Your well-prepared speech built according to our basic plan should minimize your audience's need to disregard distraction. The admonition to try out your speech in the actual venue where you will present it becomes even more important in this context. Such rehearsal gives you a chance to check on such things as

acoustics, room arrangement, heating or air-conditioning, windows, other possible sources of outside noise, and so on.

Systematically following the seven sure-fire steps presented in this chapter will carry you well along your path to successful speechmaking. Review the steps before beginning work on each speech. Avoid shortcuts. Your listeners will thank you.

3
CONQUERING STAGE FRIGHT

*I*n 1973 R. H. Bruskin Associates polled Americans on what they feared most. Heading the list: *speaking in public.* Fear of death appeared on the list, but in seventh place. One student explained: "I can understand that difference in ranking; once you die, you no longer have to give public speeches!"

People who speak or otherwise perform in public unanimously suffer from stage fright. Operatic tenor Luciano Pavarotti once confessed to a reporter that he felt the pangs of fear before every performance. Further, he said, "Find someone who is not nervous before a performance and I'll show you someone who is not speaking the truth."

You might think that college speech professors would become immune to stage fright, but you would think wrongly. In 1969 I personally observed two speech professors, both friends of mine, *pass out cold* while delivering scholarly papers before meetings at our national convention in New York. Stage fright not only affects everyone, but it lasts a lifetime.

Some speech teachers (and textbooks) hardly mention stage fright. They notice that the symptoms decline throughout the academic term, so they take the attitude of "Why bring up that uncomfortable subject?" They fail to realize that speech students reduce stage fright reactions mostly by getting used to talking to the same friendly classmate faces. When those speech students go off to speak to new, strange audiences, stage fright will return with a vengeance.

But stage fright feels so awful. What can we *do* about it?

The Symptoms of Stage Fright

To cope with any emotion, you first need to understand it. This chapter focuses on helping you learn about and deal with stage fright. To explain it, we must begin with its symptoms.

The symptoms of fear occur anytime the organism faces a perceived danger. Any danger, regardless of its basic nature, causes the same symptoms in all people. Everyone has experienced fear, so you will recognize these symptoms.

At the first recognition of any danger, you feel a sudden spasm of energy (from adrenaline) called the alarm reaction. If the danger persists, your body undergoes a series of changes. Your heart begins to pound. (You may recall Poe's story "The Telltale Heart.") You feel breathless; your breath comes and goes in little short pants. Your face

> *"Humans possess a wonderful organ, the brain; it starts working the minute you get born and doesn't stop working until you get up to make a speech."*

flushes. The palms of your hands and the soles of your feet break out in a cold sweat (you literally get "cold feet"). You feel a sinking sensation, or butterflies, in your stomach. Your mouth goes dry and cottony. You find it difficult to control your voice: it feels as if it will break, squeak, or croak. Your mind goes blank ("Humans possess a wonderful organ, the brain; it starts working the minute you get born and doesn't stop working until you get up to make a speech."). You tremble, mostly in your arms and legs. Your skin may break out in goosebumps.

All this physiological activity interferes with your concentration as you try to make a speech. So what do you do? You feel terribly awkward. You shift from foot to foot, trying to find a comfortable stance to stabilize your shaking knees. Your arms and hands feel oversized, so you try to hide them behind you, under your armpits, under the lectern, or in your pockets. You look anywhere but at that audience sitting out there, as if by not seeing them you can make them disappear. You shrink behind the lectern as though trying to hide. You talk as fast as you can in order to get the speech over with. Your numbed brain cannot keep up with your racing words, so you fill voids with "Uh," "Um," or "You know."

Why does this happen? Why does your body run at 90 mph when you want it to slow down to idle speed? Well, all this goes on for sound biological reasons.

The Origins of Stage Fright

Your body's autonomic nervous system produces many automatic reactions besides fear responses. If you exert your body in a warm room, your autonomic nervous system will order up perspiration. Sweat naturally air-conditions you as it evaporates; if you lost your ability to sweat, you might die of heatstroke. If you get overly chilled, your muscles involuntarily contract and expand to stimulate blood flow and warm you up; we call that shivering. If you go without food or water long enough, your body will tell you that you need to eat or drink. In each of these cases your body responds to changing conditions and adapts itself to better survive.

So, why does your body respond the way it does to *danger*? Well, before humans became civilized, forming societies with soldiers and police and firefighters to protect them from danger, they had to face danger on their own—and often. Our primitive ancestors had to cope with natural disasters such as forest fires, volcanic eruptions, lightning storms, and earthquakes. They had to learn to perform dangerous feats like fording or swimming rivers and climbing mountains in order to hunt game for food. They had to fight other people to protect their territory, their homes, or their families. And they constantly had to guard against predatory wild animals.

Dealing with any of these dangers would come easier if one had extra strength and energy. And those humans who lived long enough to pass on their genes were those who developed the fear syndrome of symptoms which, taken together, provide the body with extra strength and energy.

> *Those humans who lived long enough to pass on their genes were those who developed the fear syndrome of symptoms that provide the body with extra strength and energy.*

Consider one of those ancient humans, a primordial man plodding along some Old World path. Rounding a turn in the trail, he comes face-to-face with a saber-toothed tiger. What can this man do to keep from becoming the tiger's lunch? Unlike other animals, he has no wings to fly away, no shell to withdraw into, no protective armor. Our primitive man has only two options: he can flee, or he can fight. Extra strength, endurance, and physical adaptability would enhance either activity. So his system begins to meet the life-and-death challenge.

While a burst of adrenaline provides his first instant rush of energy, his autonomic nervous system springs into action. It orders the heart to begin circulating blood rapidly and the liver to release a reserve form of food energy called glycogen, which the body must oxidize for energy. Oxidation requires air, so his autonomic nervous system switches his breathing apparatus into high gear. As glycogen oxidizes in the panting lungs, our man's heart pumps it out as sheer energy to the awaiting muscles needed for running or fighting. These muscles, primarily in the arms and legs, become energized.

The threatened man's body needs blood for this muscle-energizing process, not for the process of digestion, so the digestive process stops operating, causing a sinking feeling (butterflies) in his stomach and drying up his mouth, as salivation (part of the digestion process) ceases.

Blood rushing through the capillaries makes his skin blush. Sweating relieves his body of weight and waste products, streamlining it for running or fighting. It also makes our caveman slick and harder for a predator to hang onto. Goosebumps raise his hackles, actually making his hair stand on end, so he looks larger and more ferocious to the tiger.

With all this bodily activity going on, talking becomes pretty difficult. Air rushes up and down our man's throat so rapidly he can't slow it down to form words. In his larynx (voice box) antagonistic-pair muscles jerking back and forth against each other make voice control nearly impossible. Talking requires upper brain activity, too; and his mind has gone blank.

Why do talking and thinking become so unimportant in this situation? Because these activities arrived late on the evolutionary scene. If our hypothetical caveman decides to try to talk the tiger out of snacking on him, he won't live out the day.

Those of our ancestors who developed the emergency system to make them better runners and fighters passed this system on to us in their genes.

To sum up, the various physiological symptoms of fear originally developed as a way to energize the body to survive some emergency. This process, natural and normal, proves necessary for survival. Imagine, if you can, someone who never suffers from the symptoms I've described—someone who fears no personal danger whatsoever. Just how long do you think he or she would live, fearing nothing or nobody?

You may say, "I understand the reaction to real, physical danger. But why does all this happen when I just think about giving a speech? Why does the thought of facing an audience make me react as if I have exposed myself to death or dismemberment? Should I expect the audience to blow me away or to come after me with a black-jack?"

No, you do not face physical danger when you speak in public. Nevertheless, your body recognizes the situation as threatening. You do indeed face danger—not physical danger, but *psychological* danger, which is no less real than physical danger.

Self-image and Stage Fright

We humans have left behind us the natural life to which we once adapted so well—that of hunting and gathering. We now live in artificial societies governed by symbols and sounds, which allow us to tinker with concepts, notions, ideas. This kind of living paints on each of us a thin veneer of what we call *civilization*, and it complicates our behavior far beyond that of our ancient ancestors. Unable to behave as our natural instincts dictate, each of us establishes and maintains an elaborate system of personas, masks, or self-images.

For instance, each of us has an *intellectual* self-image—we each regard ourselves as pretty smart. And we want our fellows, especially our peers, to share this belief. But when we speak in public, we expose our intellectual self-image to possible damage through criticism. Do you want people to walk away from your speech saying things like, "Did you hear what that idiot said? Can you imagine anyone with any sense saying such things?" Of course you do not; you want them to think, "What a brilliant speaker; she really covered that topic well!"

We also have a *social* self-image. We enjoy thinking of ourselves as being likable. Well, speaking exposes your social self-image to possible criticism, too. You fear that you might let slip some of those words in your vocabulary that you reserve for a few intimate friends and that these verbal slips may cause you social castigation.

Third, we each possess a *sexual* self-image. Most men want to think of themselves as masculine and want others to do so, too. Most women wish to retain their femininity and want others (especially men) to so recognize it.

Our society expects men to show masculine qualities: courage, bravery, fearlessness. They must avoid the degrading epithets of scaredy-cat, coward, yellowbelly, wimp. And the American male must not show "negative" emotions in public: pain, fear, remorse, dejection. On the other hand, our society allows women to show all kinds of emotions in public, including fear.

Society's differing expectations for the male and female roles make for different stage fright responses from men and women. On written questionnaires measuring stage fright, such as the Personal Report of Confidence as a Speaker (PRCS), women admit to more stage fright than men do; however, on observational measures of stage fright (such as audience ratings or recorded heart rate), men generally demonstrate more fear than do women.

Years ago a two-hundred-pound football player was one of my worst stage fright victims. He could barely get through a short speech. One day I tape-recorded the speakers and, at the end of the period, played back a short sample of each speech. When my football player heard his voice on the machine, he had a powerful emotional reaction. His eyes watered, his face flushed, his ears nearly burned off his head. Afterward he asked me if he really sounded like that, saying that he didn't recognize his own voice. I explained that he hears himself mostly through bone conduction but that others hear him through air conduction, and that he sounded like himself just as much as the other speakers had. The guy then grinned from ear to ear—he literally radiated self-satisfaction. "Just great," he said. "I have a real *baritone* voice. I actually sound like a *man!*" This poor fellow had felt for years that he had a thin, feminine, "sissy" voice to contrast with his manly physique. So 95 percent of his stage fright left him in one fell swoop.

Some people have a distorted cosmetic self-image; they think that people won't like their looks.

Eventually we all develop a *professional* self-image. I can feel threats to mine—not before a class of undergraduates, but when I face the judgment of my peers. When I go to a professional convention and report on my research, I fear the potential for criticism from my fellow scholars, and I get nervous just like any freshman speech student. My colleagues who fainted during their presentations in New York probably could attribute their collapse to a threat to their professional self-images.

Still other self-images can become objects of concern. Some people have a distorted cosmetic self-image; they think that people won't like their looks. One young man in my speech class spoke in a garbled mumble because he didn't want people to see what he hyperbolized as his "crooked teeth." One's *economic* self-image may become threatened in a speaking situation. I feel calm when talking to a student or a colleague but feel somewhat nervous talking to my dean or university president. I certainly want *them* to like me: they "pay" me!

Knowing how an audience can affect various self-images can provide true understanding of just how stage fright operates. I remember reading a journalist's interview with the distinguished English actor Sir Cedric Hardwicke. "I suppose," said the reporter, "that, after forty-six years on the stage, your first-night jitters are a thing of the past." Sir Cedric's reply: "You know, it gets worse every year."

Hardwicke's statement seems illogical: all that experience should have allayed all his nervousness before the lights. But if you think about the idea of self-images, you will realize that Sir Cedric's professional image, his *reputation*, had grown over the years; he thus had more to lose each year if he blew his lines. We expect the beginning, inexperienced actor to make fluffs now and then, but the great Sir Cedric Hardwicke? Never!

> *Can we call the stage fright we feel in response to our endangered self-images real? Can we accept it as normal, natural, vital for survival? You bet we can.*

Let me make a most important point here. Earlier I wrote that we must consider the fear reaction to physical danger as normal, natural, even vital for survival. Can we claim the same for the fear response to psychological danger? Can we call the stage fright we feel in response to our endangered self-images real? Can we accept it as normal, natural, vital for survival? You bet we can.

Given the culture we live in, rich with symbolic interactions with our fellows and complicated by highly intricate social, legal, and political interrelationships, fright at the prospect of giving a public speech should seem as natural as salivating at the sight of food. In fact, if giving a speech to a valued group of people does not make you nervous, you should begin to doubt your sanity. To paraphrase Kipling: "If you can keep your head when all about you are losing theirs, perhaps you don't understand the seriousness of the situation."

Can you imagine a person who cares nothing about self-image? What would you call someone who doesn't give a tinker's damn about what people think of him intellectually, socially, professionally, cosmetically, economically, and so on? How about "crackpot," "misanthrope," "screwball"?

Truly, in our artificial, civilized world, we find it absolutely necessary to develop, maintain, and protect a variety of self-images. And it thus becomes quite normal, necessary, and vital for our survival to recognize a threat to any of these self-images and to react biologically as if we find ourselves in physical danger. And if we have impaired our "normal" capacity to react with fear to a self-image threat by using drugs or alcohol, we open up our behavioral repertoire to saying and doing things that will hurt us. Sober, we would restrain ourselves from angry or obscene words; intoxicated, we may say things to friends, supervisors, or a spouse that would put us in the doghouse. Under normal circumstances, we might perceive when our audience grows restless; doped up with tranquilizers, we might drone on until we anesthetize *our listeners*.

By now you probably accept stage fright as normal, natural, and vital to survival. So what can you do to overcome it?

Some Remedies for Stage Fright

First, you will never *overcome* stage fright if by that term you mean "no longer experience it." As long as you stay alive and retain most of your sanity, you will experience some stage fright when a speaking situation threatens one of your self-images. You cannot disregard that fact. But you can reduce the extent of your uncomfortable symptoms, with work and practice. You will learn to handle it. As one woman put it after completing a course in public speaking: "I still have butterflies before I speak, but now they all fly in formation."

If you have followed my reasoning thus far, you have already taken the first step toward lowering your level of stage fright. You understand and believe that stage fright constitutes a normal, natural, needed-for-survival part of living. And you know that all people experience it; you do not suffer alone. And you need not "fear fear itself."

All too often, this scenario occurs: A young man has to give a speech. When the teacher calls his name, he rises and approaches the podium. He feels nervous; after all, he knows that his self-images will soon lay exposed. The nervousness occurs normally, but he does not know or believe that. He feels his shakiness and thinks, "Oh my gosh! I'm shaking and sweating. Everyone will see that and know I'm scared!" This thought accelerates his fear. He says to himself, "Uh oh. I'm getting *worse!* I'm shaking more, my voice will squeak, I'll look like a coward!" This observation further increases his trepidation. His symptoms double. And so perceived fear produces more fear, on a self-accelerating spiral to communicative disaster.

But with the right set of attitudes and beliefs about fear, our novice speaker reacts differently. Called on to speak, he strides to the lectern. Recognizing his slight fear reactions as normal, he observes to himself: "Lucky me! Normal! Natural! Sure, I feel a bit nervous, but that will give me just the extra edge of alertness and energy I need to do a bang-up job here today! The audience will notice my slight shakiness, but they know about that from experience, and expect it. Besides, in a minute or two, after I have gotten into this speech, I will have calmed down to normal and will have this speech really cooking." Our speaker, through his attitude and knowledge, has avoided the self-accelerating threat/response/increased threat/response cycle that can wreck a speech.

Besides your attitude toward fear itself, you will find another set of attitudes important in reducing stage fright: your attitudes toward *yourself.* The key: learning to understand yourself, your strengths and limitations, and to accept yourself with those strengths and limitations. In other words, your self-images should correlate closely with reality. Always try to do well, but don't expect to always come out best. As Bonaro Overstreet wrote in *Understanding Fear in Ourselves and Others*, "Perhaps the most important thing we can undertake toward the reduction of fear is to make it easier for people to accept themselves; to like themselves."

You can also take several specific actions to minimize initial stage fright reactions and symptoms. Do them in relation to what you know about the causes of the problem.

Reducing the Size of the Threat

You will find that the amount of fear you feel exactly equals the size of the threat you face. Size of threat = *amount of fear reaction* represents as much an equation as $2 + 2 = 4$. And you know from your math training that reducing one side of an equation automatically reduces the other side. So if you reduce the size of the threat, you will reduce the size of the fear reaction. How do you reduce threat? I suggest three ways.

First, speak on a topic that you know well, one that you have spoken or written about before, that you have studied for a particular reason, that you have an interest in. For instance, I feel pretty comfortable speaking to groups about any one of several topics in the area of communication. I can discuss the psychology of humor (my research specialty) easily before groups. I would feel at home speaking on several aspects of photography, a some-time hobby of mine. But I would feel scared to death if I had to hold forth on "Latest Advances in Nuclear Fission" before a physics department colloquium.

Second, prepare well for speaking. Most stage fright merely represents lack-of-preparation jitters. It comes from fear of failure, because the speaker knows that he or she has not put in enough time and energy to ensure doing a satisfactory job. Did you ever go to an exam ill-prepared? Didn't have time to read all those outside assignments? Didn't get around to outlining the book chapters? Couldn't study because you had other things on your mind? If so, you probably remember going into that exam with more than a little fear in your heart.

Most stage fright merely represents lack-of-preparation jitters. It comes from fear of failure, because the speaker knows that he or she has not put in enough time and energy to ensure doing a satisfactory job.

On the other hand, I hope you have felt the contrary experience that comes from having studied well. Think of a time when you knew the material backward and forward. That teacher couldn't ask a single question you wouldn't be able to answer. Your preparation made for dry palms and a placid cardiovascular system as you entered the testing arena; it made you confident that your instructor wouldn't be able to stump you. You aced that test.

These effects of preparation also hold true with speaking. If you have faithfully followed the advice and preparatory steps outlined in Chapter 2; if you have worked diligently to find interesting and varied materials for your speech; if you have rehearsed and honed it before live audiences several times and, as a result, feel that you have a really important message for your audience that you can put across with authority and clarity, your chances for failure will dramatically diminish. And so will your stage fright.

If, on the other hand, you wait until the eleventh hour to begin work on your speech, then throw it together in a panic, you have every right to expect a terrific case of the jitters as your speaking occasion approaches. Remember: You ought to *earn* the right to speak—by hard work.

A third method of reducing the size of the threat of speaking: Come to the speech rested and in good physical condition. Eat nutritious food, and avoid any food or drink likely to upset your nervous or gastrointestinal systems. Get a good night's sleep the night before. Of course, if you wait until the eleventh hour, such care of yourself becomes impossible. One of my students, giving his final speech for the course, failed miserably. He became so nervous he could not remember his words. He resembled a punch-drunk boxer, eyes rolling in his head. One eye glowed blood red, as if the white had been scratched out by a fingernail. Next day he came to my office and seemed dumbfounded at his performance. He had expected to do so *well*. "Honest," he said, "I worked on it all night; I didn't even go to bed!"

Countering Physiological Reactions

Your autonomic nervous system has prepared your body to contend with physical danger, either to fight it or to run from it. But you must merely give a speech, not run or fight; your body has overprepared. You have more strength and energy than you need for speaking. So get rid of some of it, in one of the following ways.

Your autonomic nervous system has prepared your body to contend with physical danger . . . but you must merely give a speech, not run or fight . . .

First, before you even get up to speak, alternately tense up and then relax some muscles. Crunch your toes down into the floor and feel how much energy your leg muscles burn up. Then relax your toes and feel the tension drain away. Do the same with the muscles of your arms and chest. Do some isometrics. Place your palms together in front of you and press them together vigorously, then relax them. You have used up lots of energy. Grip the sides of your chair seat and try to lift yourself straight up, then relax. If you can wait offstage while someone introduces you, you can practice lifting the piano there, or do some deep-knee bends while awaiting your entrance cue (I did the latter in the minister's office moments before walking into the church auditorium to get married).

You can also use up some of that excess energy

while you speak, through gestures, directed movement, shrugs of the shoulders, changes in facial expression—in short, by "getting loose," showing *animation*. I realize that a beginning speaker almost instinctively tries to stand as still as possible during a speech. You do so because you subconsciously know that by moving and gesturing you bring attention to yourself. One of your instinctive behaviors, running away, comes into play here; the tendency to stay still helps you "hide," makes you less visible. But as a speaker, you should *want* to draw attention to yourself. You have chosen to stand up and talk while others sit and listen. And if you stand there like a stick, moving only your mouth, crouching behind the lectern as low as possible, you will not only look unnatural and artificial, you won't use up that excess energy throbbing through your body.

A third way to try to bring your bodily processes into a more comfortable homeostatic balance: Try to catch up on your need for oxygen. Many people report that taking several deep breaths before rising to speak makes their breathing more normal. But try this a time or two at home before attempting it on your first speech; for some people a few such deep breaths only makes them dizzy.

Replacing Emotion with Intellectual Activity

Remember that the numbness in your cerebral cortex as your speech draws near results from your lower brain's taking over and preparing your body for a physical instead of a social or psychological danger. Mother Nature thus decrees that you should act, not think or talk. You want to reverse this process.

A well-known psychological principle says that emotional activity can replace intellectual activity. We sometimes call the act of becoming emotional "losing our heads." But the reverse can also happen: intellectual activity can replace emotional activity. For instance, if you sit and watch a scary movie but concentrate on wondering how the filmmakers made the special effects so convincing during the more exciting parts of the movie, I doubt that you will become as frightened as the other movie patrons.

This principle works in speaking. If you can get off to a good start in talking (an intellectual activity), your cerebral cortex will begin right away to retake command of your total organism. How can you ensure getting off to a good start? Begin with an introduction that you absolutely cannot forget.

One type of introduction you can't forget: the story of some event that happened to you that illustrates the point of your speech. This event occurred in your actual experience. You have recounted it numerous times before. How could you possibly forget it?

As a beginning speech student, I once gave a speech on the idea that "Great change can come when you least expect it." I began like this:

> In August 1945, I found myself at age thirteen in my first experience of Boy Scout summer camp. We were told at breakfast that Friday morning that the radio had reported that the United States had just used a new weapon of war on Japan, then our enemy. They said to keep an ear open for any unusual bugle calls during the day, and if we heard one, we would gather at the flagpole and celebrate the end of World War II. That bugle call never came, and our buses took us home the next day. That Saturday afternoon Churchill and Truman jointly announced via radio the war's end. The atomic bomb had ushered in a new era.

By the time I had reached "That Saturday afternoon . . ." my breathing had returned to near-normal.

Some speakers use the simple trick of beginning a speech by reading something—perhaps a short poem, an item from a newspaper or magazine, a clever quotation, an anecdote, or a brief letter. I do not advocate reading your entire speech, but a short reading at the beginning revs up your brain and restores cortical control; and such readings quite acceptably launch good extemporaneous speeches. A young man in my class gave a speech on the Equal Rights Amendment and the women's movement in general. He began by reading:

> *Women, it is now quite clear, are very much like men,*
> *Except, of course, for here and there, and sometimes now and then.*

Another student began a speech by saying that just that morning she had received a note in the mail, which she read:

> I know that today you give that big speech, and I know you will do an outstanding job of it. With your superior intelligence, quick wit, indomitable personality, and deep and profound insight into the human condition, you will deliver a masterpiece of oratory.
>
> Love,
Mom

You can also increase intellectual activity by having an easy-to-remember speech. To do this, you need to use as many mnemonic (memory) devices as possible, including good organization. Humans remember organized material much better than unorganized material. More on this matter when we come to Chapter 5. Phrasing the

*I*f you can approach each assignment as a genuine opportunity to communicate worthwhile information and ideas to a group of people you like and admire, if you feel that you truly have worthwhile goods to deliver, your stage fright will diminish.

purpose of your speech in easily remembered words also helps you (and your audience) remember your speech. For instance, a scholastically successful student of mine gave a speech on the formula for maintaining a near-perfect grade point average: The four R's: *Read, Reflect, Recite,* then *Review.*

Countering Emotion with Emotion

We often express our ambivalence about something by saying that we have mixed emotions. What does this mean?

Psychologists tell us that we cannot feel two quite different emotions at the same time. We can feel each of two emotions alternately, but not simultaneously. Try feeling sorry for yourself at the same time that you laugh at yourself. You can't do it.

So, replace fear with some other emotion as you begin your speech. Some speakers begin with a little humorous anecdote to gently poke fun at themselves. The speaker who began with the "letter from Mom" did so, with great effect. You can't take yourself too seriously (a good definition of stage fright) as you make jokes about yourself.

You might also begin your speech with a kind of righteous indignation over the topic of your speech. "Here's a problem that we must solve," you repeat to yourself over and over.

Become audience-centered. Develop a real concern that your audience will understand and perhaps even act on your message. You can't remain very self-centered (another definition of stage fright) if you concentrate all your energy and attention on your audience.

In conclusion, I hope you will reconsider a point made in Chapter 1. If you approach each speech merely as an assignment, you might experience a higher degree of stage fright. If, however, you can approach each assignment as a genuine opportunity to communicate worthwhile information and ideas to a group of people you like and admire, if you feel that you truly have worthwhile goods to deliver, your stage fright will diminish. You will work hard, look forward to stepping in front of the class, and do a good job. You will feel that you have done your audience a genuine favor by sharing yourself with them, and you will not feel the need to conclude your speech with that old bromide, "Thankyew." Furthermore, when you finish, you are likely to feel successful, to have had fun, and to feel pleased with yourself.

4

SECURING MATERIAL FOR YOUR SPEECH

eople want to hear interesting and useful content. You must provide it. That content must come from somewhere. This chapter tells you where you can find it. It also tells you what *kind* of content to look for.

If you expect to speak on your particular area of expertise, finding material will present no real problem. You will have much of it in your head; you may find the rest at arm's length, on your bookshelf, in your files, in your diary, and so on.

Do others call you the best gardener in town? Then your personal library probably bulges with seed catalogs, gardening how-to books, almanacs, and the like. Do you work as a social worker, dealing constantly with alcoholics, drug users, and the homeless? Then you probably possess a wealth of information on these topics. Do you adhere to vegetarianism? And must you verbally defend this lifestyle often? Then you probably own a large batch of evidence on the humaneness, healthfulness, and satisfaction of vegetarianism.

Experts find no trouble gathering enough important and useful material for a speech, but they might have difficulty picking and choosing from what they already have available.

A nonexpert doesn't have a lot of specialized knowledge of a topic and might not have a lot lying around on bookshelves and in magazine racks. If you fit into this category, you need to find that specialized knowledge somewhere. In fact, even an expert finds it necessary to dig up *some* information for a speech. Finding information usually means going to the library.

Other sources exist outside the library, of course. For instance, I always recommend that my students keep up with the happenings in the world around them. I instruct them to read, thoroughly, at least one good newspaper daily; to study at least one good weekly newsmagazine, such as *Time, Newsweek,* or *U.S. News & World Report;* and to keep up with world, national, state, and local news via radio and television newscasts and documentary programs.

Keeping abreast of events not only makes one a better-informed citizen, but it can prevent embarrassment in a public-speaking situation. For instance, I once heard a young speaker plead for more state laws barring racial intermarriages (miscegenation) because of the difficulties that children of such marriages face. The young woman did not know that two years previously the U.S. Supreme Court had ruled such state laws unconstitutional.

You can always go to a newsstand or bookstore for information.

Or you may find, or know of, a nearby expert on your topic whom you could interview and perhaps borrow printed information from. You could invest in a telephone call to interview a more distant expert. If you work for a large commercial, governmental, or educational organization, you might find that you have access to that organization's considerable research-and-development department. But gathering material for a speech usually requires going to the library.

A Guide to the Library

Libraries contain vast amounts of information. Use them.

Libraries vary greatly in size, holdings, arrangement, and sophistication. Research libraries, in particular, grow more computer-accessible every year. I can now sit in my office and access the University of Georgia Main Library from my computer and learn the availability and status of most of its books and any of its periodical holdings.

But to give you some idea of what to look for and how to do so, let me describe a library exercise that I assign my students. I feel that once they have completed the exercise, they can find their way around our library and should have no trouble locating information on any speech topic. Remember that this exercise remains unique to the main library of the University of Georgia and will not fit your own. But most libraries offer some sort of orientation, whether in the form of printed material, self-guided tours via audiocassette players, or staff-led tours.

Early in the term I hand my students a written assignment that directs them to go to the main library and perform certain tasks.

The student first goes to the reference room, usually the largest station of any library. There the student must find the reference shelf containing the *Readers' Guide to Periodical Literature,* find the names of five periodicals beginning with the letter S, and write them down on the assignment sheet.

The *Readers' Guide* indexes articles (alphabetically by subject matter and then by title) in hundreds of periodicals, from Aging through *Mademoiselle* to *The Yale Review.* The index provides all the bibliographic information you need to find the complete article in the published periodical. Part of a sample page of the *Guide* is presented on the next page.

SENSES AND SENSATION—See also—cont.
    Time perception
    Touch
SENSOR PAD
    Court backs FDA's device definition [unapproved medical device] D. Farley. il *FDA Consumer* 26:43-4 Ja/F '92
SERIAL MURDERS *See* Murder
SERMONS
    That's interesting. M. E. Marty. *The Christian Century* 109:175 F 5-12 '92
SERRANO, IRMA
                    about
    La Tigresa. A. Coe. il *pors Film Comment* 28:64-5 Ja/F '92
SERVICE, VOLUNTEER *See* Volunteer service
SERVICE INDUSTRIES
    See also
    Robots—Service industry use
SERVICE STATIONS, AUTOMOBILE *See* Automobile service stations
SERVICEMEN
                    Retirement
    See Retired military personnel

Youth—Sexual behavior
    Men and the morning after: the naked truth. W. D. Leight. il *Mademoiselle* 98:72-5 Ja '92
SEXUAL DIMORPHISM *See* Dimorphism (Biology)
SEXUAL DISORDERS
    Sexual problems by prescription. T. L. Crenshaw. il *The Saturday Evening Post* 264:64-5+ Ja/F '92
SEXUAL ETHICS
            See also
    Adultery
    Sex education
SEXUAL HARASSMENT
    Conduct unbecoming a preacher. J. Jordan-Lake. il *Christianity Today* 36:26-30 F 10 '92
    Harassment blues. N. Munson. *Commentary* 93:49-51 F '92
    Nina Totenberg: queen of the leaks [A. Hill's leaked testimony] A. L. Bardach. il *pors Vanity Fair* 55:46+ Ja '92
    Our process (our show) [A. Hill-C. Thomas hearings as compared to film Advise and consent] D. Thomson. il *pors Film Comment* 28:7-10+ Ja/F '92
SEXUALITY *See* Sexual behavior

Reprinted by permission of *Reader's Guide to Periodical Literature* and the H.W. Wilson Co.

To some readers of this book, this information presented on *Readers' Guide* may appear utterly elementary. But many college students remain unfamiliar with this most basic and useful resource.

The next part of the assignment in the reference room asks the student to access each of four computer systems. One accesses material in the ERIC system; another electronically indexes the material in psychological journals; a third (called InfoTrak) indexes popular periodicals also indexed by *Readers' Guide*; and a fourth indexes recent books in the library's card catalog. One item from each computer-assisted source must appear on each student's assignment sheet. My librarian friends assure me that libraries will only become more and more computerized.

The student next must find a work by call number Ref/Z1002/B5685 (here at Georgia) and write down how many volumes of the work exist. The work, *World Bibliography of Bibliographies*, can lead the student to just about any bibliography on any subject.

On the reference tables the student must next find the *Education Index* and write down the titles of three articles published since 1985 on the use of television in teaching. Thus the student should know how to find information in any professional or general periodical dealing with any educational subject, such as busing's effect on school integration, the use of honor systems, or the criteria for evaluating teachers.

Having found this index, the student must then find three other special-subject-matter indexes, one of which indexes material in the student's major field (or probable major). The student may find these indexes by prowling the reference tables, by looking through the subject index of the card catalog, or by seeking help from the reference staff. The titles and publication sources of these three indexes must accompany the written library assignment. Students will find such indexes as The Index *to Journals in Communication, Psychological Abstracts, Sociological Abstracts, Applied Science and Technology Index, Engineering Index, Index to Legal Periodicals, Industrial Arts Index, Social Sciences and Humanities Index, Biological and Agricultural Index,* and *Public Affairs Information Service*. Knowing about these indexes, the student can now find specialized, original information on nearly any subject.

The student must then find the subject card catalog, locate three books on the subject of "sharks," and write down their titles. This portion of the card catalog lists the library's books and other publications alphabetically by subject matter. Then the student must find the author and title portion of the card catalog and find the call number of the book *Understanding Laughter: The Workings of Wit and Humor* and enter that number on the assignment sheet. The student should now know how to use the *real key* to the library, the card catalog. He or she can find published material by any one author, of any one title, or on any one subject. Of course, by the time you hold this book in your hands, card catalogs may have disappeared, replaced by keyboards and glowing computer screens. (When I attended college we didn't even have photocopy machines!)

Next, the student must go to the reference desk and ask for a specific volume by call number (which at Georgia means Ref/HG/ 4057/19__[current year]), titled *Standard and Poor's Register of Corporations, Directors, and Executives* (usually abbreviated to *Standard and Poor's*). This tome lists much information about every corporation in America, including the addresses of corporate offices and the names of the officers. The student's assignment: Look up and record the name of the president of Fisher-Price Toys, plus the name of the company that owns Fisher-Price. The student should now know how to contact virtually any officer of any corporation providing any service or manufacturing any product in the country. Through these contacts the student can seek information or make complaints about the company. Knowing specifically whom to contact, by name, enhances the chance of a reply.

Most of our students do not know that the telephone directories of most American cities exist on microfiche in our library. To impress this fact on them, I have them find, in the reference room, the address and home telephone number of James W. Gibson of Columbia, Missouri. This exercise teaches the student that a wide variety of experts around the country can easily become accessible via telephone.

Suppose you wanted to know which colleges use the semester and which the quarter system, or which colleges do and do not have honor systems or coed dormitories or student cooperatives. To acquaint my students with how they can obtain such information, I direct them to find our collection of microfiched college catalogs and look up the opening date of the next summer term of the New School for Social Research in New York.

To demonstrate that students can find out the history of a word and its changing meanings, I have them look up the *Oxford English Dictionary* (call no. at Georgia: Folio/PE/1625/.O87/1989), a massive scholarly etymological work. They must look up the word *humor*, find meaning number II.4, and write down the date when the word first appeared in print with that meaning.

As you might imagine, the student has by now put in considerable mileage in the reference room and should know how to get around in it and how to find a veritable cornucopia of more information.

The student must now go to our library basement, where we keep a number of important sources, including our microfilm collection, our current and microfilmed periodical literature, and the current newspapers from all over the country and the world.

The student must now learn how to find "All the news that's fit to print," in the current and back issues of the *New York Times,* on microfilm. The student must find the *New York Times Index* and record the titles of three recent articles on current New York City crime statistics. This source indexes the *Times* much the same way that the *Readers' Guide* indexes general periodicals—alphabetically by subject matter. A part of a page from that index appears here.

Finally, the student must find the microfilm copy of the *New York Times* published on his or her birth date and record three headlines for other events that occurred that day. Now the student can find and read on a microfilm reader any issue of the *New York Times* and any of a large number of newspapers and magazines stored there on microfilm. (Georgia even has on microfilm all back issues of *Playboy.*)

```
VIOLENCE. See also                          WANG LABORATORIES INC. See also
Assaults                                    Data Processing (Computers), Ag 28
Bombs and Bomb Plots                          Wang Laboratories Inc says Federal District Court
Crime and Criminals                         found two Wang patents valid and that Toshiba
Demonstrations and Riots                    Corporation and NEC Corporation and their US
Murders and Attempted Murders               subsidiaries must pay royalties on infringed products
New York City—Social Conditions and Trends, (S), Ag 16,D,3:1
  Ag 25,31                                  WANNISKI, JUDE. See also
Prisons and Prisoners, Ag 17                Union of Soviet Socialist Republics (USSR), Ag 31
Terrorism                                   WAR AND REVOLUTION. See also
Torture                                     Armament, Defense and Military Forces
VIRGIN ATLANTIC AIRWAYS. See also           Arms Control and Limitation and Disarmament
Airlines and Airplanes, Ag 16               WAR CRIMES AND CRIMINALS. See also
VIRGINIA. See also                          Lebanon, Ag 27
Atomic Energy, Ag 28                        WARD-JACKSON, ADRIAN. See also
Capital Punishment, Ag 23,24                Acquired Immune Deficiency Syndrome (AIDS),
VIRGINIA POWER CO. See also                   Ag 23
Atomic Energy, Ag 28                        WARMUS, CAROLYN. See also
VIRUSES. See also                           Murders and Attempted Murders, Ag 17
Acquired Immune Deficiency Syndrome (AIDS), WARNER-LAMBERT CO. See also
  Ag 20,29,30                               Smoking, Ag 22
Herpes Viruses                              WARNING SYSTEMS. Use Security and Warning
VISAS. See                                  Systems
Immigration and Emigration                  WASHINGTON (DC). See also
Travel and Vacations                        Abortion, Ag 18
VISTA (SARATOGA SPRINGS, NY,                Airlines and Airplanes, Ag 27
DEVELOPMENT). See also                        Washington, DC, buys new office building to house
Housing, Ag 18                              Mayor's office, City Council, other agencies while
VOICE OF AMERICA. See also                  District Building is renovated; building lost bid, under
Union of Soviet Socialist Republics (USSR), Ag 23  contested circumstances, to house National
VOLCANI CENTER (ISRAEL). See also           Aeronautics and Space Administration; photo (S),
Fruit, Ag 31                                  Ag 25,X,13:4
VOLCANOES
```

The student next must journey to the second floor, where we keep our large collection of government documents. He or she must find who publishes the *Monthly Catalogue of U.S. Government Publications* and write it down in the report. Then the student must ask a librarian on that floor what kind of assistance he or she can provide for students interested in such information.

Our library's third floor houses a special collection, including rare books and the Georgia Collection— books about Georgia and Georgians, and *by* Georgians, including past and present telephone directories of all areas of the state. I have the student find one item, explain its presence there, and then find and record the telephone number of Glenn Novak of Carrollton, Georgia.

Finally, the student must find the journal with the call number PN4071/S8, photocopy a page from an issue printed in the past three years, and turn in the copy with the assignment. The journal: *Communication Monographs*, formerly titled *Speech Monographs*, a professional journal of the speech discipline. I also have the student find a professional journal in his or her (proposed) major field and photocopy a cover of one issue to turn in. Some of the titles submitted include *Public Opinion Quarterly, Journal of Broadcasting, Journalism Quarterly, Bulletin of the Atomic Scientists, Business Quarterly, Forest Science, Horticultural Research, Legislative*

Review, Music Review, Poultry Digest, and *The Pharmaceutical Journal.*

Once my students complete this library exercise, I have confidence that they know how and where to find plenty of information for their speeches. If you will take a similar tour of *your* library, I feel sure that you will also become confident about doing research for speeches.

Supporting Material

After you know where and how to look for material for your speech, you might ask, "What *kind* of material do I look for?" Of course, much of your speech will consist of *you*: your ideas, your generalizations, your attitudes, your knowledge, your experiences, and so on. But what kind of material do you want to find through interviews, phone calls, or the library? Most of what you will want we call *supporting material*, specific information that will support (or help to explain or prove) the ideas you will try to put across to your audience. Let us consider the several kinds of supporting materials: facts and figures, examples, comparison and contrast, testimony, repetition and restatement, definition, description, wit and humor, and visual aids.

Facts and Figures

What does the word *fact* mean? Something we consider true? Not exactly. How can we define *truth*? As Edward Bunker once stated, "Facts and truth are often cousins—not brothers." So, how *can* we define *fact* for our purposes here?

When a man learns of a crime after its commission and does not report it, we call him an accessory after the fact. Here *fact* refers to the crime; it means actual occurrence, or existence. And a "statement of fact" is thus a declarative statement that affirms an occurrence or existence. "The world exists in the shape of a spheroid" is a statement of fact. And we call the statement "The moon consists entirely of green cheese" a statement of fact, too, since it asserts a certain kind of existence. Of course, we know that scientific study proves the first statement "true" and the second "false."

Statements of fact used in speeches should as much as possible reflect truth that careful and systematic observation can prove. They should also specify rather than remain general. Rather than saying something like, "Several years ago when I went out West . . . ,' you should say something more like "In August of 1979, when I drove through the Yuma Desert of Arizona . . ."

Figures present facts about number and quantity. Again, you should state your figures as specifically as possible. Instead of "Our trip was really long, and we burned a lot of gasoline," say something like "We drove 5,324 miles on our trip and used 253 gallons of gasoline." Bernard Baruch once said that "Every man has a right to his opinion, but no man has a right to be wrong in his facts."

Good, experienced speakers usually pepper their speeches liberally with specific facts and figures. Such use of factual material convinces audiences and usually causes them to think, "Wow, that speaker really did some homework!"

William L. Winter, executive officer of the American Press Institute, impressed listeners at the National Association of Government Communicators in 1990 with a fact-filled speech thoroughly documenting the economic plight of the modern news media. To make his main point, "The simple fact is that in today's tough economic environment, there is much bad news for the media," Winter provided more than enough factual data for support:

> The newspaper industry is enduring the worst economic period it has seen in many decades. The retail environment, marred by the crash of such giants as the Campeau Corporation and the mergers and acquisitions of the late 1980s that left us with far fewer major retailers and thus far fewer advertisers, has depressed newspaper revenues significantly.
>
> Newspaper circulation continues its very slight climb. But household penetration—that is, the ratio of total households to newspapers sold—is tumbling dramatically. In 1946, there were 130 newspapers sold every day in this country for every 100 households. By 1987 that number had dropped to 69 newspapers for every 100 households. That is the statistic that troubles newspaper executives more than any other. . . .
>
> The number of people who say they read a newspaper daily has dropped from 73 percent in 1979 to less than 55 percent today. . . .
>
> Our nation's illiteracy rate is high, and getting higher. There are about 60 million adults in the United States today who are functionally illiterate—that is, who cannot read at even a ninth-grade level and whose lack of language skills keeps them from functioning effectively in our society.
>
> A study of the American Society of Newspaper Editors suggests that by the year 2000 the United States could have a pool of 90 million citizens whose lack of language skills could render them virtually untrainable.[1]

---

[1] William L. Winter, "Putting the World in Perspective: The Economic and Competitive Environment of the News Media," *Vital Speeches of the Day,* March 15, 1991. Reprinted by permission of Mr. Winter.

On October 4, 1990, Rosalyn Wiggins Berne of the University of Virginia Darden School spoke before the FOCUS group of Women's Week in Charlottesville, Virginia. To prove her point that the current conditions for women in America differ radically from those in our immediate past, she used the latest statistics then available to her:

The number of working women with children under age one increased 70 percent during the past decade. Seventy-three percent of employed women are of child-rearing age, and women with children under six are the fastest growing segment of the work force. The number of divorced, widowed, or separated working women with children under eighteen years of age increased 76 percent between 1971 and 1982. In 1984, 11 million men and 6 million women were the only wage earners in their families. Among all American families, nearly 1 out of 5 is maintained by a woman, with one-third of them having incomes below the poverty line. Today, fewer that 9.9 percent of U.S. households consist of a man working outside the home and a woman at home taking care of the household and children.

This is the reality, but it is also a reality that women have greater opportunities than ever before for achieving economic and professional success.[2]

We generally call the kind of numerical data presented by Berne *statistics*. And when considering statistics, we must remember Benjamin Disraeli's complaint: "There are three kinds of lies; lies, damned lies, and statistics." Of course, many find it easy to lie with statistics. Too many people gullibly swallow any "factual" material presented in statistical form because it sounds so "scientific."

Bosh. Before accepting statistics as "truth," do a little poking. To come up with a statistic, someone must count something in some way. Find out who did the counting and how he or she did it. Suppose I told you that I took a poll here on campus and found that two-thirds of the students I questioned thought that the U.S. should double its income tax rate. You would probably ask me whom I polled, right? I reply, "I asked the first three people who walked out of the International Student Service Office, and two out of three I asked said they favored the idea."

Examples

Did you ever sit, listening to a speech or lecture on some complex and abstract phenomenon, your brow knit in concentration as you strained to follow the speaker's ideas? And then the speaker said something

[2]Rosalyn Wiggins Berne, "Keeping Our Balance in the 90s: Women at Work, Women at Home," *Vital Speeches of the Day*, November 1, 1990, p. 56. Reprinted by permission of Ms. Berne.

like, "Let me give you an example. Just three years ago right here in this very town . . ." Ah! Then you could sit back, smile, unknit your brow, nod, and think, "OK. Now I see." Examples can evoke this sort of response. As columnist Jenkin Lloyd Jones has said,

> Skilled speakers go easy on abstractions and heavy on specific example. Unless an audience is constantly dragged back to a world it knows and understands it will drift off. Jesus understood the power of parable, and Abe Lincoln often made a political point leap to life by beginning, "There was an old farmer down in Sangamon County . . ."[3]

Like many writers, I distinguish between two kinds of examples: *illustrations*—the longer, narrative stories that make the speaker or writer's point concretely—and *specific instances*—brief, self-explanatory or instantly recognizable examples.

I find illustrations useful in my speeches and class lectures (even my students seem to appreciate some of them). One of my favorites:

> During the summer of 1979 my wife and I camped on the south rim of the Grand Canyon. We decided to spend some time on the shuttle bus that circles the rim; it stops at each scenic overlook where tourists can board or debark and spend as much time as they like. After one such stop the hefty female driver said over the loudspeaker, "Will everyone please get their arms inside the bus so we can proceed?" Nothing happened. She raised the volume: "We can't proceed until *everyone* gets their arms inside the bus!" We did not move. Now she grew angry: "Would the young man in the back *please* get his arm inside the bus!" All eyes turned to the college-age man on the port side with his arm and even his shoulder and head out the window. He did not move. Face red and eyes ablaze, the beefy driver slammed down the mike and stomped toward the rear of the bus, fists clenched. As she heaved to near the young man, he turned to her, smiling, and withdrew a 3 x 5 card from his pocket and displayed it to her. It read: "Hello. I am German; sorry, but I speak no English."

I naturally use this story to illustrate that we often misunderstand people's behavior and that it pays to pause, to reflect, to look before you leap.

The story of the young German can be called a literal or factual example: it actually happened. But sometimes you can make your point by using an illustration that could happen, or could have happened. Such a hypothetical illustration can clarify a problem or event we might otherwise find difficult to comprehend. For instance, several years ago an ex-Washington bureaucrat noted that the gov-

[3]Jenkin Lloyd Jones, "Short Course in Public Speaking," *Greenville* (NC) *News*, November 28, 1970. Quoted by permission of Mr. Jones.

ernment usually tries, unsuccessfully, to solve social problems with money. He used a hypothetical illustration, which I paraphrase:

You set up a new bureau in Washington to get cigarette smokers to quit smoking. We do it with money, so: suppose we offer, to anyone who quits, a cool ten thousand bucks. That ought to do the trick with some!

So what happens? Anyone who would like to pick up a quick ten grand takes up the smoking habit for a while, then quits, and claims his money. Voila! Our quit-smoking campaign has promoted cigarette-smoking!

OK, that didn't work. So we change the rules. Now, in order to collect the ten big ones, you have to prove you have smoked coffin nails for, say, four years! Who would take up a dangerous, filthy habit for four years just for money?

Smart thirteen-year-old kids on the wrong side of the poverty line look ahead and see they will never have the money to make it to college even if they can stick it out four years in high school. But ten grand would make a great start toward the tuition gap. So the junior-high kids take up puffing nicotine to guarantee their college education. Our antismoking campaign has created a generation of urchin smokers!

Because illustrations, either factual or hypothetical, explain issues in such a down-to-earth, realistic, flesh-and-blood manner, no wonder so many speech experts consider them probably the most potent form of support with a general audience. You need look no further for proof of illustration's perceived persuasive impact than the evening news. The public may have difficulty fathoming the recession that plagues the country; but when the TV news crew interviews a forty-three-year-old father of three, unemployed for fourteen months since losing his $55,000-a-year job as an engineer, our economic plight becomes starkly believable. Look for good illustrations to highlight each of your speeches.

Whereas an illustration might be sufficient standing alone, specific instances work better when presented in groups, for a cumulative effect.

My late friend Laurence J. Peter invented the Peter Principle, which asserts that an employee in a hierarchy will rise to the level of his own incompetence; that is, he will eventually get promoted or succeed to a higher position with duties or responsibilities quite beyond his abilities. To explain and prove his point, Peter cited ten specific instances:

Socrates: A competent teacher who reached his level of incompetence when he became his own defense attorney.

Julius Caesar: One of the greatest generals of all time, who was too trusting in his relationships with politicians.

Nero: A competent fiddler who achieved his level of incompetence as an administrator.

Alexander Hamilton: A brilliant scholar and financier—although at one time he was jealous of the combat record of his former law partner, Aaron Burr, he later challenged him to a duel.

Benedict Arnold: When his courage and competence as a patriotic officer were not appreciated, he reached his level of ineptitude by shifting allegiance to the British.

Ulysses S. Grant: Victorious U.S. general of the Union forces in the Civil War, he served two scandal-ridden presidential terms.

Gen. George Armstrong Custer: Flamboyant glory-seeker who achieved his level of incapacity when he attempted to wipe out an Indian encampment at the Little Bighorn.

Warren G. Harding: A newspaper publisher who became president of the U.S. and gave dirty politics a bad name by surrounding himself with some of the most dishonest and corrupt chiselers of all time.

Adolf Hitler: The consummate politician who found his level of incompetence as a generalissimo.

Richard M. Nixon: Author of a successful book, *Six Crises,* was later unable to communicate convincingly a simple message such as "I am not a crook."[4]

See how hard-hitting a string of specific instances can seem? You may find such strings or lists difficult to come by, but your search may pay off handsomely. Of course, your specific instances must appear to the audience as either instantly recognizable or self-explanatory, since they represent a kind of shorthand; if not, you need to convert them into stories—into illustrations.

I have judged a number of public-speaking contests sponsored by civic organizations. I remember once voting to award first place to a

[4]Adapted from David Wallechinsky, Irving Wallace, and Amy Wallace, *The Book of Lists* (New York: Bantam Books, 1977), pp. 14–15. Reprinted by permission of William Morrow Publishing.

young man whose speech made a single point: that success does not depend exclusively on a college education. His speech comprised his main point, reiterated several times, and a string of examples—men and women who reached prominence in business, industry, government, and the arts, without having even attended college.

Comparison and Contrast

Speakers and writers use comparisons to show similarities; they use contrast to emphasize differences.

Comparisons generally serve one of three purposes: to make meaningful something relatively meaningless; to explain something unknown in terms of something known; or to explain something new and therefore "suspect" in terms of something old and "acceptable."

For instance, consider the term *one billion dollars*. Can you actually conceive of such a sum? Of course, you "know" that a billion dollars equals 1,000 times a million, and half of *two* billion dollars. But how really *meaningful* can "one billion dollars" seem to you? After all, you and I have experience dealing with a few bucks at a time; we do not receive and pay out dollars by the billions. (Perhaps this reasoning influenced a former secretary of defense to say that "It's difficult to spend a billion dollars and get your money's worth.")

To make this huge sum more meaningful, let's compare it to amounts that we can more nearly comprehend. Suppose we had $1 billion to spend and that we decide to spend $100 per minute, 60 minutes per hour, 24 hours per day (without stopping to eat, sleep, or go to the bathroom). How long would our bankroll last at this rate of spending? For just a little over nineteen years.

A microbiology major in my speech class once spoke about the electron microscope housed in his department. In order to emphasize the fact that many, many microscopic organisms inhabit each human, he pointed out that "Each of you has a greater number of separate, living creatures on and inside your body than all the human beings that have ever lived." His comparison made his fact so real that many in the audience felt like squirming and scratching.

People seem suspicious of new and untested ideas, but the realization that a new proposal differs little from an old and accepted approach soothes and reassures. For instance, the American populace became edgy in 1990–91 as the U.S. and "coalition" military buildup began after Iraq's invasion of Kuwait. Fear that huge numbers of American casualties would result from a ground war with

Iraq made some Americans squeamish. But our leaders' (and media's) constant comparison of Iraq's Saddam Hussein to Adolf Hitler, as a war-mongering, potential conqueror of the world "who must be stopped" helped rally public opinion behind what eventually became Desert Storm.

In the 1960s American students staged demonstrations on college campuses across the nation. These protests, some of which produced violence and counterviolence, deeply disturbed many people, who asked themselves, "How can students so violate their traditional roles as peaceful, thoughtful, passive, empty vessels needing fill-ups of knowledge?" Such people lacked awareness of the history of student protest: they did not know that in 1811 a riot at Columbia University resulted in the students taking over the church in which Columbia had scheduled commencement. They did not know that in 1807 Princeton had suspended half the student body for misbehavior, or that general riots had become a standard for the times at the University of Virginia in 1827. Student riots and protests of the 1960s may have disturbed many people, but not because of their historical novelty.

Contrast, as mentioned earlier, points out differences; its use can achieve striking results. Janet Martin, vice-president of a large Canadian bank, speaking before the North Toronto Business and Professional Women's Club, used contrast to emphasize the strides that women had made in marketplace employment:

> The 1970 undergraduate class at the University of Toronto's faculty included 33 women—just slightly over 1 percent of the students. In the 1990 class, there were 465 women, or almost 17 percent. . . . within the banking industry . . . women make up the majority of the industry's work force. Three out of every four bank employees are female. And almost half, or 48 percent, of middle and upper management positions are occupied by women. This is an improvement from four years ago when only 39 percent were managers.[5]

Testimony

When you think people won't believe you, you borrow the words of someone who agrees with you—someone your audience will believe. Canada's associate minister of national defence Mary Collins used the words of FDR when she wanted to impress on her American audience the solemnity of the 200th anniversary of the Bill of Rights:

[5]Janet Martin, "Room at the Top," *Vital Speeches of the Day*, LVII, #11, March 15, 1992. Reprinted by permission of *Vital Speeches*.

Fifty years ago, when he established a national Bill of Rights Day, President Franklin D. Roosevelt reminded Americans, and the world, of the cost of the rights and freedoms being celebrated. "Those who have long enjoyed such privileges as we enjoy," he said, "forget in time that men have died to win them."[6]

Everyone has used testimony for "proof" at one time or another, whether in a scholarly term paper in school or in a knock-down, drag-out argument like "OK, if you don't believe me, just ask (choose one: my Dad; my teacher; Mr. Jones next door; my Grandma; my boss; my big sister)!" But testimony has two other uses as well. You can use it to simplify complicated, technical points or to spice up your speech with quotations.

In 1955 college debaters argued about whether we should stop nuclear testing in the atmosphere. The affirmative debaters argued that radiation in the atmosphere from atom bomb testing could endanger humans. To prove such danger would involve using a wealth of complicated, technical data. To save time the debaters simply quoted experts in the nuclear field who claimed that radiation levels soon would become intolerable to humans. As I write this, proponents of the Star Wars antiballistic missile system proposed by the Pentagon argue that the system will work; as proof they simply cite the recent success of U.S. Patriot missiles against Iraq's SCUD missiles.

Many skilled speakers use quotations to brighten and spice up their speeches. An apt quotation that says just what you wish you had said, and in a manner you would never have thought of, delights your audience and marks you as a literate and sensitive human being. So you should have at your elbow when working on your speech at least one book—or better, several books—containing apt quotations. Many such books list snatches of poetry and condensed wisdom alphabetically by subject matter. You can find just what you want quite easily.

Suppose you decide to develop a speech on "friendship." In my own library you could find many apt quotes to flesh out that speech. You could open to "Friendship/Friends" in my *Peter's Quotations*, by Laurence J. Peter, and find a number of pithy remarks:

> True friendship comes when silence between two people is comfortable.
> —*Dave Tyson Gentry*

[6]Mary Collins, "The Responsibilities of the New World Order," *Vital Speeches of the Day*, LVII, #15, May 15, 1991. Reprinted by permission of *Vital Speeches*.

You can always tell a real friend; when you've made a fool of yourself he doesn't feel you've done a permanent job.
—*Laurence J. Peter*

Instead of loving your enemies, treat your friends a little better.
—*Ed Howe*

True friendship is like sound health, the value of it seldom known until it be lost.
—*Charles Caleb Colton*

The Great Quotations, compiled by George Seldes, offers an anonymous Near East proverb:

A friend is one who warns you.

My dog-eared old paperback copy of *Best Quotations for All Occasions*, edited by Lewis C. Henry, offers:

Be slow to fall into friendship, but when thou art in, continue firm and constant.
—*Socrates*

Among nearly four pages of quotes, editor Edward F. Murphy, in his *Crown Treasury of Relevant Quotations*, includes these:

Friendship with oneself is all-important, because without it one cannot be friends with anyone else in the world.
—*Eleanor Roosevelt*

The reward of friendship is itself. The man who hopes for anything else does not understand what true friendship is.
—*Saint Ailred of Rievaulx*

Books of quotations such as these pay back the writer and speaker far more than their modest monetary cost. Take advantage of them, and your speeches will sparkle with glints of wisdom, wit, and charm. (For additional sources to enhance your speeches, consult my article "Snappy Sources Shape Spicy Speeches," in *The Toastmaster*, January 1989.)

Repetition and Restatement

You may have never considered repetition or restatement as a form of supporting material, but it remains undeniable that reiteration to the point of redundant overkill can successfully plant ideas into listeners' heads. Advertisers certainly use it, don't they? Advertising copywriters condense a sales pitch into a simple, compelling idea, called a unique selling proposition, and then assault our senses with it over and over again. Who can forget which beer engenders the argument, "Less filling!/Tastes great!" Doesn't every American know which diet cola has "Uh Huh!," which cigarette the ads proclaim as "springtime fresh," or which automobile reflects "The Heartbeat of America"?

Because repetition and restatement *do* work so well, you should repeat and restate the main points of your speech (the ones you want your audience to remember) as often as you can without sounding utterly monotonous. And repeating a catchy phrase that encapsulates your message can produce fantastic results. We remember the most vivid of Martin Luther King, Jr.'s speeches by its title and its ringing, oft-repeated phrase, "I Have a Dream." Marc Antony's emotional funeral oration over the body of Julius Caesar raised the mob to fury and mutiny partly from his increasingly ironical use of "And they [Caesar's murderers] are honorable men." Thirty years ago a young woman in my class gave a speech complaining that we adults overorganize the lives of our children, never allowing them to just act like kids. She called her speech "The Plot Against Childhood," and repeated the title at appropriate places throughout the speech. The phrase and the speech remain memorable for me to this day, a full generation later.

Reiteration works. It does. It certainly does. Use it. Use it often.

Definition

"Definition" may also seem misplaced in the category of supporting material, but speakers and writers often use definition in arguing or explaining. Consider the term *patriotism*. Look how others have used it as argument, both positive and negative:

> To love is . . . the real duty of patriotism, whereas, in the mouths of many of its noisiest professors, the point would rather seem to be to hate.
> —*John Ayscough*

> A real patriot is the fellow who gets a parking ticket and rejoices that the system works.
> —*Bill Vaughan*

> There's one beneficial effect of going to Moscow. You come
> home waving the American flag with all your might!
> —*Mary Tyler Moore*

Defining can serve other purposes than persuasion. It might help
your audience to understand. As Joseph H. Odell wrote in his
Unmailed Letters:

> Few of us pause for definition even in our most serious discussions, and
> when we do we are amazed, not that there is so much bitter misunderstanding
> and acrimony in life, but that there is so little.

Description

Description might also not seem much like a supporting material, but
it may powerfully bolster a particular point after all the other kinds
of support have been tried and have failed.

For instance, take the idea of "driving safely." How many times
have we read the statistics on death and injury on our highways?
How many slogans have been tried ("Arrive alive"; "Drive defen-
sively"; "Watch out for the other guy"; "Slow down and live"; "The
life you save may be your own"; and so on) with little effect? We
simply listen, ignore, then go on our merry way slaughtering and
maiming thousands on our highways each year. But law enforcement
officials have had such great success with an article first published in
Reader's Digest in 1935 that they've handed out more than 5 million
reprints. Why? Because they believe the article scares speeders and
other reckless drivers into taking more care on our highways.

Reader's Digest reprinted the article in a collection in 1940 and in
the magazine again in October 1966. What makes up the article's
supporting materials? Almost nothing but pure description of what
happens when people combine high speed with poor driving judgment. I won't risk upsetting your stomach by quoting the descrip-
tions of the car crashes contained in that article. It was written by
J. W. Furnas; look it up for yourself if you dare.

I do offer a milder descriptive and persuasive passage: an award-
winning radio commercial. A man speaks these words with a firm,
authoritative voice while, in the background, we hear the loud, raspy
gasping of a person struggling to breathe.

> Every day you inhale fifteen thousand quarts of air—all of it polluted. This
> polluted air contains: sulfur dioxide, a chemical linked with chronic bronchitis;

carbon monoxide, which, in sufficient quantities, will kill you; acrolein, a chemical used in tear gas in World War I; benzopyrene, which has produced cancer on the skin of mice. Our polluted air also contains unconscionable amounts of dirt and soot. It comes to the point where either you do something about air pollution, or air pollution may do something to you.

If you've had your fill of polluted air, send your name to Citizens for Clean Air, Box One Million, Grand Central Station, New York.

Wit and Humor

Researchers have conducted a number of empirical studies to determine whether wit and humor serve as support in otherwise straightforward speeches to inform or persuade. My book *Understanding Laughter* discusses many of these studies (out of print; try your library or interlibrary loan). I summarize the findings of these studies here.

1. Adding humor to a persuasive speech has not been found to affect persuasion one way or the other, unless audiences perceive the humor as inappropriate to the subject matter or as offensive (for example, sick humor). If offensive, humor detracts from effectiveness.

2. Appropriate humor used in speeches to inform rarely helps an audience learn material in the speech but it probably makes the audience like the speaker more. This greater liking could enhance the speaker's credibility and therefore his or her persuasiveness.

3. The addition of sarcastic or satiric wit to an otherwise straightforward persuasive speech does not noticeably enhance or detract from the speech's persuasiveness.

4. "Straight" satiric messages, such as those by Art Buchwald, Art Hoppe, or Russell Baker, can change attitudes (persuade), but only if the audience understands or catches on to the **serious** points intended by the author. Variables such as ego involvement with the topic and the topic's importance to the audience complicate the persuasive effect of satire. Considerable evidence indicates that many people might enjoy satire but still not understand the serious theses intended by the authors.

5. The use of mildly self-deprecating humor can enhance a

speaker's image without damaging his or her general credibility. Such humor must remain mild, however, and audiences must perceive it more as "wit" than the more earthy "humor."

6. Speakers who attempt humor but elicit no laughter suffer lower credibility ratings than if the jokes had gotten laughs.

In short, the evidence suggests that most speakers would do well to leave humor out of their speeches unless they intend purely to entertain an audience (see Chapter 10) or else have enough experience to know how to use humor really well. At any rate, the speaker should serve up humor sparingly. (For another, more detailed discussion of this topic, see "Advice to the Beginning Speaker on Using Humor—What the Research Tells Us," *Communication Education,* 34, April,1985, 140–144.)

Figure 1

Visual Aids

Adding visual aids to your speech can help make your points clearer, more vivid, or more persuasive. A picture may or may not be worth a thousand words (it depends on the picture and the words), but if visual aids can help your audience "see" your points better, by all means use them. Figure 1 shows a speaker explaining the structure and workings of the human larynx, using a large-scale model of the human

Figure 2

voice box to make understanding easier. Figure 2 shows another speaker demonstrating his point with a handmade poster. Such visuals, premade at home, usually prove superior to attempts to reproduce visuals at the chalkboard as one speaks. Such aids look better, and the speaker can use them while facing the audience.

Figures 3 through 7 show some other types of visual aids you might use to give your speech a professional look. Figure 3 shows an exploded drawing, excellent for demonstrating how a mechanical device fits together and operates. Figure 4 shows two circle graphs, or pie charts, useful for presenting percentage data. Figure 5 presents a

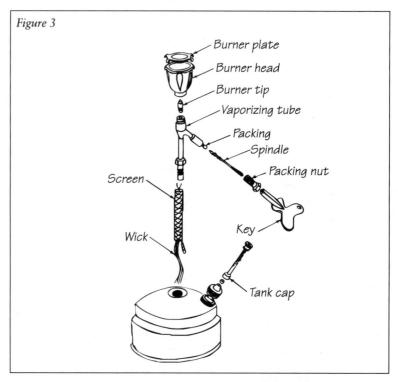

Figure 3

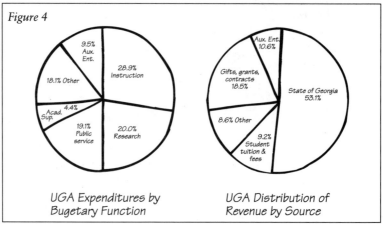

Figure 4

UGA Expenditures by
Bugetary Function

UGA Distribution of
Revenue by Source

bar graph, excellent for showing relative amounts or rates. And Figure 6 shows a multiple-line graph, a fine method of comparing and contrasting two or more trends (but not too many, please!). Figure 7 represents a good example of the cutaway drawing, highly effective for showing the inside workings of mechanical systems.

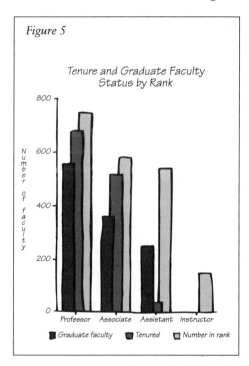

Figure 5

Tenure and Graduate Faculty Status by Rank

Number of faculty

Professor Associate Assistant Instructor

◼ Graduate faculty   ◼ Tenured   ◻ Number in rank

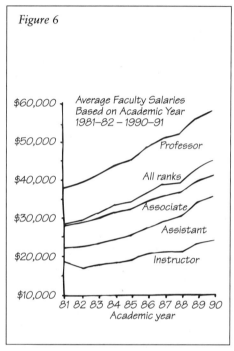

Figure 6

Average Faculty Salaries Based on Academic Year 1981–82 – 1990–91

Professor

All ranks

Associate

Assistant

Instructor

81 82 83 84 85 86 87 88 89 90
Academic year

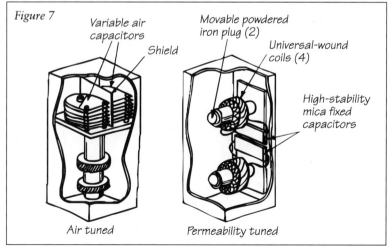

Figure 7

Variable air capacitors

Shield

Movable powdered iron plug (2)

Universal-wound coils (4)

High-stability mica fixed capacitors

Air tuned

Permeability tuned

*E*quipment that does not work on cue frustrates student speakers and their audiences: speakers discover that the electrical outlets they planned to use are inoperative; brilliant, creative posters made at home don't show up well from more than five feet away...

Although well-chosen visual aids can produce a veritable blockbuster of a speech, their ineffective use can turn a fair speech into a fiasco. Over my years as a professor, I have witnessed hundreds of student speeches, many greatly enhanced with visuals. But I have also seen dozens of speeches ruined by the inept use of visual aids. Equipment that does not work on cue frustrates student speakers and their audiences: speakers discover that the electrical outlets they planned to use are inoperative; brilliant, creative posters made at home don't show up well from more than five feet away; projectors jam or their bulbs burn out at crucial moments; electrical cords turn out too short to reach an outlet across the room; demonstration materials slip and fall from the sweaty hands of the fearful; speakers suddenly discover that, with a projector on and the lights out, they can't read their notes; trembling beginners spill liquid and granular material, creating guilt, embarrassment, and a mess for the next speaker; posters rolled up into a tube for transport refuse to straighten out and stand up for viewing; audiences cannot hear the speaker's voice over the whirring motor of the slide projector; speakers remove borrowed equipment from its case only to find a model they have never seen before; speakers find that two inches of cellophane tape will not secure a heavy poster to a dusty chalkboard. And so on. Can you believe all this? Well, I have witnessed all these disasters. Therefore, I propose the following list of dos and don'ts.

1. Make posters, drawings, lettering, and so on large and dark enough for even people in the back of the room to see. Check it out. Set it up thirty or forty feet away; can you see it plainly?

2. Keep visuals simple. The audience cannot comprehend anything too complex, and a "busy" visual will distract. Each person in the audience might look at a different part of the

complicated chaos, whereas you want them all to attend to the same point at the same time. That's why you speak and they listen.

3. Remember, the audience should see the visual aid; you should look at it as little as possible. Look at the audience.

4. Fight your nervous urge to "play with" any visual aid you may have in your hands. Show it, then set it down or hide it behind the lectern or under the table. Don't threaten to skewer people in the front row with a pointer as you fence with the air, and don't use the pointer for extra calisthenic exercises as you speak.

5. Use visual aids only when necessary. Keep them out of sight; bring them out to use them, then get them out of sight again.

6. Rehearse your speech with all your visuals and props. Make sure you know how to use them. If possible, rehearse with them in the room in which you will speak.

7. Don't allow a projector to defeat you. Each has a noisy motor to cool the bulb. You must speak over that noise, so practice doing that. To make yourself, not the projector, dominate the scene, darken the room only halfway and stand up front; use a remote-control switch on a long cord for your slide projector, or use a friend as your projectionist. Make sure you have enough light to see your notes, or provide your own light. Make sure you have a spare projector bulb in case one burns out.

8. Keep the audience's attention focused on you and your point. This means, for instance, not passing things around the audience, which creates a buzzing bunch of individuals with numerous foci of attention. A single handout for each member of the audience works OK, however. For instance, I once had a student who handed out identical copies of U.S. Army maps of Vietnam and used them to explain how a forward observer could direct artillery fire on the enemy by map quadrant.

You should not drag in visual aids simply to have them. Some speeches probably cannot profit enough from the use of visuals to make up for the time, effort, and expense they might create. On the other hand, some concepts absolutely require some visual representation for accurate communication. Use your own good sense, and maybe even ask for some advice from time to time. And when you do choose to use visual aids, nothing works so well as preparation, preparation, and preparation.

5
ORGANIZING YOUR SPEECH

uiz time: What do a successful business venture, an effective political election campaign, and a good speech have in common? Answer: Good organization. You need to organize your speeches well—for three reasons.

First, as I noted in Chapter 3, you can remember your speech much better when you have organized it well. In addition, your audience will remember your speech when you organize it well—and they must remember the speech if you want them to act on it.

Second, audiences appreciate the logical order in a well-organized speech. If your listeners can follow from point to point, seeing that B follows A and that C follows B in logical progression—and if they can deduce the total pattern of your thoughts—then they will appreciate your speech aesthetically. After all, most people have sat through many a miserably organized, hard-to-follow speech. Give them one they can comprehend without effort and they will applaud both themselves and you for it.

The third and most important reason for good speech organization is that it will help ensure your speech's effectiveness.

What do I mean by "effectiveness"? You will remember from Chapter 2 that each speech should have one clear-cut purpose and that to accomplish that single purpose the speaker will usually emphasize just two or three main points or ideas. Proper organization presents those two or three main points in memorable order and should also repeat those main points often enough to reinforce their retention. I cannot stress the importance of this point enough. People cannot learn and remember a great deal of material from a speech. If you make a speech whose success depends on the audience's learning seventeen specific facts, the speech will fail. But if all your organization and presentation of details help the audience remember the two or three generalizations (your main points) they must remember for the speech to produce results, your chances for success dramatically increase.

To help the audience remember those two or three generalizations, you should organize your speech according to the partitioning pattern. Let's look at that pattern, first in the abstract, then as applied to some topics.

The Introduction

You can begin your speech in one of many ways: establishing rapport with the audience through reference to them, the occasion, or yourself; giving a personal greeting; defining some key term in your speech; explaining why you chose your title; referring to a previous speaker; presenting a brief history of the topic; telling an anecdote, humorous or otherwise, that illustrates your central theme; narrating a dramatic incident; or quoting from a newspaper, magazine, book, or poem. No doubt many more ways exist.

However, any speech introduction should accomplish two objectives: (1) to tell your audience why you wish to speak to them on *this topic*; (2) to reveal to them your specific purpose.

In revealing your specific purpose you ought to go one step further and relate the main points you will make in your speech. In other words, your introduction should lay out the main organizational pattern of the speech so that your audience can begin to know what you have in mind. In abstract outline form, then, your introduction should look like this:

Rationale: I find it a pleasure to stand here today. I have chosen to speak to you today on ——— because ———.

Thesis: I decided to speak on this topic today because I hope to (inform/convince/motivate) you that/to ———.

Partitioning: In order to do this, I will present three major ideas.

My first point will concern . . .

My second point will involve the idea of . . .

And my third point will show that . . .

This kind of introduction provides your audience with an initial motivation to listen carefully and reveals your game plan.

Of course, sometimes you will not want to reveal your exact thesis or main points, such as when you speak on a controversial topic that might provoke hostility in your audience. Suppose, for instance, I began a speech this way:

I believe you will agree that tonight I speak on a topic absolutely vital to every man, woman, and child in this country—because it touches the pocketbooks of each and every one of us.

For tonight, I intend to convince you that the United States should impose an additional tax of one dollar on each gallon of gasoline sold at the pump. In order to do this I will present three main arguments:

First, I will enumerate a number of compelling reasons concerning our gasoline supply, demand, and possible replacement with alternative fuels.

Second, I will prove that a one-dollar-a-gallon rise in taxes will solve a number of our national financial problems.

And finally, I will show that the one-dollar-a-gallon tax will prove more feasible than any other solution to our gasoline supply/financial morass.

What would happen? All those opposed to the tax (probably the vast majority) would begin mentally arguing with me the minute I finished stating my purpose. Their attitude? "All right, Buster, you just *try* and convince me of that nonsense!" In Chapter 9 we will take up the proper way to introduce such a volatile topic. For now, suffice it to say that for the vast majority of your speeches you should begin with the rationale for the topic, the thesis statement, and the partitioning of that thesis into its main points before you go on into the body of the speech itself. Follow the example of John B. Donovan, president of Donovan Public Affairs, speaking to the Westchester County Chamber of Commerce in White Plains, New York:

Good evening. This is an exciting event. It's a great way for businesspeople to get together and to do the activity that will lead to their success—communicating directly with their prospects.

An expo like this is a comparatively new way of communicating. I want to share with you some information about certain forms of communication that many of you haven't considered yet. You haven't considered them either because you haven't been forced to consider them or because you're supposed to have a certain gift for them. *I'm talking about public speaking in its various forms, including first, going on television; second, making a speech; and third, making a presentation.* [Italics mine]

Let's look at the television variety first. The single most . . .[1]

The Body

The body of your speech contains the meat of your presentation. Here you present your main points, along with the supporting material for each, and in the prearranged order you have chosen. Repeat and restate each main point as often as possible without excessive redundancy. For instance:

You remember from my introduction that my first point today concerns the fact of the overcrowding and underfinancing of our schools. Now, why do I call our schools overcrowded? Just let me quote some comparative figures. . . .

So, I think you see now the serious problem of school overcrowding, even when considering the most conservative of figures and future estimates. But can

[1]John B. Donovan, "Power to the Podium," *Vital Speeches of the Day,* LVII, December 15, 1991. Reprinted by permission of *Vital Speeches.*

I prove that our schools remain underfinanced as well? I think so. Let me quote from the report on . . .

This speech, when fleshed out, should establish the first main point of the speech. To help the audience follow your line of thought, you need to include a smooth *transition* to your next point.

Why use transitions? Because audience members appreciate them and because the audience enjoys the "shifting of gears" you provide for them. You warn them, through a transition, that you have finished one segment of the speech and plan to start the next.

We become accustomed to these little gear-shifting signs through our reading. As we read, we see that chapter headings, centered or side headings, boldface paragraph heads, and even the beginning of new paragraphs with their indented first line all indicate a shift of emphasis or direction. Because these visual signs do not appear in a speech, the speaker must provide them verbally, in the form of transitions.

> *To help the audience follow your line of thought, you need to include a smooth transition to your next point.*

An effective transition accomplishes two purposes: it summarizes the previous main point and forecasts the next, such as:

So, now you can understand about the overcrowding and underfinancing of our schools. The dual nature of too little space and not enough money makes a tough problem out of it. And this brings me to my second point: that we can solve both these problems with a modest adjustment in our millage rate. Why, if we would raise our rates by only one mil, it would mean that . . .

Your last transition could summarize all previous main points and then forecast the last one:

OK, you agree on the overcrowding and underfinancing of our schools. I hope you also agree now that a one-mil rise in taxes will relieve the problem greatly. Now let's go on to explore the question, "Do we find the tax hike *the* most advantageous and practical solution?" Well, I think I can show you that the tax hike *will* prove the most advantageous and practical solution; and I have three reasons for believing that . . .

The Conclusion

Your conclusion should, at the very least, accomplish two goals: summarize the main points (again!) and restate your purpose or goal.

I hope that tonight I have convinced you of the overcrowding and underfinancing problem of our schools; that a one-mil raise in taxation will solve this dual problem; and that we can find no solution more practical and advantageous than this one.

Therefore I again ask for your support of the school board in raising our school taxes by one mil.

Besides performing the necessary duties—summarizing the main points again and restating the thesis—the conclusion might also include other material. Several techniques exist for rounding out the speech on a high note. These include a prediction of what the future might hold, a factual or hypothetical illustration embodying the thesis of your speech, a wise or pithy saying, a vivid quotation, a call to action, a statement of your own personal intent, or a challenge to the audience ("Have you the courage to stand up and lay your name on the line with me?").

> *When you begin that final summary, the audience will say to itself, "Ah, here's the windup."*

In summary, the partitioning pattern I strongly recommend here gives the audience a rationale for listening to the speech; reveals your purpose and your main points for achieving that purpose; presents each main point in a logical sequence, bolstered with appropriate supporting material; separates the main ideas and reinforces them with sound transitions; and summarizes again the main points and restates the thesis in the conclusion. And when you begin that final summary, the audience will say to itself, "Ah, here's the windup."

Once you have restated your thesis after the summary, and perhaps after you have rounded it off with one of the above techniques, you should speak your last words with a downward inflection of finality, then stop. Everyone will know that you have ended the speech; you will not have to clue them in with some tired cliché such as "Thank you."

The rural preacher in an old story must have favored this partitioning pattern. His flock had no difficulty at all in following the folksy sermons he dispatched every Sunday. One Sunday morning a parishioner asked the gentleman, "Parson, your sermons always sound so organized! Tell me your secret." The preacher obliged. "Well, first I tell 'em what I'm gonna tell 'em. Then I tell 'em. Then I tell 'em what I done told 'em."

If you will do the same, you can't go very far wrong—at least in terms of organization.

Arranging Main Ideas

You can choose from a variety of ways to arrange main ideas. Sometimes the topic itself will suggest the arrangement, other times not.

Almost any informative speech of a how-to-do-it, or *process,* nature will suggest that you use a *chronological* order. You simply arrange main ideas in the order in which they occur

Purpose: To inform the audience about how to secure a passport.

Main points:

   I. Obtain a certified birth certificate from your county clerk.
   II. Find a qualified photographer and get two duplicate photos of yourself made.
   III. Get a passport application from one of several places that supply them, such as a U.S. Post Office.
   IV. Send the completed application, the birth certificate, and the photos, with a check for $55, to the address provided on the application form.

Other topics adapt well to an ordering by *size.* For example, in discussing the four poisonous species of snakes in the United States, you might begin with the species most prevalent in the country and end with the one least prevalent, or vice versa.

Still other topics might fit some sort of *spatial* or *geographical* order. For instance, you might divide a topic such as "The House I Hope to Build Someday" this way:

   I. The general living area
   II. The bedroom wing
   III. The working space
   IV. The grounds

Any number of speech topics fit into some sort of *causal* pattern. Such a pattern would include both causes and effects; you might begin with the cause of a phenomenon, then discuss its effects. Or you could reverse the order and speak of the effects, then the causes.

The *problem/solution* order lends itself in an almost lawlike manner to any topic involving the solution of a problem. The arrangement for such a speech inherently involves the discussing and answering of three questions, in chronological order:

I. Just what, if any, problem exists?
II. What solution(s) can solve the problem?
III. Will the solution we choose solve the problem in the most practical, efficient manner?

You will read more about this arrangement in Chapter 9, when we will add "arousal" to make it the Problem/Solution/Arousal (PSA) plan for persuasion.

A more-or-less miscellaneous order exists for your use when no other seems to fit your subject matter: we call it *topical*. It involves simply dividing your subject into logical categories, or topics. For instance, when speaking to various groups about humor, I have used the following topical order:

I. Slapstick or physical humor
II. Verbal jokes and wisecracks (including one-liners)
III. Puns and other verbal witticisms

The Outline

Let us look at a few rules you should follow in constructing your outline, then I will present a model outline that follows these rules— a model that you would do well to emulate in your own efforts.

1. At the top of your outline you should write down your speech's purpose, or the goal you hope to achieve, in terms of what response you want to get from your audience (remember step 2 from Chapter 2):

The purpose of my speech: to get the audience to agree to my plan.

2. You should divide your outline, like your speech, into three parts: the introduction, the body, and the conclusion. Begin with the body first, and divide it into the main ideas you will need to get across in order to achieve your purpose or goal (step 3 from Chapter 2). State these main ideas in complete, usually simple, sentences, usually with an active verb. Word these main ideas (like all ideas stated in the outline) as you would say them to an audience (not as notes to yourself). Make your main ideas simple, logical divisions of your

purpose; they should reflect back a simple, consistent, unified thought pattern. In fact, check to see that the set of main ideas, if accepted or understood by your audience, will result in successful achievement of your purpose. For example:

I. My plan will benefit workers.
II. My plan will benefit management.
III. My plan will benefit consumers.

(Note that Roman numerals denote main ideas.)

3. As you divide your main ideas into subordinate ideas, indicate them with capital letters, and use complete, simple sentences for these points. Show the descending order of generality of ideas and supporting materials by indenting properly (see the example that follows). Such indenting shows that the subheads at each level directly relate to the heads just above.

When you divide a section into subheads, make sure a true division actually exists (don't divide and get just one piece). Thus, if you have a *1*, you need a *2*; if you have an *a*, you need a *b*; and so on.

I. My plan will benefit workers.
   A. It will benefit workers in unions.
      1. Fact A proves this.
      2. Expert A agrees with my conclusion here.
   B. It will also benefit nonunion workers.
      1. Fact B proves this.
      2. Expert B agrees, also.
      3. When implemented, the plan benefited non union workers in both Canada and England.
         a. In Canada wages went up 4 to 5 percent.
         b. English workers made more money for working shorter hours.
   C. Even white-collar workers will benefit.
      1. Expert C testified to this effect.
      2. A poll of white-collar workers in London indi cates satisfaction with the plan.

Transition: So you see, my plan will definitely help workers. Now let me show you how it will enrich management.

II. My plan will help management . . .

Please note another feature of the good outline: transitions appear on the outline between main points.

After you finish outlining the body, with main ideas, subordinate ideas, supporting materials, and transitions, you proceed to develop and outline your introduction and conclusion.

Now, as promised, I present a model outline for you to emulate. You will find others in Chapter 9 and in the Appendix. Chris Evans used this outline for a speech in my class at the University of Georgia

.Purpose:	*To inform the audience of what to consider when choosing a quality bicycle.*

INTRODUCTION

Rationale:	*Happiness*: "Pedaling past the gasoline pump line." America now faces a bicycle boom that could rival that of the early 1970s. Do *you* know what to look for to get the most for your money in a bicycle?
Thesis:	Before buying a bicycle, you need to know three basic principles.
Partitioning:	Determine your purpose for buying a bike and the environment in which you will ride it.
	Choose a proper retailer from whom to buy your bike.
	Become familiar with the bike's major components in order to determine overall quality.

BODY

   I. Select a bike according to your own purpose for having one and where you will ride it.

      A. For flat terrain and short distances you would only need a one-, three-, or five-speed bike.

      B. For longer recreational riding and moderate to tough hills, you would wisely choose a ten-speed.

      C. You might want a bike you could carry onto a bus or train, or into the office.

         1. You can buy folding bikes for train and travel, but will find them expensive and maybe uncomfortable.

         2. You could carry a *lightweight* nonfolding bike up and down stairs in your building.

Transition: After deciding what kind of bike you want, you must decide where to buy it.

   II. Choose a proper retailer—carefully.

     A. Purchase it where you can also get parts and service.

     B. You will find more satisfaction in a regular bike shop than in a department store.

       1. Bike shops have bikes of higher quality.

       2. Bike shops have bikes that will fit *you* best.

       3. Bike shops assemble their machines more carfully.

       4. These shops have parts, and welcome your repair and adjustment business.

Transition: After you decide on the type of bike for you and find some reputable shops in your area, you need next to look for quality.

  III. Examine the bike's components to determine overall quality.

     A. Bikes come in two basic types: racing and touring.

       1. Racing style means connections at sharper angles, which shorten the wheel base to about forty inches; this gives quicker steering, less shock absorption, and more responsiveness.

       2. In the touring style, the frame angles extend the wheel base to about forty-six inches, promoting greater stability for straight-line riding.

     B. Carefully check the *frame,* the single most important component, which determines the bike's efficiency and handling.

       1. The best frame consists of fine alloys, which make it strong yet light.

       2. Heavier, less expensive frames consist of high- and low-carbon steel.

       3. The good frame will look carefully *aligned;* check this with the wheels *off*.

       4. The joints of the frame determine quality, too.

         a. Manufacturers *braze* lightweight metals.

         b. They *weld* the heavier, cheaper metals.

         c. The very best bikes have overlapping braces at the frame joints.

     C. Consider the wheels, another major component.

1. Unless riding rough streets, choose lightweight rims.
2. High-pressure tires lessen pedaling effort, but reduce traction and comfort on bumps.
3. Lower-pressure tires make it harder to pedal but give more traction and comfort.

CONCLUSION

So if you decide to get in on the biking boom, remember to take care in deciding on the right bike for you, choose the right retailer, and check that bike's components for quality.

Happy biking!

6

USING EFFECTIVE LANGUAGE

While reading *Time* magazine at home one day I came across a brief mention of a man who had died "of his own hand (defenestration)." The first thought that jumped into my mind: "Defenestration? What a way to do yourself in!" But then I picked up my pocket dictionary to look for the word. Finding nothing under D, I turned to the F's and found *fenestration*—seems it has to do with "window arrangement." Did he jump out a window?

Next morning at the office I consulted my *unabridged* dictionary. Sure enough, *defenestration* means to "throw out of the window." It comes from the Latin *fenestra,* meaning "window." Our suicide threw himself out of a window, apparently.

Why should I begin a chapter on language with such an example? Besides the fact that few people know the word *defenestration,* this example points out a crucial difference between the language of writing and the language of speech.

With a written message, you can take your own sweet time trying to figure it out. You can reread it as many times as necessary. You can look up unfamiliar words in the dictionary. You can ponder over a passage, then read it again. You can ask others to read the message and ask them to tell you what it means to them.

But when it comes to a spoken message, you have no time to ponder an unfamiliar word, to turn a sentence's thought over and over in your mind until you unravel the idea hidden within. We refer to speech as a linear medium; it just keeps on going. If you stop to think over a sentence or phrase, you get left behind. As another speech teacher said many years ago, written language must appear *ultimately* intelligible, but spoken language must appear *instantly* intelligible.

Differentiating between Written and Spoken Language

Scholars generally agree that real differences exist between good oral style and good written style. And empirical studies tend to support their conclusions. The specific differences these experts find between good written and oral expression include the facts that oral style:

1. Uses shorter sentences.

2. Uses a smaller vocabulary. In an essay you might write the word *hence,* but would you use that word in conversation or a speech unless you wanted to sound pedantic?

3. Uses shorter words, words with fewer syllables. General audiences find these words easier to comprehend.

4. Uses more contractions. Your English teachers probably forbade you to write *don't* rather than *do not*. But you rarely say it this way, unless for emphasis. Mom says, "You *do not* use words like that in this house!" but "You *don't* like liver and onions, do you?"

5. Uses more colloquial and nonstandard words, which come and go with the seasons. *Red dog* gave way to *blitz*, but you would use neither in an English theme.

6. Uses more self-referential words (*I, me, myself, mine*) and more pronouns in general. In an English assignment or scholarly paper, you might refer to yourself as "this writer," "this researcher," or "the author of this essay." (Or as the presiding officer of a parliamentary body would say, "The Chair recognizes Ms. Martinez."

7. Uses more qualifying words, such as *however, but, except, if, anyway.*

8. Uses more extreme or superlative words, such as *all, none, always, every, never,* and so on. We use words more carefully when we write, compared to when we speak.

9. Uses more repetition. Speakers repeat words, syllables, sentences, phrases for impact, since listeners cannot go back and "relisten."

10. Uses more terms expressing personal bias, such as *apparently, it seems to me, in my opinion,* and so on. This usage tends to counteract the effect of the more extensive use of superlatives (more on this later in the chapter).

11. Uses less precise enumeration, especially with large numbers. You might write "$9,684,586.45," but you would probably *say* "nearly 10 million." An audience can grasp that figure instantly. If you included the precise number in your speech, they might remember only the 45 cents at the very end of the number.

12. Uses more guidelines for the listeners' mental processes. These include transitions (discussed in Chapter 5), enumeration (first, second, third, etc.), internal summaries ("so, as you can see, these figures I just recited add up to a real problem . . ."), and what we call *guideposts* ("And now we turn to the most important question yet to ask ourselves . . .").

13. Uses an organizational structure that stresses and repeats main points more often than does written style (as in the partitioning tactics explained in detail in Chapter 5).

As you see, speech should sound much different from written material that you hear read aloud. So how do you guarantee that you will talk to your audience in an oral style they can comprehend and appreciate? Two distinct ways exist, depending on how you prepare your speech.

F ew speakers have the skill and training to read as if they really understand the words as they mouth them.

First, if you prepare your speeches for extemporaneous delivery, as explained in the step-by-step method of Chapter 2, you should have no difficulty with the problem of oral versus written style. If you know your material well and choose your words from your head as you stand before your audience, your style will come out as oral, as conversational. Unless, of course, your speech contains phrases, sentences, or paragraphs that you originally wrote into your speech and unconsciously memorized as you rehearsed.

Second, some experienced (and many inexperienced) speakers feel that they simply must have a manuscript before them with every word already chosen in advance (in this case, we say, "the thinking has already been done"). Stage fright usually motivates this desire. Politicians and businesspeople almost always seem to read their speeches from manuscripts, which results in our hearing a lot of speeches we do not especially enjoy.

We don't enjoy most manuscript speeches for two simple reasons. First, someone wrote them (and maybe *not* the speakers) in a style that sounds, not like speeches, but like "essays on their hind legs." Second, few speakers have the skill and training to read as if they really understand the words as they mouth them. It takes a good actor to do this.

Along with these two monumental disadvantages of the manuscript speech, there do exist some advantages: you can't forget your speech (unless you left it in the pocket of your other coat); you can hand out copies to the press in advance, for publicity purposes; you'll have a very good idea of how much time it takes to deliver; you can't be misquoted; and if you get sick, someone else can read it.

So, if you absolutely must use a manuscript, try to keep it from sounding like that "essay on its hind legs."

Instead of just writing it, *say it* first, then write it. Gather your materials, outline the speech, and then speak it into a tape recorder, as if talking earnestly to a friend over a cup of coffee or a beer. Talk to the recorder in your normal conversational tone; that way you will eventually *converse* with your larger audience. Then copy the speech from the recording. It should come out in your own oral style. Next you can polish up the language a bit; remove the *you know*'s and the *uh*'s and the incomplete sentences and syllable repetitions. Then you can rehearse from your manuscript so that it becomes as familiar to you as the feel of your teeth on your tongue.

A good example of how this process works appears in a film, produced by Time/Life, called "How to Make a More Effective Speech." It features a genielike pixie called "Master" (played by Tony-Award-winning actor Robert Morse) who teaches a middle-aged executive named A. J. Bagshaw (played by John Randolph), a complete novice at speechmaking, how to compose and deliver a speech his boss has assigned him. The terrified Bagshaw, with Master's help, learns to state his purpose, gather his material, organize it logically, shout it into a tape recorder, and have his secretary transcribe it into a manuscript. He cleans up his fluffs, rehearses the speech numerous times before several different audiences of one (his wife, his secretary, the company's head of research and development), and even tries it out wearing his old tuxedo. His maiden voyage into oratory proves a rousing success, and A. J. brims with pride and self-satisfaction to the point where he nearly pops the buttons off his dinner jacket.

Choosing the Appropriate Word

Some people suffer from the misguided perception that somehow the language of public speaking must differ widely from that of normal conversation. "Oratory" must ring with polysyllabic words, stentorian phrases, and larger-than-life abstractions referring to heroic and mighty events in the History of Humankind.

Nonsense. Few people can get away with such puffery; a fine line exists between eloquence and hot air. As a beginner, you should not try to balance on that line. Just use the small, common, easy-to-understand words that you normally use in conversation, and make yourself understood. The U.S. Department of Agriculture might refer to an "individually operated, hand-held earth excavator." You should call it a "spade." Why would a sports commentator refer to a football game as played on "a natural surface" instead of "on grass"? The U.S. Secretary of Health and Human Services might prefer to refer to his department's "program misuse" and "management inefficiency," but you should call it "fraud, abuse, and waste," words that the department recently struck from its vocabulary.

All right, so you agree; you should keep your language simple. But don't misinterpret. Sometimes you still need to work on your language to make your speech effective.

For instance, you may consider a speech complete except for one or two unsatisfactory words. Perhaps you want to replace a particular word that sounds nearly right with one that you think sounds *exactly* right. Well, not *right*, exactly, but "more correct." Well, no, *correct* won't do, either. Let me see. Where did I leave my thesaurus?

When I look up *correct* I find "adj., accurate, strict, perfect, true, unerring. See *RIGHT*." Hmmm. Let's look up *right*. There, page 431: "Right . . . becoming, suitable, proper, correct, meet, fitting, seemly, appropriate." I found it! I wanted *appropriate*.

See what I mean? Sometimes you will need to dig into a thesaurus to find the word that will "make" your speech. With luck, you will work on a word processor and will have a thesaurus built right into your system, at your fingertips.

Expanding Your Vocabulary

As a speaker, a thinker, and a student, you should never remain content with your own vocabulary; the greater your vocabulary, the greater your grasp of ideas. Your vocabulary resembles a toolchest; the more tools you own and the more variety you have, the more kinds of jobs you can do.

To motivate you to vary and expand your vocabulary, I print here a speech by one of my former students, Kingsley Corbin. Read it for the language and ideas, then come back later and look at it as a good model speech to actuate using the problem/solution/arousal (PSA) plan you will find in more detail in Chapter 9. (*Note:* Labels in the left margin specify the steps and substeps in the PSA sequence.)

SWELL YOUR VOCABULARY, STRETCH YOUR MIND

Introduction:
Interest
material

You would have to call the father of a good friend of mine a real optimist. Last quarter, when my friend's grades from college arrived in the mail, his dad looked at the three F's and one D and said to his wife, "Well, at least we know our son doesn't cheat in school or take any of those mind-expanding drugs!"

Purpose

Well, today I want to talk to *you* about expanding *your* minds—but not through drugs, through vocabulary.

Partitioning
of main points

Specifically, I want to talk to you about problems you face with a poor vocabulary and then show how you can improve the situation. And I hope to motivate you to try my cure.

Problem step

If you consider yourself an average adult, your vocabulary exceeds that of a child of ten by only one and a half. Get that? The average adult's vocabulary remains only about one and a half times as large as that of a ten-year-old! And this means something else: it means that your vocabulary increases at a rate of only one-hundredth of the rate it did when you studied in the lower grades of elementary school. Now, if these accusations sound insulting, I apologize; I apologize especially because they refer to me, too! I used to think I had a good vocabulary until I took a little test a few weeks ago; I found out that my vocabulary rated a little better than average.

I say these things only to get you to face the facts about vocabulary development that educational testing studies have turned up in recent years. I'm talking about hardworking scientists interested in the power of words, too, not research by some theoretical profs over in the English Department.

Now, we college students probably have vocabularies stronger than the average adult, but I know you would agree with me that a better vocabulary would sure come in handy for each of us.

Support:
Illustration
Statistics

For instance, proof exists that vocabulary indicates one aspect of intelligence. Learning power definitely improves as vocabulary increases. In one study, two high school classes took part in an experiment. One class took normal courses, and the other took them plus a rigorous vocabulary training course. At the end of the experiment the grades in the class with the vocabulary training exceeded the others considerably. And not only in English; their grades in all courses, including math and sciences, came out higher. Also, Professor Lewis Terman of Stanford University has found that vocabulary testing measures intelligence as well as the standard, accepted Stanford-Binet IQ tests do.

And limited vocabulary doesn't just affect schoolwork. It may affect career success later in life. Dr. Johnson O'Connor of the Human Engineering Laboratory of Boston and the Stephens Institute of Technology in New Jersey gave a vocabulary test to a hundred young men studying to become industrial executives. Five years later, without exception, every one of those who passed in the upper 10 percent—that is, those in the upper 10 percent in vocabulary—had attained executive positions. On the other hand, not a single one of those scoring in the lower 35 percent of the vocabulary test had become execs.

Internal summary

So there you have it. If you folks have good vocabularies, you will probably do well here in school and later on when you go into your careers. And if you don't have good vocabularies, you may have to settle for a C average and a

Transition

mediocre job after school. But if you have a weak vocabulary, must you accept just mediocre grades and a mediocre job? Not really. You can do something about it. *Now.*

Solution step

You *can* improve your vocabulary and do it a whole lot faster and easier than you might ever have imagined. You can do it by using any number of useful books on vocabulary training. I just happen to have a couple right here: [holding up] *Thirty Days to a More Powerful Vocabulary* and *Word Power Made Easy.* You can buy them in our campus bookstore or at any of the bookstores downtown.

These books have short quizzes to give you an idea of how good or bad your own vocabulary is. I found out, to my chagrin, that mine ranked far below what I thought it would. Then I read how my vocabulary would affect my grades and probably my career after school, and I really began to read them in earnest.

How it solves the problem

These books don't define words the way a dictionary does. These books don't "read" like dictionaries. They tell stories about words. They show how words relate to objects and to other words, and they make a fun game in doing so. The more I read, the more I wanted to read.

Examples

About a month ago I read in *Thirty Days* the story of the word *obsequious,* which means "excessively polite behavior designed to get something out of you," sort of. Shortly after, I took my girlfriend to dinner, and about halfway through I noted our waiter acting in quite an *obsequious* manner in his desire to get a big tip out of me. I didn't have to use the expression "excessively polite" or "unnaturally and overly fawning" or some such. That new word then became part of my growing vocabulary.

It works

These books are based on two simple principles: (1) words are verbal symbols of ideas; and (2) becoming more familiar with more words makes you familiar with more ideas.

Overcoming objections

These books, cheap paperbacks, cannot break your budgets. Either one costs less than three packs of cigarettes

Also, they don't take a lot of time. You can carry them around in your pocket or purse and read them in spare moments. I read half of one chapter on the campus bus from Russell Hall to North Campus, and the other half on the ride back.

Plus, you will find them easy to read. Either book reads a lot easier than the textbook for this class and provides a lot more fun. Since reading them, I have seen words in my regular classroom readings that I would have just skipped over a couple months ago. Just last night, while reading my psych book, I came across the word *misogyny*. Two months ago that word would just flicker past my eyes meaninglessly as I read on; but now I know from a little word game in one of these books that *misogyny* means "hatred of women." And man, that does not describe *me*. I *love* women!

Arousal step   Can you picture yourself making A's and B's in all your classes beginning next quarter because you understand more clearly what you read in your textbooks and hear in your lectures? Or can you imagine becoming the manager of a business or a top executive in a company simply because you have a clearer understanding of the instructions and ideas given you by a higher officer? Being on the dean's list and catching the brass ring in the business world sure beats mediocre grades and treadmilling in the old rat race. You must choose; which would you prefer?

Conclusion   So, what'll you have? Mediocrity, or excellence? Strive to improve your word power. Any good vocabulary book like these will do the job for you— and provide you with some fun at the same time. You might think, "Well, I can

Action to take   do that anytime." But don't put if off. Begin right away. Get down to the bookstore and pick up *Thirty Days to a More Powerful Vocabulary*. Then, when spring quarter starts, you will almost have finished it and be ready to take the University of Georgia by storm. *Do it!*

Achieving Vividness

If the federal government erected a memorial to President John F. Kennedy, which of his words do you think the artists would chisel at its base? Probably, "Ask not what your country can do for you—ask what you can do for your country." JFK immortalized this sentence, a figure of speech called antithesis, in his inaugural address.

Which phrases of Winston Churchill will the world most remember? I would vote for his "We will fight on the beaches, we will fight on the landing grounds, we will fight . . ." We call this rhetorical tactic repetition and parallel structure. Martin Luther King, Jr., used the same tactic to drill into the conscience of America: "I have a dream . . ."

We mostly remember speakers for a few vivid, ringing words, some catchy phrase or figure of speech, or an unusual juxtaposition of ordinary words. Franklin D. Roosevelt's "a date that will live in infamy" and "the only thing we have to fear is fear itself" come to mind as examples.

Some of my students' speeches stick in my mind because of a figure of speech, a freshly coined (for me) word, or some play on language. One young man made his speech memorable when he referred to communism as "the cause that represses." Another young man brightened his speech about his native state of Vermont with "If autumn in Vermont were a woman, every man would want to leave his wife." A young woman at the University of Nebraska, whose family recently had moved to the highly urbanized East coast, complained about having lost the advantages of rural and small-town life. She said, "The national flower of this country should be the concrete cloverleaf."

You, too, can spice up your speech and make it memorable with just one or two such jewels. Like me, you may find it difficult to make up your own verbal flashes, but you can certainly find such bright highlights for your speech. I have already mentioned reference books filled with quotations (see Chapter 4). But you can also collect them from your own reading, or even from such sources as the *Reader's Digest*'s "Toward More Picturesque Speech" page. Look for them as magazine and newspaper fillers, also. Wide reading helps, too.

Just as one can make up for a deficient vocabulary by consulting a thesaurus or book of quotations, one can make a speech come to life with borrowed figures of speech. These figures of speech include allegory, alliteration, analogy, antithesis, epigrams, epithets, hyperbole, metaphor and simile, metonymy, oxymorons, understatement, rhetorical questions, personification, onomatopoeia, and irony.

Allegory

Though not very common in speeches, allegory can effectively pinpoint human foibles and shortcomings, through indirection, as with a cloudy mirror. An allegory tells a story with a moral, thesis, or hypothesis that, the speaker hopes, the audience will see as easily applicable to the speaker's target. For instance, suppose you would like to refer to a gentleman who owes all of his status to dumb luck, to simply occupying the right space at the right time. You could use my grubworm allegory:

Mr. —— reminds me of the tale of two grubworms. They lived in the ground together, and one day a spade came down and carried off the chunk of soil in which they lived. As a man carried the spadeful of dirt, one grubworm fell off into a dark, dank, barren crack in the sidewalk. The second grubworm fell off a few feet away into a pile of fresh manure, where he prospered.

One day the starving grubworm managed to crawl out of the dark, dank, barren crack in the sidewalk and drag himself over to the manure pile, where he spied his former friend. "Oh, Brother Grubworm," he cried, "I have fallen on hard times. But you have grown prosperous, fat, and healthy! Tell me, Brother Grubworm, how did you do it?"

The prosperous grubworm replied, "Oh, just brains and ambition, Brother Grubworm; just brains and ambition!"

Alliteration

The old political epithet of "Rum, Romanism, and Rebellion" comes to mind as a good example of alliteration—the repetition of the same sound in consecutive words. It sometimes pays to use alliterative words in the title of your speech and to repeat the title often. I vividly remember a speech from many years ago titled "The Communist Criminal Conspiracy." Song titles containing catchy alliteration abound: "Tea for Two," "It Takes Two to Tango," "Bewitched, Bothered, and Bewildered," "Philadelphia Freedom," "Da Doo Ron Ron."

> *It sometimes pays to use alliterative words in the title of your speech and to repeat the title often.*

Analogy

Analogy relates one thing or attribute to another; often the two things have nothing in common literally, only figuratively. You could say, for example, that capping the federal budget now would resemble locking the barn door after the horse had run off. We realize the dissimilarities between the budget and the horse running off, but we see that too much of our money has already disappeared, too. I once criticized a student speaker for "showing about as much enthusiasm in that speech as I find in a K mart checkout clerk's 'Cash or charge?'" Abraham Lincoln urged voters, "Don't change horses in the middle of the stream," meaning don't change presidents in the middle of a war.

Antithesis

Antithesis, already mentioned in connection with John F. Kennedy, contrasts ideas, usually by a simple switch of wording. A good antithetical statement can ring in the heads of your audience for a long time. I remember one speaker saying, "What we need is a congressman who not only will count votes, but whose votes will count." Sociologist Robert Lynd aptly summarized our ambivalence toward the ubiquitous telephone. He described it as "the greatest convenience among nuisances and the greatest nuisance among conveniences."

Epigrams

Epigrams —brief, witty statements with an unexpected turn—abound in collections of quotations. For a speech to a group of authors I gleaned the following:

> No author is a man of genius to his publisher.—*Heinrich Heine*

> Almost anyone can be an author; the business is to collect money and fame from this state of being.—*A. A. Milne*

> What an author likes to write most is his signature on the back of a check.—*Brendan Behan*

Epithets

Epithets express some quality or trait of a person as a kind of "name-calling." Ring Lardner wrote about Alibi Ike, a ballplayer who constantly made excuses for himself even when he did something well. After Jim Croce popularized the song "Bad, Bad Leroy Brown," about a guy supposedly "meaner than a junkyard dog," the football fans of the University of Georgia promptly dubbed the defensive unit of the Georgia Bulldogs the "Junkyard Dogs."

Sometimes epithets carry so much magic that they endure like granite even though false.

Sometimes epithets carry so much magic that they endure like granite even though false. Chicago, for instance, became known as "The Windy City" primarily because of an overly talkative, or "windy," congressman from there; Chicago actually ranks about thirty-fifth in average wind velocity among American cities. Although America spawned no greater military officer or braver warrior than Douglas MacArthur, who constantly exposed himself to enemy fire in order to see the activities at the cutting edge of battle, his reputation became tarnished for many by the name hung on him by troops from his Bataan/Corregidor days, "Dugout Doug."

Hyperbole

Hyperbole occurs when exaggeration greatly exceeds the bounds of ordinary credibility. Hyperbole does not seek to misrepresent, as ordinary exaggeration might, but to *emphasize*. One hyperbolic song lyric claims "I cried a river over you." Billy Sunday, the prohibitionist preacher, yearned for an America so dry (liquorless) that "You'll have to prime a man before he can spit." An old-timer in the drought-stricken American Southwest complained, "I wish it would rain just once—just once, mind you. Not for myself, but for my grandkids. I've *seen* rain." The tall tales we enjoy usually depend for their effect on hyperbole, and so do many of our insult one-liners: "He's so cheap he'd skin a flea for its hide and tallow"; "She's so ugly that when she enters a room, the mice jump up on the chairs"; "He has a face that you don't want to remember but just can't forget."

Metaphor and Simile

Metaphor refers to someone or something as being akin to someone or something that it resembles. We refer to a highway location that produces traffic jams as a bottleneck. We often use such terms without thinking of the metaphor. As Harry Reasoner pointed out on TV, he once heard a traffic reporter refer to "the biggest bottleneck" he had ever seen; if he had had the metaphor in mind, he would have called it "the smallest bottleneck."

Unconscious use of metaphor occurs regularly and habitually. We refer to an exciting book as "real dynamite"; we call our home "our castle"; we refer to an attractive female as "a real doll."

One danger of using metaphors results from the fact that many come across as old, overused, and thus trite. If you can invent your own telling metaphors, so much the better. The creative eye that can see a heretofore hidden relationship and uncover it will find ready favor with any audience. It requires native inventiveness to see an original relationship and to transform it into vivid language. Writer Shana Alexander excels at this talent. Look how she described the bail hearing of kidnapee-turned-urban-guerrilla Patty Hearst:

> I saw her first from the back, facing the judge, one tiny hand hooked in her jeans. Standing there before the high bench, she looked slouching and tough, a transvestite Dead End Kid in lilac tee shirt and dyed red hair. The only way to see her at all in the packed courtroom was to rise on tiptoe for a quick peek. Other spectators did the same, and throughout these tense proceedings the surface of our human throng rose and fell like a pot of bubbling oatmeal.

Alexander also described sex therapists Masters and Johnson, as they chatted on a TV talk show, as "a happily married couple, just plain Bill and Gini, the Ma and Pa Kettle of Gynecology." She perceived Robert Mardian, of the Watergate scandal, as "a man of Teflon, cold and perfectly smooth."

An infrequent but real danger of metaphor arises when a speaker overdoes things. Years ago then-Congressman Gerald Ford got carried away with a "ship" metaphor in attacking the Democratic president. The following transcription of that metaphorical spree comes from the 1968 CBS-TV presentation, "The Strange Case of the English Language." Commentator Harry Reasoner interrupts regularly:

> REASONER: Congressman Gerald Ford got carried away with a "ship" metaphor one night.
> FORD: The president's only explanation was, "When a great ship cuts through the sea, the waters are always stirred and troubled." Apparently the president has been standing on the stern [pause for laughter, then applause] looking backward at the wake, wondering which of his officers to dump overboard next. [More laughter, then applause]
> REASONER: So far, so good. The metaphor worked, so he went on with it.
> FORD: The ship of state is wallowing in a storm-tossed sea, drifting toward the rocks of domestic disaster . . .
> REASONER: . . . and on with it . . .
> FORD: . . . tossed by the waves of a worldwide fiscal crisis. The captain should return to the bridge . . .
> REASONER: . . . and on with it . . .
> FORD: We need a captain who will seize the helm, call up full power, break out new charts, hold our course steadfast, and bring us through the storm.
> REASONER: Three minutes later he was still going on with it.
> FORD: It's time for all hands to man their action stations. Let's not give up the ship . . .
> REASONER: . . . people were beginning to feel seasick . . .
> FORD: . . . America has weathered many a terrible storm, rescued many a weaker vessel, and we'll do it again.

Similes do somewhat the same job, but with a weaker connection, usually using the word *like* or *as;* "Trying to talk sense to him is like trying to nail jelly to the wall."

Metonymy

Metonymy uses one word to suggest or mean another, much like a metaphor. We speak of the White House when referring to word from our president. We say a man has a five o'clock shadow when he really needs a shave. "Dog breath" refers to halitosis.

Metonymy includes euphemism—substituting a more pleasant

synonym for its harsher cousin. "Passing on to his reward" sounds nicer than "dying" (or, the dysphemism, "croaking"). And we do not usually "rest" in "rest rooms."

Oxymorons

Oxymorons combine contradictory words. We might call a particular act a "cruel kindness" or vice versa. We note that the world contains a great many "educated fools." Almost everyone knows one "poor little rich girl." Some cynics characterize the terms "military intelligence," "honest politician," and "brilliant professor" as oxymorons.

Understatement

Understatement, the opposite of hyperbole, also attracts attention and stresses the speaker's point. In the movie *Dr. Strangelove,* a general (played by George C. Scott) discusses the possibility of a nuclear exchange with Russia. He declares that "I don't say we won't get our hair mussed" in the resultant nuclear holocaust. Wags sometimes refer to World War II as "that minor disagreement among nations."

Rhetorical questions either require no answer or else answer themselves; they might take the form of declarative statements in question form.

Rhetorical Questions

Rhetorical questions either require no answer or else answer themselves; they might take the form of declarative statements in question form. They help a speaker hold the audience's attention. Our schooling has conditioned us to snap to alertness the moment someone (like a teacher?) asks a question. We immediately begin searching among our brain cells for the answer. In school, the teacher would ask something like, "And now, who can tell us the year of the Norman invasion of England?" then quietly scan the class for the one face betraying the student who does not know the answer. Years of this kind of conditioning trigger an automatic stimulus/response behavior; the question acts as the stimulus, and alert, conscious thinking becomes the response.

When a speaker says, "And, do you know just why our representative voted that way?" we respond, mentally, with "No, just why did she?" in active involvement. The same kind of leap to a higher arousal level occurs when the speaker himself answers the rhetorical question: "*Did you know* that lettuce, a completely metabolic food, uses up more calories in your eating and digesting it than it contains?"

Do you now see how rhetorical questions and other figures of speech can enliven your speeches? Do you *really*?

Personification

Personification involves speaking or writing about an inanimate object as if it possessed humanity. "The tree limbs waved at us frantically during the windstorm."

Onomatopoeia

Onomatopoetic words sound like the things they stand for. Bells "tinkle"; brooks "babble"; "zipper" gets its name from the sound it makes; "plop-plop, fizz-fizz" reminds us of Alka-Seltzer dissolving in water.

Irony

Irony involves saying one thing, but sarcastically meaning the opposite. "That great American patriot, Benedict Arnold"; "Comedian Don Rickles, 'Mr. Warmth'"; or "Johnny Carson, the Great Stone Face."

E-Prime

Earlier in this chapter I differentiated between written and oral style. I wrote that oral style contains more extreme or superlative terms than does written style. The reason I gave: we write more carefully than we talk. And, for a number of reasons, we ought to exercise more care when we use "allness" terms in our talking. Why? Simply to make our language more nearly fit reality. Because, really, does it actually rain "every time" you plan a picnic? Does a blind date or a previously untried food "always" disappoint you? Do "all" college athletes lack academic ability? Do you "never" get your way when arguing with your (parents/sibling/spouse/girlfriend/boyfriend)? No, no, no, no. If not, then, why talk as if you could answer yes, yes, yes, yes?

As stated earlier, the use of "to me" terms tend to take the worst out of our "allness" terms. But we need to do better at this. The cause of this problem arises from the fact that the design of our language itself does not reflect reality very well. We learn to use the lazy "*is* of identity" to overcategorize and overgeneralize. When we say that "Joe is lazy," we tend to convey the point that Joe is lazy *now*, has *always been* lazy, and *always will be* lazy. You would reflect reality more accurately by saying something like, "I have seen Joe sitting around a lot and I rarely see him working/studying/reading/exercising." You may have seen Joe *only* at rest or taking it easy.

> *Refusing to use the verb* to be, *especially* is, *forces the writer/speaker to make statements more representative of actual reality.*

General semanticists call language that uses no form of the verb *to be* "E-Prime." Refusing to use the verb *to be,* especially *is,* forces the writer/ speaker to make statements more representative of actual reality, much like a good map provides its user more help if it actually fits the territory it represents. It also tends to force the use of active verbs and the active voice; it discourages the use of passive verbs and the passive voice. Try it sometime. In case you have not yet noticed, I wrote this entire book (except for directly quoted material) in E-Prime (unless I slipped up here and there or else an editor sneaked in an *is* or *are*). No forms of the verb *to be* here!

To summarize, you can make your speeches memorable by using vivid language and figures of speech, but sparingly, as you would use spices in cooking. Otherwise keep your language simple and conversational. Remember, you should always think of public speaking as *enlarged conversation.*

Reading a book on psychotherapy recently gave me a pleasant jolt as I read about the author's own discovery along these lines. He had successfully practiced public speaking since the age of four. He had won many speaking medals in both grammar and high school. He had debated competitively for his college. And yet, after one of his speeches on psychology, a friend, who had not understood much of the speech, asked the author some questions about the lecture:

When I got through answering them, he said, "Why don't you talk as simply as this when you talk to an audience?"

I said, "It [oratory] has to be larger than life; you have to get their attention." But then I thought about it and made a decision to try [the conversational mode]. I would speak to any audience the way I speak to anybody else in ordinary conversation.

That author who decided to change his speaking style? Harold Greenwald, world-famous speaker, psychotherapist, and best-selling author. He found the plain talk formula so successful that he decided he would also speak to his clients in plain language. He finds such plain talk far more effective not only for communication in therapy sessions but in establishing empathy with the client. He also feels it establishes his authenticity with the client far better than does donning the traditional mantle of superiority over the patient.

Chat with your audiences; converse with them. They'll love it.

7

DELIVERING YOUR SPEECH

I f you would follow all the advice given so far in this book—carefully organize your speech, prepare it for extemporaneous presentation, strongly and sincerely desire to communicate information and ideas of real worth to your audience, and believe that you "have a speech to give" instead of "have to give a speech"—then you would have little need for a chapter on how to deliver a speech.

TV news often shows people demonstrating about some cause and raising their voices against the forces they consider "the enemy." Would you say that any of their delivery seems out of place, awkward, or inappropriate? Probably not. Because they sincerely want to get their message across, they don't worry about their "delivery."

Several years ago my local county commission held a public forum on a proposed ordinance that would ban door-to-door sales. The proposed law probably found its impetus in local folks' desire to keep away salesmen hawking encyclopedias, religious books, magazine subscriptions, or the latest "miracle" kitchen implement at their doors. News of the open hearing spread rapidly by telephone and word of mouth, and a large crowd attended the meeting.

One untrained, unprofessional speaker after another stood up to speak against the proposed ordinance. "Do you want to absolutely halt the sale of Girl Scout cookies in this county, and earn the displeasure of every voter associated with the Girl Scouts?" "Do you really favor stopping the guys from Boy Scout Troop 2 from financing their yearly operations by selling 50-pound bags of lawn fertilizer house-to-house each spring?" "Can you really want the Lions Club to cease its yearly campaign of selling brooms and mops to raise money for the visually impaired?"

The people who raised these questions showed no problems with speech "delivery," and their messages came across like gangbusters. The ordinance disappeared into oblivion.

But beginning speakers still expect advice on how to look and sound before an audience. So here goes, although since I sit here before my computer, writing words that you will see months or years from now, I'm limited in the help I can give you. I recently coached a tenth grader going for the state championship in an oratorical contest sponsored by a national civic organization (he won second prize). To achieve this success we had held face-to-face sessions, aided by videotaped practice sessions—activities that you and I cannot share.

But even without proximity in time and space, I can offer some ideas, concepts, and tips to help you improve your speech delivery—at least in your early speeches as a beginner.

Vocal Delivery

In previous chapters I suggested that you think of your speeches as "enlarged conversation." Let's consider how you should use your voice as you converse with your audience.

Rate

How fast do you talk in conversation? Probably 120–150 words per minute, an ideal rate. And what happens when you go faster? How do you think people perceive you if you race along at 200 or more words per minute? Nervous? High-strung? Emotional? Probably. People typically think that a rapid speaker (public or private) uses sheer speed and volume of verbiage to compensate for a lack of worthwhile content. "Fast talker" remains a negative epithet in our culture.

And what if you talk too slowly? You know the common stereotype of the slow talker: dim-witted, stupid, uneducated, indecisive, backward. Get the picture? Keep your pace up for interest—and to gain respect from your audience—but don't make it too fast.

Volume

What do you think of a person who talks too loud? How about overbearing? Domineering? Dictatorial? Insolent? Bullying? Good enough for starters. And what about the speaker with a voice so soft that you nearly develop "earstrain"? The one whose voice barely vibrates your eardrums? How would you describe this poor soul? Timid? Diffident? Faint-hearted? Fearful, weak, pliant, shy, bashful, demure?

The proper balance, of course, involves speaking loudly enough for audiences to hear easily but not so loudly that you seem overbearing. Remember, in public speaking you will need to converse a little more loudly and more forcefully than you would to your partner across a card table. As one writer has suggested, you should project your words to an imaginary, slightly deaf little old lady in the sixteenth row. It just takes more energy to speak to twenty or a hundred people than it does to one or two. After you have done a little public speaking, this fact will seem self-evident. But don't shout at your audience, unless you need to make a particular point emphatically. Do you enjoy getting yelled at?

I cannot give a written formula for finding out whether you speak at an inappropriate rate or volume. You need to try out your speaking rate and volume when you rehearse before your live audience of one or two. Ask them, "Do I speak too fast for you? Too slowly? How about volume? Too loud or too soft?" Then adapt accordingly.

> *An earnest, communicative attitude can do a lot toward concealing any minor defects of voice or articulation that a speaker may have.*

Quality

I assume that the quality of your voice falls somewhere within the normal range—not too high or low in pitch, not too gruff or squeaky—and that you can pronounce and enunciate the forty-six or so phonemes (individual single sounds) that make up the English language. If your voice does *not* fall within this normal range, you probably already know it, and nothing I can write here has a chance of changing it. If you have a serious voice or diction problem (which takes your voice out of the range of normalcy), you need the help of a professional speech therapist to correct it.

Likewise, I assume that you do not have the charming, mellifluous voice of a TV news anchor.

In other words, I assume that you have a normal speaking voice that, although identifiably yours, would not draw attention to itself while you earnestly present a speech on a matter of concern to you.

When a way of speaking calls attention to itself, thus interfering with what the speaker *says,* we use the label "speech defect." But an earnest, communicative attitude can do a lot toward concealing any minor defects of voice or articulation that a speaker may have. A young man in my class, a better-than-average speaker, once wanted to hear his taped presentation in the privacy of my office. After the playback he remarked, "I never before noticed that little lisp I have on *s* sounds." I replied, "I never did either." Then I reminded him that one of the twentieth century's most accomplished orators had a pronounced lateral lisp—but that almost nobody noticed it because they always listened so carefully to what he said. That orator? Sir Winston Churchill. And according to historians, another pretty fair country speaker named Abraham Lincoln had a "high, reedy voice," and he didn't do too badly with it.

Pitch

Pitch refers to how high or low your voice registers on the musical scale. People perceive a high-pitched voice in a man as "feminine," and a deep, low voice in a woman as "mannish." Again, I assume your pitch falls within the normal range for your age and sex. If not, you can do little about it, since size of the vocal folds determines pitch. You can, through practice and the help of a tape recorder, raise or lower your pitch three or four notes, but to do much more you would need professional help. Otherwise, we all pretty much have to live with the pitch dictated by the length and thickness of our vocal cords.

Variety

Vocal variety represents one of the ways a speaker can "hold an audience without a rope." Your rate should vary from quite fast, while running over a minor or trivial point in your speech, to a pronounced crawl on an important point you wish to emphasize, as in "And now—the one—the most important—*the* single excruciatingly *vital*—point to remember is: Do not—under *any* circumstance—touch—that—red—switch!"

An experienced speaker also uses the "pregnant pause" for emphasis and variety. A sure sign of the inexperienced speaker shows in his or her even, fast rate of speech, without a trace of pause (to get through in a hurry?).

The experienced speaker also varies his or her volume according to the importance of the material. Some points will literally need shouting (or near-whispering) for emphasis. You can further enhance overly loud or soft vocalizations with accompanying facial expressions, postures, and gestures.

A good speaker also diversifies vocal quality. "The enemy that bores from within!" might come at the audience raspingly, gutturally, whereas you might use theatrical, pear-shaped tones for hyperbole: "And now—I present the one—the only—the most fabulous single idea of the century . . ."

Little can be said about variety of pitch. If you have pitch variety, we say you have vocal melody; if not, we call your voice monotone. Listeners prefer melody to monotony. You should use rising and

> *Vocal variety ... can stimulate your audience like caffeine.*

falling inflection—your voice might fairly screech on "Can you *imagine* that?" while your pitch might drop to its lowest point on a note of solemnity: "And, thus, his wasted life came to an end, after barely twenty-four years."

In short, your voice must vary to fit the differing emotional and intellectual levels of your speech. Voice and content must coincide, must fit together— must say the same thing. Your voice should reveal, not hide, your emotional and intellectual involvement with what you say.

Vocal variety in your speech can stimulate your audience like caffeine.

Visual Delivery

We can apply points already made about vocal delivery to visual delivery—how you look as you speak. First, as with your vocal delivery, you should vary your visual delivery. Do not stand the same way, or in the same place. Use different postures, gestures, and facial expressions. A lively, varied visual delivery, combined with vocal variety, will keep your audience attentive.

Like vocal delivery, visual delivery must fit your words and ideas; if it contradicts the verbal message it can cancel it out. Your audience will have difficulty accepting your serious point if you deliver it with a smirk on your face; few will feel motivated to take the action you call for as you stare out the window, avoiding eye contact with the audience you supposedly hope to motivate.

The way you look when giving a speech, like the way you sound, should resemble the best conversational delivery. When conversing with someone on a serious topic, we usually expect the other's posture to indicate alertness, interest, and yet comfort. We want our conversational partner to look at us, to communicate meaning and emotion by gestures, facial expressions, changes in posture, shrugs of the shoulders, and so on.

Before briefly discussing each of the important aspects of visual delivery, we should consider the concept of empathy, treated in Chapter 1 (in regard to "negative egocentricity").

We react with empathy when we feel the same way the other person does. When we sit in the stands at a football game and see the tailback collide head-to-head with an opposing tackle with a great THWOCK! we cringe in empathy. Our pain and nervousness as we suffer through a trembling public performance by a friend or relative also exemplifies empathy.

But empathy can apply in positive situations as well. Whenever you get up to speak, your audience cannot help but empathize with you in some way. If they perceive that your nervous, jittery behavior stems from lack of preparation, they, too, will feel nervous and jittery. But if you step to the lectern and demonstrate calm, poise, and relaxation, your audience will stay calm, poised, and relaxed, too. If, during your speech, you remain alert, communicative, alive, so will your audience. You cannot help but communicate when you stand before an audience, and you cannot help but stir up in your audience, through empathy, the same feelings you undergo. Jenkin Lloyd Jones once blamed "stage fright," a "virulent affliction of the young," for causing much negative communication. "The frightened speaker transmits his agony to the audience," he said. "Sympathetic audiences cannot concentrate on what is being said, and the whole affair is a fiasco."

Let's look at some aspects of visual delivery that elicit positive empathy.

Eye Contact

We consider eye contact absolutely essential to effective speaking. You must look into the eyes of each person in your audience, over and over again. People feel "talked to" when a speaker looks them in the eyes. You must, therefore, know your speech well, to avoid leaving the eyes of your audience too often to look at your notes. If you must constantly stick your nose into your notes—or, worse yet, your manuscript—the audience will likely think: "If the *speaker* can't remember what he wants to say, how can he expect *us* to!"

Posture

Your posture should best fit the adjective *alert*. You should absolutely radiate alertness. Remember, the more alert you seem, the more alertness the audience will pick up through empathy. Thus you should not keep your hands in your pockets or tucked into a belt; you should not hold your hands behind your back or clasp them together in front of you; you should not wring your hands above the lectern; you should not lean on or drape yourself around the lectern; you should not even stand tentatively on one foot, perhaps with the other crossing behind or balancing on toe tip behind you while you keep your hands on the lectern for balance.

Instead, you should stand tall and erect, on both feet, with the weight of your body more on the balls of your feet than on your heels, with a slight tilt forward toward the audience. Your feet should remain slightly apart, with one slightly forward of the other, for good front-to-back and lateral balance. As a professor of mine once said, "Stand so that if you should faint or die suddenly, you would fall *toward the audience*."

If you have no lectern, hold your notes in front of you with one hand and let the other hang naturally at your side; it will stay there, ready for any gesture you may feel the urge to make later (it won't be hidden away in a pocket, for instance). If you have a lectern, place your notes on top of it, and place your hands lightly next to them, "at the ready" for a gesture.

Facial Expression

You will want to make your facial expressions match your words and ideas. A big, warm smile in the introduction, when establishing common ground with the audience, hasn't hurt a speaker yet. On your more serious points, however, you can sneer, scowl, shake and bob your head, and so on, to fit what you say. Of course, I recognize that the younger generation might not consider scowling or sneering very *cool*; they might consider public emotion of this sort the very antithesis of approved behavior. But audiences still appreciate a speaker who can evoke varying emotional responses with language and appearance, including apt facial expressions.

Gesture

Normal speakers use gestures to emphasize or express feelings. Good speakers' gestures add to, rather than detract from, their intellectual and emotional meanings. Most experts emphasize that a speaker's gestures should be natural, unaffected, and within "cultural norms" (should not draw attention to themselves).

As "Master" in the Time/Life film on making a more effective speech says about gesturing, "Don't do it unless you feel it."

Dress and Appearance

I must touch on one other aspect of nonverbal communication that goes along with vocal and visual delivery; academic jargonists currently call it *artifactual communication,* meaning simply your physical appearance: how you look and dress.

Ordinarily a speaker should dress to fit the situation. Dress formally for a formal situation, informally for an informal one. The basic rule remains the same as for vocal and visual elements: Neither your dress nor your appearance should interfere with reception of the substance of your message. Avoid all extremes, unless you intend them to be part of your message. For instance, I once gave an afterdinner speech as the program at a formal banquet of young bankers while wearing a jacket, tie, and . . . . Bermuda shorts. My dress fit my thesis: that bankers should wear Bermuda shorts in public, in order to counter their conservative image. I made that speech in 1956, when men did not wear shorts outside their own backyards. (Midway through my speech I had to stand on a chair in order to show my own abbreviated trousers above the speakers' table.)

You cannot fail to communicate something by your dress and appearance, intended or not. Since the age of thirteen I have worn a short crewcut. I intend no message with my hair, but some might perceive me, at least at first, as an out-of-date old codger. Others might perceive me as a neo-Nazi. But I keep the haircut merely for comfort and convenience. (I can comb my hair with a washcloth!) A young man with long, stringy hair may think he communicates the message, "There goes a bright, free spirit, not owned by *anyone*!" But others may react differently: "There goes a weirdo hippie bum who doesn't give a darn what people think of him." A woman speaker wearing ragged jeans, dilapidated sandals, a dirty, tie-dyed T-shirt, and no makeup may present a similar unintended message.

In general, I advise (but do not require) students to dress up for speeches; I tell them to dress as if going to a job interview. I also tell them, and they usually agree afterward, that a well-dressed appearance increases their self-confidence and positive thinking toward the speaking occasion.

Leadership

Let us now think of public speaking as a leader-follower relationship. Consider yourself—the speaker—as the leader, and the audience as your followers. You have made yourself the expert on your topic;

you, not the audience, chose (or became chosen) to stand up and speak on this topic. The audience supposes that you will lead them to understanding or conviction or action; therefore, you must become their leader and behave like a leader.

Interestingly enough, a recent book[1] puts forth the proposition that communication comprises the very basis of leadership. And certainly, leaders must communicate with their constituencies.

You must begin your leadership function before you actually begin your speech. Will a master of ceremonies or a toastmaster introduce you? Then sit alertly and listen to that introduction. It may contain something you can respond to in your own introduction, thereby demonstrating your versatility, alertness, and quickness of mind. One such speaker listened to the glowing praise heaped on him by the MC. Then he rose, took the rostrum, and said, "The MC said so many nice, flattering things about me that I suddenly feared that I had just died."

Whether introduced in glowing terms or merely announced as "the next speaker," you must now begin to demonstrate leadership. Stride purposefully and confidently to the lectern; don't drag yourself up there as if you wished to escape notice. Smile. Look as if you plan to start enjoying yourself.

Once you reach the lectern, express to the audience, nonverbally, that you eagerly look forward to speaking—but not before you satisfy yourself that the speech will begin on its very best legs. Do not hurry. Place your notes and other materials on the lectern and arrange them as you want them. Then look up and over the entire audience for a few moments before you begin speaking. This tells the audience, "Here I stand, up here; there you sit, down there. When I assure myself that you have prepared yourselves to listen, I shall begin talking." This behavior establishes the leader-follower situation from Minute One.

When you open your mouth and capture their interest and attention with that lip-smacking introduction you have prepared, you will find yourself on your way.

A well-organized speech full of useful and interesting information, delivered with enthusiasm, will maintain your leadership position throughout. You must then end your speech on a note of authority.

As in show biz, end with a big finish. Have a strong summary/

[1]M. Z. Hackman and C. E. Johnson, *Leadership: A Communication Perspective* (Prospect Park, Ill.: Waveland Press, 1991).

conclusion, repeating your main point. Then hit the last line hard, ending with a strong, downward inflection of the voice, as in: "And if enough of us act soon enough, we can still save ourselves, our country, and the future of our children."

Now you pause and begin picking up your notes, or whatever. The audience will immediately know, because of your last sentence, that you have ended your speech. You don't need to thank the audience for their patient listening to your speech. Doing so suggests that you don't think too much of your own speech and that you owe the audience your thanks. Indeed, the audience should thank *you!* You worked hard on your speech, suffered the pangs of stage fright, and have done the audience a tremendous favor. A real leader expects the audience's thanks. (After I made this point once in a class lecture, a student a few days later concluded his speech as I had recommended, with a strong sentence and downward inflection; he paused, then said, "You're *welcome!*" He got a good laugh, but he really had the right idea.)

"OK," you say, "an experienced pro can do that. But what about us poor, scared novices? How can *we* exude leadership with our knees knocking and our cerebral cortexes fading away into the sunset?" You have a right to ask, and you deserve an answer.

My answer: you simply must make the personal decision to do it. Use the James-Lange theory of emotion and decide to act and behave like a leader; according to that theory, the more you can behave and act like a leader, the more you become a leader. The way you behave and act will influence the way you feel. On the other hand, of course, if you behave and act like a loser, you will turn out feeling like and becoming a loser, in the minds of the audience.

Franklin Delano Roosevelt's political career appeared ended when he contracted polio (infantile paralysis). To keep his name before the public, he asked his wife, Eleanor, to fill in for him on his extensive public-speaking schedule. Eleanor, a private and shy person, cringed with terror at the thought of all those public speeches. But out of fierce loyalty to her husband, she hitched up what courage she could manage and gave it her best shot. She did not succeed completely, at first, but she worked at it doggedly. She got better and better. We now remember her as one of our country's top public speakers, as well as for her other outstanding attributes. My *Crown Treasury of Relevant Quotations* quotes her as saying, "I believe that anyone can conquer fear by doing the things he fears to do, provided he keeps doing them until he gets a record of successful experiences behind him."

To really succeed as a public speaker, then, you must make the decision to try leadership. If you find this decision too difficult to make, do not expect great success as a public speaker.

Finally, I offer a few don'ts:

1. Don't scratch your ear, nose, stomach, or *anything else* while speaking.

2. Don't jingle your keys in your pocket.

3. Don't play with anything while talking—a pencil, a ring, your notecards—unless you want to project an image of nervous immaturity.

4. Don't look at your watch, then lay it on the lectern. I consider this a useless sign to the audience that a speaker intends to end on time; I cannot remember once observing a speaker do this and then finishing within the time limit.

5. Don't fiddle with your wardrobe; don't twist buttons, pick at imaginary lint, or smooth your lapels.

6. Don't constantly push or throw your hair back out of your eyes. If you must do so, you apparently have to look down at the lectern too often; learn your speech better, or fix the hair with some mousse, spray, or a haircut. Would an NFL quarterback let his hair get in his eyes so that he had difficulty seeing his receivers?

7. Don't use the lectern to support your body.

8. Don't constantly remove and replace your glasses "for effect." If you have visual problems, get different glasses (maybe bifocals). The audience may begin counting the number of times you remove and replace your glasses instead of listening to your speech.

9. Don't scare front-row audience members by randomly waving a pointer before their faces.

10. Don't apologize for much. If you sound hoarse from a cold, for example, the audience will recognize your courage for going on anyway.

8
SPEAKING TO INFORM

Speeches to inform *teach*. To teach means to impart new information or knowledge. Elementary? Yes. But it would surprise you to know how many "speeches to inform" I have sat through that resulted in near-zero learning. In this chapter we look at five main reasons why speeches fail to inform, discuss several ways to create and maintain interest in informative speeches, and then examine the several types of speeches to inform.

Why Speeches Fail to Inform

Let's look at each reason why speeches fail to inform, and consider how to avoid it.

Language Too Specialized

To convey meaning, a word or statement must stir up in the minds of the audience the same picture held by the speaker. Words completely unfamiliar to the audience cannot succeed at such stirring up. I once heard a student speak on the technical aspects of how to ignite a hydrogen bomb. His multisyllabic vocabulary and nuclear short-hand completely baffled his audience.

Simply avoid unnecessary technical words or jargon. Do not let those specialized words slip out, unless necessary; if you *must* use new vocabulary, define terms carefully. Simple common sense can tell you what jargon will not convey meaning. Of course, if you follow the advice in Chapter 2, you will try the speech out beforehand on some people comparable to your audience, and get their reactions. If they can't decipher your jargon easily, look for clearer, simpler language.

Content Too Broad

Some speakers try to cover the moon, the sand, the stars, and outer space in a single short speech. They cannot. Could you teach an audience, in a six-minute speech, how to play bridge? Or backgammon? Or chess? Or the tactics and outcomes of all the major battles of World War II? No, but some folks try to!

Content Too Obvious

To inform, you must provide *new* information. If you repeat only what the audience already knows, you merely bore them. Can you imagine a college student giving a formal speech to other college students on "How to write a check on your checking account"? It happened in one of my classes. I also once heard a speech on how to operate three types of can-openers, including the lowly church key.

You can avoid speaking on a too-elementary topic or one already known to the audience with some careful audience analysis. The level of your audience's information on your topic becomes the most important characteristic you should know about them. You want to avoid both speaking over their heads and talking down to them.

You may have difficulty finding out an audience's information level in advance. Maturity and experience in audience analysis usually improves this ability. Generally, you will find it a good idea to assume that the audience has some knowledge but not as much as you, so speak on a kind of middle ground. Watch the audience carefully as you speak, looking for telltale signs of quizzicalness or boredom. And leave time for lots of questions afterward, if possible, to find out firsthand the knowledge level of the audience.

It would help even more to find some representative members of the group and question them beforehand about their information level on your topic; you could then generalize this level to the audience as a whole. Or talk to the leaders of the organization to which you will speak; they can probably give you a fairly accurate profile of the group's knowledge on your topic.

Of course, as a student speaking to students, you ought to know fairly instinctively your fellow students' knowledge level; after all, you must consider yourself an *expert student!*

Content Too Hard to Remember

Quickly now—recite the Ten Commandments. You can't? You have heard about and read about them all your life, off and on, and you *still* can't remember all ten? Well, then, how well would you remember a speech on "Ten Things to Remember When ——ing"? Could you recite all ten things right after the speech? After a week? Six weeks? A speaker who attempts to teach such a list greatly overestimates the capacity of the audience's nervous system.

You can overcome an audience's inability to remember many seemingly unrelated details in several ways.

First, remember that the human nervous system resembles an electronic computer in some ways, but not in others. Both receive data as input, store it, and then reproduce it, on call, as output. The difference lies in the fact that the computer, when properly operating, stores and can retrieve every bit of information it takes in. A human being can have difficulty remembering a seven-digit number long enough to dial a telephone!

Another difference between computers and humans: computers remember unrelated as well as related material. People better remember *related* material. Consider the following sequences: 2965 5802 4624 8695 8853 *or* 1776 1864 1898 1914 1941. Which set of numbers, would you rather have to remember for a final exam, the randomly picked set or the five dates for the beginning of major wars, arranged chronologically?

The point? If your speech's effectiveness depends on the audience's remembering a long string of facts, points, or ideas, especially if they do not strongly relate to one another, you will fail. The human brain simply cannot absorb that kind of detail, store it, then reproduce it. You must (1) limit the information you present orally and (2) organize the information around just a few main points, or generalizations, that the audience *can* remember.

Consider an example that I use a lot.

When I taught at the University of Nebraska, I usually heard one speech per semester on "Twenty-Seven Tips for Wintertime Driving." The speaker would dutifully list these tips, maybe from least important to most important, maybe alphabetically, maybe in order of costliness, with the barest introduction and conclusion as "bookends." Who can remember twenty-seven tips? Or twenty-seven *anythings*?

Organizing such material around three guiding principles that any numskull driver who had lived through a Nebraska winter could remember would greatly improve the speech's chance for success. For example:

    I. Winter weather punishes your car, so take extra care to keep it in good running order.
      A. Tip
      B. Tip, etc.
   II. Winter conditions slow you down, so provide more time to get where you want to go.
      A. Tip
      B. Tip, etc.
 III. Sudden storms from the plains and unexpected heavy

snows in town mean you need to keep certain survival
gear in your car trunk.

A. Tip

B. Tip, etc.

One more important way for you to help your audience remember a lot of detail: Create handouts. Duplicate your list or diagram or whatever, and hand it out at the appropriate time. (Don't your teachers do this a lot?) For instance, a student of mine gave a speech on our city's "drinking problem," defined as its citizens lack of knowledge about the happy hours and other drinking bargains available in town. At the end of his speech, as he had promised, he handed out a complete list of times and places to drink for less. I often speak on "The Phylogenetic Theory of Humor Development"; when doing so, I hand out a one-page diagram of humor's "family tree," which everyone can follow as I go through the theory.

Once again: If you will try out your speech beforehand on a representative audience, you will learn quickly enough from their feedback whether they found you guilty of any of these pitfalls for the informative speaker.

Content Not Interesting

Do people constantly hunger and thirst for information? Do many folks generally suffer from perpetual curiosity about everything and anything? Of course not. Do you? Most people think of learning as *labor;* they associate it with what we call "schoolwork" (an unfortunate by-product of our educational system). So when you get up to speak about shoes or ships or sealing wax, don't expect your audience to ravenously lap up every crumb of information you drop.

Because few people lust insatiably for any and all information they can clamp their nervous systems onto, you may wonder why anyone would have the least interest in hearing about your topic. An expert on the listening process once said, "There are no uninteresting topics, only uninterested listeners." This means that you, the speaker, must assume the task of *creating* audience interest in your subject. You must create such interest in your introduction, and then sustain that interest throughout the presentation.

Because creating and maintaining interest is so important, let's look at some ways you can do so in your informative speeches.

Creating and Maintaining Interest

Let's face it. Any semiliterate can look up a bunch of information and then recite it to an audience. But it requires some skill and work to make that information palatable. You must make your audience *want* to learn your information. You can do so in three ways.

Audience Analysis

First, adapt your information to what you know or can find out about the interests your audience already has. Let me give you some examples.

Having done some research on and written a book about humor, I have the reputation as an expert on the topic. As such, I get invitations from various groups to speak on that topic. I then go to some pains to find out what I can about the interests of each group to which I will speak.

When asked to speak at a luncheon for psychologists and psychiatrists from our college's health service, I asked of their program chairman why these folks met every two weeks. He told me they met to discuss their mutual interest in mental health. So I adapted my presentation to them and focused on "Mental Health and the Sense of Humor." When a group of pharmacy professors and graduate students invited me to speak to their biweekly seminar on improving teaching, I spoke on "Teaching with Wit and Humor," reviewing the research findings on the topic and illustrating one concept I personally teach with humor: "The Role of Selective Perception in the Communication Process." This latter consists of a slide-and-talk show using mostly "Beetle Bailey" and "Family Circus" cartoons.

Invited to speak at a home economics faculty/student/alumni banquet, part of a weekend convocation exploring the theme of "Handling Stress in Modern America." I spoke on "The Sense of Humor and Stress." For a Rotary Club meeting I spoke on "Laughter: The International Language," since Rotarians think very much internationally (they sponsor international student exchanges, etc.). For the Georgia Authors' Club I chose as my topic "The Origin and Evolution of Humor." I assumed that authors would have an interest in any aspect of humor, but especially in those features that help explain why people think and behave as they do.

Another suggestion: Assume that you yourself will sit there in the audience. Ask: "What would *I* like to hear regarding this topic?"

I refer to this process of audience analysis and self-questioning as "finding the right psychological hook on which to hang your speech." It takes a little time, thought, and maybe even some ingenuity. But if you want to become a successful public speaker, you need to make the effort to find that hook. And not only must you find it, you must *use* it, preferably in the introduction of your speech, to grab the audience while they sit poised at their most attentive moment. This hook becomes the rationale for audience interest first mentioned in Chapter 5. For example:

> I'll bet most of you have been dazzled at least once by the tricks of a professional magician. You see that ball, or that veil, or that rabbit appear seemingly from *nowhere*, and you ask yourself, "Just how in the world could he *Do* that?" Right? Well, today, I plan to give away one of that magician's secrets. I will show you how a stage magician uses *misdirection* to trick an audience.

Good Organization

You can keep your audience interested in a second way: by keeping your speech tightly organized. As emphasized in Chapter 5, people remember organized material better than unorganized material. Educators say that organization is a *mnemonic,* or memory, factor. And if your audience can follow your points as parts of a perceived logical whole, they *learn;* as they learn, they become increasingly pleased with the entire process. They begin to share your mastery of the topic. And for most people, this "Aha!" experience can exhilarate the senses and produce a response not unlike the famous "Eureka!" of Archimides when he discovered the principle of specific gravity while lying in his bath.

Attention-Getting Devices

A third strategy for holding attention comes from your delivery. Use the various factors known to influence human attention, to automatically impel the human nervous system to attend. Using these factors can convert a so-so recitation of facts into a compelling experience. Let's examine each briefly.

ANIMATION   Animation means variety, movement; advertisers, movie and TV directors, and other professional entertainers consider animation absolutely vital to holding attention. Consider the most ordinary television commercial: it contains many and diverse elements of animation, such as catchy words and music, blazing colors, zoom camera shots, high-tech special effects, attractive models blatantly emoting, cute little animals or babies, dancing raisins, drumbeating mechanical rabbits interrupting other commercials, autos racing past the actor huckstering the product, and so on.

Now, *you* can't provide your audience with this much animation, but then you needn't keep your audience from changing channels or getting up to go to the fridge or the bathroom. either. But you need to keep your audience sitting there and listening, and learning. You can do so by following the points originally discussed in Chapter 7 on delivery: Radiate alertness through vocal inflection, apt facial expression, movement, and gestures. Remember that, through empathy, your audience will reflect whatever amount of alertness and interest you yourself manifest. So try for the absolute antithesis of the hypnotist, who intones monotonously, "You are growing sleepy—sooooo sleepy.

VITALNESS   Vitalness must imbue your very first words. In your introduction you must use your hook to connect your topic with what your audience considers vital. After all, typical audience members habitually ask themselves, "Why tell me this? Why should *I* know this?" You must try to answer these questions early in your speech and then continue to provide answers throughout your speech. Sprinkle little "motivators" throughout your speech:

And now, here's a way to really save some money . . .

And if you want to lose some weight without *any effort at all*, here's what you do . . .

If you want to absolutely amaze your friends with your knowledge of ———, just listen to this . . .

Next, I want to explain how you can improve your grades *without* spending anymore time at your regular studies . . .

And with gasoline as expensive as we have it today, I think you will find these gas-saving tips valuable . . .

FAMILIARITY   Familiarity compels interest because, as Joseph Jastrow has observed, humans think more analogically than logically. We like to relate something new to something old—something

> *Audience members delight in hearing a speaker mention a familiar fact, name, place, or date.*

we recognize. I once had trouble explaining to some graduate students how they could write commands to our mainframe computer to get it to run certain statistical packages. After some quizzical looks, one grad student smiled, and said, "Why, you're doing no more than teaching us a kind of new grammar and punctuation, right?"

Audience members delight in hearing a speaker mention a familiar fact, name, place, or date; the experience much resembles suddenly spotting a familiar face from home while visiting a strange city. A colleague of mine at the University of Nebraska had a well-earned reputation around the state as a high school commencement speaker. Before journeying to some Nebraska hamlet to orate at a commencement, he would soak up news about that little town from local newspapers kept on file in the state's archives on campus. Then he could delight his audience with something like: "The situation I have in mind is very reminiscent of that time last February when your basketball team's school bus got stuck in the snow on the way to Kearney . . ."

NOVELTY As the antithesis of familiarity, novelty universally holds attention. The most effective (and overused) word in advertising confronts us constantly: "New!" (Or even, "New and Improved!"). Unusual names, unusual facts, and intriguing new combinations of information surprise and delight us. The late Sydney J. Harris turned out five newspaper columns a week for over thirty years. He devoted one or two of these columns each week to bits of information called "Facts Found While Looking for Others." He eventually accrued enough of these intriguing items to put the best of them together in a book, *Would You Believe?*. From it we learn such fascinating facts as:

Louis Pasteur had such a morbid fear of germs and dirt that he avoided shaking people's hands.

Berengaria, a queen of England (wife of Richard I), never once set foot in England.

The idea of making separate shoes for the left and right feet occurred less than two hundred years ago.

CONFLICT   Conflict holds attention well but may seem better suited to persuasive than informative speech. But many informative topics can profit from a problem versus solution arrangement (much like most "informative" articles in *Reader's Digest*), pitting the scary problem against the valiant human effort to conquer it. For instance,

I. The dreaded disease hemophilia kills 85 percent of its hapless victims.
   A. Causes
   B. Effects, etc.
II. Medical science, fighting an uphill battle, believes that inroads against the killer appear imminent.

SUSPENSE   A speaker can use suspense, an element of conflict, by withholding the most important points of the speech until near the end. You can also use this technique in short illustrations and examples (as radio commentator Paul Harvey does on his "The Rest of the Story"); you can even use suspense at the level of the sentence by couching your words in *periodic sentences*, which withhold the most important part of the sentence until the end. Consider the contrast between these two sentences:

I got my wallet picked from my pocket last December while I rode the subway from Forty-second Street to Forsyth Avenue.

Last December, while riding the subway from Forty-second Street to Forsyth Avenue, I suddenly discovered that my wallet had been picked from my pocket.

CONCRETE LANGUAGE   Concrete language, discussed in Chapter 6 as making for greater clarity and vividness, also contributes to audience interest. Its opposite, abstract language, leads to hazy images and cloudy generalities; specific language produces sharp images and enhances clear thinking. Contrast the following:

ABSTRACT	CONCRETE
He's middle-aged.	He will turn fifty-two in May.
It's a long way from here.	It's five hours by car.
She went to her office.	She caught the bus to the court house, where she works in the tax office.
She's pretty sick.	She has pneumonia, and the hospital lists her in fair condition.

HUMOR Experimental studies (mostly mine) have determined that humor can add interest to a speech not very interesting to begin with but doesn't seem to raise the ratings for an already interesting speech (containing many of the other elements discussed here). A "ceiling effect" may cause this phenomenon. However, any speaker known for humor will probably attract an interested audience who might thus learn something.

I will make one more point about humor, before leaving further discussion of it to our later chapter on the speech to entertain: you need not use humor at all. If you can use it well, and if the humor fits in with your subject matter and does not demean, embarrass, or insult anyone in your audience (or anyone or thing dear to them), it probably will do no harm—and it might make the audience like you more. But don't think that you must always begin your speech with a "good joke."

Types of Informative Speeches

Speeches to inform naturally fall into categories based on subject matter. Let us consider a few such categories, some sample topics for each classification, and the best ways to organize them.

Speeches That Explain Processes

Many speeches to inform, especially of the classroom variety, fall into the category of "process" speeches; they tell how to do something or how something works. Examples:

The triple option play in football	The Heimlich maneuver
Sewing on a button	Soil testing
Putting in golf	Making your own pretzels
How an alternator works	How marshes promote good ecology
Cooking crepes	Tuning a car
Cardiopulmonary resuscitation (CPR)	

Most such speeches would follow a chronological pattern:

    I. The first major step . . .
    II. The second major step . . .
    III. Finally, you must . . .

You could arrange some topics best *topically*:

   I. Marshes generate wildlife by . . .

  II. Marshes have value for soil ecology in that they . . .

 III. Marshes benefit us by . . .

Speeches on Products or Discoveries

Have you learned of a new discovery or a new product due on the market soon? A speech on such a topic could prove highly valuable to your audience. This area could include such topics as:

The new "natural" pesticides	The French "abortion pill"
"Silverless" photographic film	New hope for AIDS victims
Laser treatment for port-wine birth-marks	Genetics: Key to schizophrenia?
The latest in scuba gear	Converting coal to motor fuel
Gasohol	Practically calorie-free ice cream
Breakthrough in solar energy	The new sugarless sweeteners
Insects as human food	Odorless garlic for cooking

Many of these topics fit the topical order. The problem-solution order works well with others:

   I. Port-wine birthmarks, especially on the face, have produced embarrassment and rejection for many . . .

  II. Laser surgery, a new technique, can eliminate such birthmarks quickly and painlessly . . .

 III. The new technique works well and costs less than you might imagine . . .

Other such topics, to show how a discovery or product came into existence, might follow the chronological pattern.

Speeches That Introduce or Discuss Ideas

Abstract ideas or concepts not easily or universally understood can make excellent topics for speeches to inform, such as:

Wit versus humor	The Entrepreneur in America
Comedy versus farce	Freedom versus responsibility
"Classic" versus "old standard"	A managed economy
Legal sense of double jeopardy	Logotherapy (or any form of psychotherapy)
The Statute of Limitations	
What is a scholar?	Adam Smith's "capitalism"
"Leadership" versus management	Circumstantial evidence

Topics such as these lead to one-point speeches, in that the speaker presents only one main point with lots of detail to explain it. Other speeches might well fit the topical order, which, you may suspect by now, comprises a catch-all or miscellaneous arrangement.

Speeches about People or Places

Unusual information about a person, place, or group can make for an interesting speech. However, the danger with such a topic becomes one of slipping into entertainment, even gossip, by not providing information that the audience will find useful in either a practical or an intellectual sense. I once heard a student argue that we need not idealize George Washington as the "perfect American" we read about as third-graders. The student pointed out numerous behavioral and character faults ascribed to the Father of Our Country (for instance, he so feared getting buried alive that he specified an unusually long period of time between his death and his interment). The speech made George seem somehow more human, thus improving our liberal arts understanding of the world and the human condition, without becoming gossipy.

> *Unusual information about a person, place, or group can make for an interesting speech.*

Speeches about groups of people might include those on the U.N. General Assembly, the Mormon Church, Rotary International, the Hare Krishna movement, and so on.

Oral Reports

Now we take up a special form of the speech to inform, the oral report, and for one important reason: you may find yourself assigned to present oral reports as part of your job after graduation. Oral reports stand apart from other forms of speeches to inform because of four characteristics:

1. Someone usually assigns the speaker to do research and then make the oral report on that research.

2. The assignment to research and make the report usually comes from the person or persons who will constitute the audience for the report.

3. Technical or specialized information makes up the content of the oral report, based on that original investigation.

4. The oral report uses its own unique pattern of arrangement.

The most common oral reports probably come from chairpersons of committees. The organization assigns the committee a task; the committee does the task; then the chair of the committee reports to the parent group. The report comprises four parts: an introduction, a description of operational processes (what the investigator did to gather data), the findings, and the recommendations.

Let me exemplify by briefly outlining a report from Wilma Braun, who chaired a committee of the Northeast Georgia Girl Scout Council's board of directors. Her ad hoc (temporary) committee screened applicants for the position of executive director of the council.

Introduction. Good evening. Your committee, composed of myself, Mr. X, Ms. Y, and Ms. Z, etc. met often and worked hard. We believe that we have chosen a fine candidate for your approval.

Methods. Our committee met ——— times. We set the following criteria by which to judge candidates: ———, ———, ———, and ———.

We advertised the position locally, regionally, and nationally in GSA publications and local papers, such as ———. Our ad read as follows: "Wanted: ..."

We received twenty-one applications by the advertised deadline.

Using the criteria stated earlier, we narrowed our list down to the two we felt most qualified; we then brought them to Athens for local interviewing.

Although we felt that both candidates had qualifications that clearly met our criteria and needs, we felt that one candidate held an edge over the others.

Findings. We concluded that Paula Christy Heighton had the most outstanding credentials and potential. We then asked her if she would accept the position if we offered it to her; she said that she would.

Recommendation. Our committee therefore unanimously asks the board to ratify the appointment of Paula Christy Heighton as executive director of the Northeast Georgia Girl Scout Council.

Because committees do so much work in this country, someday you will no doubt find yourself chairing a committee such as this and making a similar report.

But note, also, that the arrangement of this committee report differs not a bit from that used by scientists making a report on a scientific discovery:

Introduction. Previous research shows that glop produces gog when stirred in the presence of goo; however, no evidence exists that it ever produces gog when stirred in the presence of geeg. The study reported here hypothesized that glop would produce gog when stirred in the presence of geeg, but only under certain circumstances of light and temperature.

Methods. The research team used the Glichtonich Temp/Light Generator to control light and temperature. They used a GTXM4112 Glop-Stirrer, manufactured by the Diamond X company, to stir the glop. They limited the presence of geeg in the experimental apparatus to 100 mg per rem. Gog production, monitored by a Mathis gogometer with a sensitivity range of –23 to +160, drained into a 30 cc Stephens tube.

Findings. Traces of gog accrued when the glop-stirrer stirred at ——— rpm under light and temperature intensities of ——— and ———, but only in the presence of geeg in amounts of ——— or greater.

Recommendations. It seems unlikely that stirring glop in the presence of geeg will become a commercially viable method of producing gog. Our company should continue to make gog the old-fashioned way.

Someday your superiors may assign you (or you and your group) to a research task. You will carry out the investigation and, more than likely, report the results to your bosses. The oral report form comes highly recommended for that.

Because an oral report often contains a recommendation, some might think it more classifiable as a speech to persuade. However, the speaker might leave the recommendation out and simply wait for a motion from the floor as the recommendation. Or, if the report explains the study and findings of a problem assigned by your superiors, you could leave off the recommendation and let the bosses decide what to do, based on the evidence.

Most oral reports require only a brief introduction. You needn't make a big play for interest and attention to an audience already highly interested in the project (after all, *they* assigned the project). Probably the methods section will constitute the largest part of the report; it tells what decisions the investigators made, what criteria they set, and how they gathered their information. In other words, this step reveals information vital for judging whether the results seem justifiable or not. For instance, suppose I told you that I did a survey (my method) on campus and found that two out three students surveyed favored doubling the tuition at your school. Would you not demand to know how many students I spoke to, how I selected them as respondents, and how I worded my questions?

Sharing information in today's data-oriented society constitutes a highly useful and ubiquitous activity. We should all strive to practice it more successfully, whether trying to explain processes, ideas, people, places, or new and original findings. We can do so by using understandable and vivid language, tailoring our information to the interests and knowledge levels of our audiences, organizing our messages into mnemonic patterns, and delivering our messages in an animated, lively, and enthusiastic style.

9
SPEAKING TO PERSUADE

hen you speak to persuade, you give your audience information—but not just for information's sake. You provide information that will motivate them to do or believe something you wish them to do or believe, or to do or believe something with more vigor than at present.

To see how you might achieve the goal of persuading, we must look carefully at *why* people believe and do as they do.

What Motivates People?

I pointed out earlier in this book that people do and think pretty much what they want to do and think. We can make this point our key to persuasion, then: people do and believe what pleases them. To put it more explicitly, people do and believe in order to satisfy basic biological needs (such as hunger) or because they'll receive physical or psychological rewards of some kind. We call the urges to satisfy these needs and to secure these rewards *motivations*.

Observers of the human condition have compiled various lists of human motives. We can consider the following as useful as any:

1. Satisfaction of basic physical needs, including food, shelter, and sex.

2. A feeling of mastery over our environment, or part of it.

3. A sense of success in our vocation or avocation.

4. Gratification of our need to be loved and wanted.

5. Successful avoidance of worry and anxiety, and the attainment of peace of mind; this would generally include belief in and confidence of receiving support from a Supreme Being.

6. Adventure and new experience (we have been called "the curious animal").

We all acquire many attitudes, beliefs, and opinions during our lives. As Rogers and Hammerstein's song in the hit musical *South Pacific* goes, "You've got to be taught" to hate and fear. The song concerns racial prejudice, but the lyrics refer to all our attitudes and beliefs.

We learn our beliefs from our parents, teachers, peers, and religious and political leaders, but we adopt and hold them primarily because they satisfy us. They make us comfortable or otherwise appeal to one or more of our motives. We believe and continue to believe what pleases us.

How else could we rationally explain the fact that a recent survey of Americans revealed that nearly one-third did not believe that the United States had landed men on the moon and brought them back? How can we make any other excuse for the fact that most Americans believe in extrasensory perception (ESP), even though 130 years of scientific study has failed to replicate, under laboratory conditions, a single ESP finding? Why does every American driver consider himself or herself "above average" behind the wheel (a statistical impossibility)?

Religious beliefs probably produce the doubt about U.S. moon landings, despite the amazing films we all have seen on TV. Dogged belief in ESP implies some comforting corollaries for many people. As Thomas Gilovich says, belief in ESP "suggests a greater reality which we have yet to fully understand. This can be an extremely seductive 'transcendental temptation' because it opens up several inviting possibilities, such as the potential for some part of us to survive death."[1]

And, according to Gilovich, we all classify ourselves as "above average" in driving by using the criterion at which we personally excel (see his article in the August 1991 *Reader's Digest*). For instance, if we value courtesy as a driver, we consider ourselves as "above average" at driving since we show more courtesy than most.

So much for beliefs. But the same holds for actions. We do mostly what we *want* to do.

Of course, we do many things because we think we *have to* do them. We have to get up and go to school or to work; we have to obey the traffic laws (most of the time, anyway); we have to wear clothes; we have to treat nicely those people whom we actually detest; and so on. But we only "have to" do these things because we prefer doing them to the more unpleasant alternatives. We could best judge people's behavior if they knew they were not under observation and would never get caught. One interesting finding of a 1991 survey of American attitudes bears mentioning: a surprising number of respondents admitted they would be willing to kill another human

[1] Thomas Gilovich, *How We Know What Isn't So* (New York: The Free Press, 1991), pp. 172–173.

being for a large amount of money, provided they had assurance of never being found out.

That people do and believe what they want becomes for you, as a persuasive speaker, the single most important fact to know and adhere to. Thus, you must find and articulate in your persuasive speeches the reasons that your audience should want to believe or do as you wish them to. This necessity implies four other conditions.

First, if you are to persuade others, you must know your own reasons (or motivations) for believing or doing as you want others to. Then you should have no trouble in discovering those reasons or motivations for your audience.

Second, if you know the available satisfactions for believing or doing something, you probably need to actually believe or do what you urge on others. If you do *not* believe or do what you recommend to others, you probably will not articulate the really important motivations; you will also have great difficulty looking and sounding truly sincere in your appeals (unless, improbably, you can convincingly play a role, as a trained and experienced actor might).

> *If you do not believe or do what you recommend to others, you probably will not articulate the really important motivations; you will also have great difficulty looking and sounding truly sincere in your appeals.*

Sales managers do not train salesmen by teaching them how to sound sincere and enthusiastic about their product. To make them effective salesmen, the sales manager "sells" the salesmen on the quality and value of their product, so that their sincerity and enthusiasm can come "from within." Good sales organizations usually hold regular "sales meetings" to reinforce the group's commitment to their high-quality, value-laden product. Some of these meetings strongly resemble high school "pep rallies" held just before the "big game."

Let me cite one example from classroom experience. I have regularly contributed blood to the Red Cross all my adult life. I have also witnessed a number of student speakers attempt to convince their classmates to donate blood. I can always tell which such speakers actually donate blood and which do not. The speaker who does donate can communicate the deep personal satisfaction one gets from giving "the gift of life" that no billionaire can buy, no scientist can manufacture; the nondonor speaker, not having experienced that sense of satisfaction, cannot communicate that vital message.

The third condition for giving persuasive speeches requires you to answer a question: "Why do these people not already believe or do like I do on this matter?" Answering this question requires audience analysis, for a correct answer can lead to an effective persuasive strategy, but a wrong answer can result in failure to persuade.

For instance, suppose you decide that your audience does not already agree because they know too little about your topic. Then you will choose a strongly information-based approach. Or you may decide they know the topic but simply feel apathetic toward it; then your basic approach will mostly involve providing motivation to believe or act. Do they already agree with you, at least partially? Then a pep talk approach will suffice. Perhaps you learn that your audience strongly opposes your point of view; then you will need a great many compelling arguments, backed by solid evidence and strong, impelling motives in order to overcome this problem.

Fourth, you must strive to avoid offending deeply seated attitudes or beliefs of the audience. Attacks on sacred cows become exercises in futility. Never argue with a fanatic.

The Mountain Bell Telephone System formerly used a radio advertisement featuring a young man who failed miserably in analyzing his audience (a woman) and in discovering her (at least one) deep-seated attitude:

> OPERATOR: I will place that call for you, if you wish, but it's much cheaper if you dial direct.
> MAN: Oh, well, that's the point. I want her to know that I'm spending a lot of money on her.
> OPERATOR: Oh, I understand. Certainly, sir. One moment.
> (Buzz—Buzz)
> WOMAN: Hello.
> OPERATOR: Miss Lucinda Jacobson, please.
> WOMAN: Speaking.
> OPERATOR: I have a call for you placed the *more expensive* way— through an operator. It was not dialed direct. Is that OK, Sir?
> MAN: That's fine. . . . Hi, Cindy, this is Rocky. How are you?
> CINDY: You *fool!*

Take a lesson from "Rocky," and do a good job of analyzing your potential persuadees; then formulate a persuasive plan that you think has a good chance of working.

The PSA (Problem/Solution/Arousal) Plan

You encountered the overall general persuasive plan suggested here back in Chapter 6, "Using Effective Language." In fact, I outlined a speech there that demonstrates the general plan ("Swell Your Vocabulary, Stretch Your Mind"). I call it the "problem/solution/arousal," or PSA, plan.

The PSA plan utilizes very simple psychology. People go through their lives day to day, mostly content with what they already believe and do. They think and behave more or less habitually, and a great deal of inertia operates to keep them that way. People remain satisfied with their beliefs and actions most of the time. They see no reason to change.

As a persuader, you must give them a series of psychological reasons to change.

The first reason you must present should show your audience that a *problem exists.* People do not bother to change either thinking or activity unless they perceive that an actual problem exists and that it affects *them.* We even have an old saying that encapsulates this idea: "If it ain't broke, don't fix it." You must convince your audience that "something got broke."

Once you convince your audience that a problem truly does exist and that it directly affects them (or their friends, family, country, etc.), they become interested in what to do about it. So you tell them. Give them the *solution:* use facts, examples, testimony, and so on to explain and prove how it can solve the problem and convince them that no solution can beat yours as more practical, economical, and desirable. You may also have to prove and explain to them that your solution itself will not create any *new problems.* If you properly "upset" your audience by describing and relating the problem to them, then do a good job handling your proof and explaining your solution, they should come around to a pretty agreeable state of mind.

But while your audience may now agree with you on an intellectual basis, they may not yet feel motivated to change their minds or take action. You must *arouse* them to make an emotional commitment. One good way to do so involves asking the audience to imagine the future, to project themselves forward in time, psychologically, and to consider the "terrible" consequences of the problem left unsolved (we might call this the fear appeal). Then help them visualize what wonderful and marvelous consequences will result if they accept your proposition.

These three elements—the problem, the solution, and the arousal—will generally constitute the three main points of the body of your persuasive speech. Create an interest- and attention-grabbing introduction, finish with an incisive, compelling conclusion, and you have a speech to persuade.

Let's now consider each part of that speech in more detail.

The Introduction

The introduction must capture attention and arouse interest in your topic. Your first words must cross what has been called the *interest deadline*, so do it quickly. Of course, when you get up to speak in class, you have only a minimal problem. After all, everyone expects you to speak on this day and at this time. The class members sit prepared to listen to a speech. They may even have the assignment of taking notes on your speech and later critiquing it. Nevertheless, although you have their general attention, you need to focus their thought processes on your particular topic, through one or more of the methods discussed in the previous chapter.

For the "professional persuader" out there in the real world, the problem of capturing the audience's interest and attention from the very first moment of contact looms large.

But for the "professional persuader" out there in the real world, the problem of capturing the audience's interest and attention from the very first moment of contact looms large indeed. The advertiser must glue you to the TV commercial in the first seconds, or you might head for the bathroom or fridge, or open your book, thus missing the multimillion-dollar ad. The advertiser must grab onto your nervous system instantly to stop you while you are flipping through a magazine, so that you will look at, read, and absorb the full-page picture and message singing the praises of the advertiser's product. Professional speakers or politicians may face the prospect of wringing serious consideration of their topic from a group of comfortable, genial, well-fed-and-wined banquet guests. How do they do it?

TV commercials blast onto our consciousness with bright colors, vivid music or sound, whirlwind activity, beautiful women or handsome men exuding sex appeal, cute little babies or cuddly little animals, mouth-watering close-ups of succulent food, bold double-entendre statements ("Let me see your shorts," "Does she, or doesn't she?"); magazine ads do the same with the printed page, but can only suggest whirlwind activity. The speaker before the restive, bored, or well-stuffed banquet audience has a lesser task, but must start out with proven attention-getting material: a striking statement, a vivid quotation, an amusing story, a gripping human-interest anecdote, or a threat of vital concern to the audience.

The speaker need not always go for gimmicks just to gain attention and interest in the topic. It depends on the amount of interest the audience already has in the subject. For instance, one student's speech began somewhat like this:

> This town has a drinking problem.
>
> The drinking problem consists of the fact that we students have a hard time finding all the bargains in drinking that the town has to offer. In addition, on Sundays, when the bars are closed, students don't know where to get a beer without leaving town. Well, I plan to tell you where and when you can find all the happy hours and other drinking bargains; further, I'll be telling you where you can find a beer here in town on Sunday!

Such an introduction certainly caught the interest and attention of that audience!

Note that this introduction not only strives to capture audience interest and attention by appealing to extant tendencies to act, but it ends with a statement of the speaker's thesis, or purpose. Thus, the introduction performs the two necessary functions of that part of the speech: it draws interest and attention to the topic and specifies the particular purpose.

After you capture the interest and attention of your audience and focus that interest and attention on your specific thesis, you find yourself ready to start the body of your speech, beginning with the problem that needs solving.

Establish the Problem

As stated before, people rarely change (their minds or their actions) as long as they remain comfortable with their beliefs or behaviors. In the problem step you must make the audience *uncomfortable*. You must either present them with a particular problem that cries out for a solution or kindle in them some unfulfilled desire (make them want something they do not yet have). To establish the "problem" in the minds of your audience, you might use several stages in the problem-

You must absolutely succeed in the final stage of the problem step: relate the problem to the audience.

building portion of your speech. Let's illustrate these stages with two hypothetical topics: (1) the need for a new municipal water-purification plant and (2) the desirability of the sport of backpacking.

First, you must explain the nature of the problem (or desire) so that everyone understands exactly what you mean by it. If the audience does not understand the problem, they can hardly do much about it: (1) "Our city faces a severe shortage of drinking water within the next ten years because of a deteriorating water plant built back in 1928." (2) "The cushy, indoor, TV-filled lives we young Americans lead continue to turn us into a bunch of overweight, out-of-shape couch potatoes, causing us to miss out on the greatest gifts nature has to offer."

You might next illustrate the problem with actual examples from real people: (1) "Just last year the people of Jefferson City discovered they had the same problem we will have soon. In November of last year they had to start *rationing* water." (2) "Just three years ago I discovered I had become twenty pounds overweight. Climbing a flight of stairs winded me. I found myself sitting before the TV for hours, hypnotized by that 'chewing gum for the eyes.'"

Next, you might find it necessary to provide additional proof that the problem looms large, by offering more examples, facts, statistics, testimony, and so on: (1) "If our growth in population and industry continues for another three years at the rate of the past ten, our needs will outstrip our maximum ability to produce 10.5 million gallons of water per day, the amount we now use. Consider that: ten and a half million gallons—*each day!*" (2) "The AMA estimates from surveys that 34 percent of Americans age fifteen to twenty-six weigh more than medical science believes they should. The latest statistics from military recruitment physicals reveal that just over half of our young men show serious problems of physical conditioning."

And you must absolutely succeed in this final stage of the problem step: *relate the problem to the audience*. The audience might sit there and agree that a problem does exist; that the problem appears real since it occurred elsewhere; and that it appears widespread and serious. But if you allow them to think at this point, "Well, things really do look bad, but none of this applies to *me*," you lose their interest. So grab them by the lapels: (1) "Without a new water supply in this town in the next three years, you will find that *you* have suddenly become the victim of water rationing." (2) "The time has come for *you* to consider that growing roll around your middle, to break away from the TV, to get interested in the out-of-doors—while still young and without the responsibilities of a career and family."

Provide the Solution

Your problem step has convinced your audience. They understand the problem, see its ramifications, understand its implications, and (most important) feel it as their own. You have upset them. Now you get them off the hook, using four steps.

First, carefully explain the new attitude to adopt or the action to take. Make your explanation perfectly clear to avoid any misunderstanding: (1) "We must pass the city bond issue for the proposed new

Your problem step has convinced your audience. You have upset them. Now you get them off the hook . . .

water system. I ask each of you to go to the polls on April 13 and vote 'yes' for Proposition 2." (2) "I propose that you at least try a highly satisfying form of recreation: backpacking. I don't mean that you should run out and spend $500 on equipment and hit the most rugged section of the Appalachian Trail this weekend. But you can rent or borrow the minimal equipment and then try it out to see if you like it by backpacking lightly at a state park some long weekend."

Second, show that your plan will solve the problem. Show that it works. If you don't prove this point, you fail. For instance, most Americans would like to see it made extremely difficult for mental patients, career criminals, and small children to get their hands on guns. But few proposals so far offered to achieve these goals have shown any promise of really working, without enacting complete martial law—and who wants *that*?

So show that your idea does work: (1) "The Water Board estimates that the new system that Proposition 2 would provide will supply us with all the water we will need through the year 2060." (2) "Complete backpacking provides lots of fresh air and exercise, ensures a healthful nutrition plan, and gets you out where you can commune with nature. I have lost thirty pounds of flab and now can hike twenty-five miles of mountain trail per day, carrying thirty-five pounds on my back."

If possible, you should next illustrate your plan's success. Sometimes such illustrations do not exist, but if they do, they make for excellent proof: (1) "Proposition 2 will give us almost the same kind of system Jefferson City installed in 1991. They have a system *par excellence*. Let me tell you about *their* . . ." (2) "Since I have gotten into shape through backpacking, I can now venture into beautiful country that will remain unseen by 99 percent of our citizens."

Finally, in this "plan works" portion of your speech, you must anticipate and overcome any objections the audience might have to accepting your proposal. You have probably failed to persuade anyone who walks away from your speech saying something like, "That all sounded pretty good to me, *but* . . ."

Obviously the audience has objections to your proposal; otherwise they would have already taken the necessary actions and would not need persuading. What objections could they have? The usual general objections come to mind easily: it will take too much time, money, or effort; it might create other problems; the proposed solution may not work as well as some other, unmentioned solution.

Specific purposes ferret out specific objections. "Buy a Ford Escort" might meet the resistance of "It's too small," "Read *Gone with the Wind*" brings out "I don't need to; I've seen the movie seven times," or "I already read it, years ago."

I cannot overly stress the importance of this stage of the problem-solution step. Unless you overcome obvious or latent objections, persuasion does not take place. I have in my "persuasion" file a sales manual for a popular encyclopedia. The manual contains stock rebuttals to stock objections that the potential customer will probably raise. The salesperson memorizes all these rebuttals and comes to your doorstep prepared to launch into any and all of them to make the sale.

For instance, a customer will commonly object to the cost of the books. For this objection the salesperson has six memorized rebuttals to call forth at the drop of a sales brochure. For the objection, "I want to think it over" (a position the sales rep must never let stand) the salesperson can call on any one of thirteen memorized rebuttals. "Children as young as ours can't use an encyclopedia" will meet any one of four stock rebuttals. And so on.

The point? You must prepare for any possible objection and have the ammunition to overcome it. You may hold a question-and-answer period after your speech in which most of this can occur; if not, you will have to handle all expected objections in the speech itself. Again, failure to do so, where objections exist, doom the persuasive speech to failure.

You may have to work at your creative best to devise ways to overcome objections. A young man in my class once gave a lively, interesting, even fascinating speech on "Take a Trip to Europe." His talk, reinforced by his 35mm slides, made Europe seem exciting and rewarding. Unfortunately, when it came to how his college-student audience might afford such a trip, he remained silent. When asked about this omission, he lamely replied that he "didn't want to bring up this negative point and spoil the speech."

Granted, one can spend a fortune on a European vacation. But one can cut corners, too. Did our young man discuss the best times of the year for bargain air fares? How about special student rates, or tours? Couldn't young people save a lot by hiking around Europe, using Eurailpasses, staying in student hostels? How about suggesting that a student's parents, friends, and relatives be talked into pooling their resources to pay all or part of such a trip as a graduation present?

You don't wish to read *Gone with the Wind* because you already read it six years ago? Don't you know you can get a lot more out of a big book like that on a second, third, or even fourth reading? How much of the book do you really remember after six years? Wouldn't you find it great to reread the book, and thus refresh your memory in order to make reading the sequel, *Scarlett*, more meaningful?

If you have done your job up to now, you have secured your audience's collective ear. You have convinced them that a real or potential problem truly faces them, that your solution will solve the problem for them, and that they really can adopt your solution. They sit there, intellectually prepared to follow your guidance, perhaps, but will they act? Probably not. You have to do one more thing. *Motivate* them.

Arouse Emotions

To arouse an audience means to quicken their heartbeats and to raise their blood pressures and body temperatures. Excite them with the positive future prospects they will enjoy when they follow your advice. Or, contrariwise, paint a gloomy picture of what awaits them if they don't heed your words. Many times you will want the audience to imagine both the positive and negative consequences of following your lead. In this third main point of the body of your speech, you make your audience want what you wish them to want. Here you do not describe the ratio of fat to lean meat on the steak; instead you "sell the sizzle" of that mouth-watering T-bone on the platter.

To illustrate, again with our two sample topics: (1) "Allow this bond issue in April to fail, and in a few months you might wake up one morning, turn on the faucet to fill the coffee pot, and get nothing but a gurgle. Opening the morning newspaper, you might learn that *your* street gets water on odd-number days of the month only. Happy toothbrushing! But if you help get this bond issue passed, we can all look forward to all the sweet, fresh water we will need in our lifetimes. No need to do without watering the parched lawn in August; have all the water you need for laundry, your pool, carwashing, . . ." (2) "So, you can go on with your sedentary, indoor life—continue to walk only from your desk to your car to the dining table to the chair in front of the TV to the fridge. You can thus keep working toward that heart attack at age forty. *Or* you can become a backpacker, toughen up your legs and body, rejuvenate your heart, and open your senses to the wilderness. Learn what it's like to sleep and wake up beside a gurgling mountain stream, miles from the sounds of civilization. Discover the thrill of climbing to the valley's rim for a view that you have truly earned, and discover that you consider it worth the ascent . . ."

> *In this third main point of the body of your speech, you make your audience want what you wish them to want . . . you "sell the sizzle."*

After a near-lifetime of hearing student speeches in classrooms, I remain amazed by the number of speakers who either fail to offer or else give short shrift to this arousal step. The cause might stem from the wish of young people to eschew anything resembling emoting, so as to appear cool. Youngsters may also have difficulty in finding and using strongly emotional "future-pictures" to relate to their audiences. But, whatever the reason, neglect of the arousal step (or, as James M. Holm dubbed it, the projection step) greatly detracts from the persuasive potential of the speech to persuade.

Even a beginning student speaker should find it possible to construct a formidable projection step fairly easily by using his or her own experience. After all, speakers who do or believe what they urge must already possess the pertinent knowledge to so construct that step. Do you want people to buckle up their seat belts each time they enter a car, as you do? Then you should know how it feels to buckle. Even if you have difficulty putting it into words, perhaps you can find, through research, material that you can use. How about this:

Oh, I know you can find easy excuses for not buckling up on every little trip. Well, just keep on making those excuses, and you might have the kind of "minor" accident that Walter H. Cameron of Indianapolis had. Forced off the road and into a concrete abutment at only *twenty-five miles an hour*, Mr. Cameron crashed into his steering wheel with the same force as if he had fallen from *two stories*. For his dangling, unused seat belt, he paid one broken jaw, three fractured ribs, a cracked elbow, and fourteen stitches in his face and neck.

Or you can do like me. I have the seat belt habit. In a car I feel not quite dressed without first hearing that reassuring metallic click as I assure myself of greater safety. Each time I get behind the wheel I snap on that belt just as automatically as I insert the ignition key and turn on my engine. That belt reminds me that I am undertaking a dangerous task: driving but that I have become a safer driver by this action. As I take on the now-conscious task of risking my life and limb on our streets, the gentle tug of my seat belt reminds me constantly of my status as a safety-conscious, responsible driver. Do the same, and you can quietly increase your own self-pride as a safe, conscientious driver.

So, find or develop that arousal step, include it in your speech, and smell that steak sizzling.

The Conclusion

Up to now you have captured your audience's interest and attention, proven to them that some problem exists, demonstrated that your solution will take care of things just fine and dandy, and energized them to change in the direction you have advocated by arousing their emotions. Now you need to tie up your appeals in a single knot and come to an end so that your persuasion can begin to show results. You can do so in several ways, only some of which I illustrate:

Make a direct challenge or appeal: "Don't wait until too late! Do it now!" "The sale ends Thursday. Come in tomorrow!" "Supply limited! First come, first served."

Summarize or restate the thesis: "And so you see, we simply have to have that new water system. Be sure to get down to the polls on April 13 and vote 'Yes' on Proposition 2; and take your friends and neighbors to the polls, too, so they can vote for *progress*."

Use a stirring quotation: "Goethe said it for all of us: 'Nature knows no pause in progress and development, and attaches her curse on all inaction.'"

Use a telling illustration to encapsulate your theme: "Seize your opportunity today! Remember the frugal Frenchman who saved his most precious bottle of wine to toast his long life on his deathbed; when the dying man finally opened the bottle, he found that it had turned to vinegar. Drink the wine of life while you can enjoy it!"

Make a statement of personal intent: "The Student Union will sponsor an easy overnight hike from Neels Gap to Woody Gap on the last weekend of next month. I plan to enjoy that hike myself. Won't you join me?"

There you have it. A step-by-step, stage-by-stage plan for persuasive speaking. Later in this chapter we will look at how to adapt the PSA plan to various kinds of persuasive speeches.

You may remember that Chapter 6 ("Using Effective Language") included a sample speech that follows the PSA plan. This might be a good time for you to go back and review that speech.

Don't think that dreary old speech professors, out of touch with the real world, are the only advocates of the PSA plan. You can find the plan used by professional persuaders countless times throughout the day or night. For instance, many one-minute commercials on television thrive on it.

In my own classes I show a film of award-winning TV commercials that illustrate various advertising techniques. I then use a handout to discuss how each commercial either emphasizes one or more of the steps in the PSA plan or systematically clicks through each step. One that does the latter, a particular favorite with students, advertises the Volvo. We first see a house with attached garage, door open, a car's front end exposed to our view. Our attention and interest become immediately involved as, through animation, the car turns into an animal, with headlight eyes, hood-cover mouth, wheel feet, and a switching tail behind. The announcer asks, "Has your sleek wild animal turned into a monster? What with the gas bills, the repair bills, is he eating you out of house and home?" By now the "car" has begun to eat up its garage and house (the problem). The owner muzzles the monster by putting a chair in its mouth and drives it off to trade for a new Volvo (the solution), which he drives home and parks. Then the announcer points out that, freed from all those gas and repair payments, the owner can put his money into home improvement and swimming pool payments, as our hero repairs the monster's damage, puts in new bedrooms upstairs, and installs a new swimming pool (positive arousal). Then the announcer mentions "fence payments" to "protect your home from your neighbors' beasts" (and the visual field expands to show neighbors' houses, outside our hero's new fence, getting devoured by *their* cars (negative arousal). The conclusion remains covertly implied: "Buy a Volvo."

Persuasion in Campaigns

Much persuasion in our culture occurs in campaigns, extended over considerable periods of time. In the case of campaigns, individual messages may strive to accomplish only one or two goals of the PSA pattern. Some advertising campaigns and practically all political campaigns use this strategy. For instance, when the Stan Freberg Ltd., But Not Very ad agency agreed to take over the Chun King Chow Mein account, they found a major problem: almost no one knew that the canned Chinese food existed. The first step in their ad campaign, then, concentrated efforts to introduce the product to the nation by drawing attention and interest to its very existence. After getting brand-name recognition (attention, interest), the next stage of the campaign emphasized sales points.

> *Much persuasion in our culture occurs in campaigns, extended over considerable periods of time.*

Most campaigns must appeal to broad segments of a population scattered by location, intelligence level, education, age, and so on.

The campaign runs for a considerable period of time, and often goes through the three to five steps of the PSA plan. Consider the case of beginning a race, from scratch, for state governor.

When I lived in Nebraska, the governorship became vacant. A

man from a tiny town of about four hundred souls in the sand hills of northern Nebraska decided to run. The group he organized to advance his candidacy faced a formidable problem: No one outside of the candidate's small hometown had ever heard of him. So the first campaign goal was to introduce the candidate to the state's voters.

To accomplish this goal, radio jingles were composed and sung over the airwaves; these jingles taught the public to spell and pronounce the candidate's name. After the jingles had taught us his name and how to spell it (assisted by pictures in paid newspaper ads and others nailed to telephone poles), the next step of the campaign took shape: the candidate and his followers began pointing out the unsolved problems left behind by the departing governor and his unicameral legislatures. The candidate stumped the state, noting these problems repeatedly.

Next step came a series of messages designed to show how the new governor would solve the problems he had so effectively articulated. He would provide leadership, would answer the objections of his opponents, and so on.

After a weeks-long campaign of discussing the problems and how to solve them (the issues), the candidate and his organization adopted the time-tested step of arranging for brief TV commercial spots, some live media events, and public appearances designed to show off the candidate smiling and waving confidently, projecting the positive image of leadership that he would carry into the governor's mansion.

Late in the campaign the staff turned their attention to concluding the campaign successfully—by urging a get-out-the-vote wave of activity.

This particular campaign succeeded. Norbert Tieman became Nebraska's governor.

In summary, for such a long campaign the persuasion might follow the steps of the PSA plan, each step a stage in that campaign, each with a specific goal, but all of them together aiming for a final, general outcome, or ultimate objective. We could map it this way:

Stage 1 (Introduction). *Specific goal:* to make name and face of candidate known. *Technique:* make appearances, play jingles, advertise name and picture widely. *Ultimate objective:* to elect candidate governor.

Stage 2 (Problem step). *Specific goal:* to create dissatisfaction among electorate over state of the state. *Technique:* criticize rivals supposedly responsible for state problems. *Ultimate objective:* to elect candidate governor.

Stage 3 (Solution step). *Specific goal:* to convince electorate that candidate can solve state's problems. *Technique:* present platform, views, solutions. *Ultimate objective:* to elect candidate governor.

Stage 4 (Arousal step). *Specific goal:* to heighten candidate's image as inspirational leader. *Technique:* nonargumentative TV spots, media appearances, etc. *Ultimate objective:* to elect candidate governor.

Stage 5 (Concluding step). *Specific goal:* to get out the (favorable) vote. *Technique:* stir up the candidate's faithful, arrange for transportation to the polls, and so on. *Ultimate objective:* to elect candidate governor.

As mentioned above, the same series of steps can constitute an advertising campaign, especially for a new or otherwise relatively unknown product.

Types of Persuasive Speeches

You might present any of three types of persuasive speeches, classified as to specific purpose: to convince, to actuate, or to stimulate. You must know exactly which kind of persuasive goal you plan to achieve, since your specific purpose determines which type of speech you will present. And how you arrange and build the speech depends on the type of speech you will give. Let us consider each type in turn.

Speeches to Convince

Two characteristics distinguish the speech to convince: (1) It argues a controversial proposition, meaning one on which reasonable and informed people will disagree. In fact, the speaker must assume that at least part of the audience will disagree with his or her thesis; otherwise they would not need any convincing. (2) The speaker attempts only to modify the audience's attitudes, opinions, or beliefs, rather than to motivate them to take action. In other words, the speaker tries to get the audience to form, modify, or strengthen their attitude toward some moot proposition, such as "We should view gambling as morally wrong." With a topic like this, the speaker merely hopes to convince the audience to agree with the speech's thesis; the speech can succeed even if the audience does not decide to fly to Atlantic City or Las Vegas to begin wrecking the gambling casinos. Speeches to convince fall into three categories, depending on what type of proposition each argues. Again, you must exercise your critical judgment on what type of proposition you will argue in your speech, because once again, the type of proposition determines to some extent how speech construction should proceed.

Speeches to convince argue propositions of policy, value, or fact.

QUESTIONS OF POLICY   The speech to convince on a proposition of policy argues that we should (or should not) immediately adopt a certain policy, rule, or law that will govern our behavior in the future. For this reason, we say that a proposition of policy always concerns the future. Some propositions of policy:

The federal government should (or should not) control and license all ownership of guns.

Congress should (or should not) revive the Equal Rights Amendment and submit it to the states for ratification.

The federal government should (or should not) decriminalize the recreational use of marijuana.

Congress should (or should not) repeal the Delaney Clause.

The government should (or should not) legalize laetrile.

Our state should (or should not) legalize gambling (a lottery, pari-mutuel betting, dog racing, etc.).

The government should (or should not) double the money it spends on AIDS research.

At a bare minimum, the policy speech must deal with at least three stock issues: need (or lack of need), why a solution will (or won't) work, and practicality (impracticality). These issues or propositions *inherently* constitute the proposition or issue of policy. They take this form:

1. Serious problems do (do not) exist in relation to X.

2. The proposed plan will (will not) solve these problems (even if such problems did exist).

3. The proposed plan will (will not) solve the problems in the most practicable manner (but, in fact, will produce additional problems, etc.).

Notice that, with this "stock issues" arrangement, the speaker arguing *for* a new policy would have to prove *all three* propositions to succeed at persuasion (with no problem, no solution becomes necessary; if no solution seems needed, who cares about its practicability?). Note, also, that to be against a new policy, one need prove only *one* of the three issues (if no need, no problem; if the plan would not solve the problem, even if one existed, it won't get adopted; even if the problem existed and the plan would solve it, that plan won't get adopted if seen as impracticable or productive of additional problems. Debaters call this the even-if negative case).

> *The stock-issues arrangement consists of the PSA plan minus introduction, conclusion, and arousal step.*

You might also notice that the stock-issues arrangement consists of the PSA plan minus introduction, conclusion, and arousal step. But the entire PSA plan works best for a proposition of policy because it includes the features missing from the straight stock-issues case (introduction, arousal step, and conclusion), as in the following:

INTRODUCTION: Voltaire once said that "The art of medicine consists of amusing the patient while nature cures the disease." He was not referring to the problem of America's medically uninsured.

PROBLEM: Thirty to thirty-five million Americans do not have nor can afford medical insurance; they face possible financial ruin.

SOLUTION: Senate Bill X proposes a limited "socialized medicine" plan for these people. It will work, and prove the most practical plan, too.

AROUSAL: What would you do if you lost your job, or if your employer canceled your health coverage? Wouldn't you like basking in the security of knowing that, even if you became seriously ill, the federal government would pay your medical bills?

CONCLUSION: So Senate Bill X should come into law. (*Optional:* Get busy. Write or call your senators and urge them to vote for this bill.)

The major advantage to this arrangement for the speech to convince on a proposition of policy lies in the fact that emotional arousal will help secure audience compliance with the speaker's purpose.

QUESTIONS OF VALUE The speech to convince on an issue or proposition of value concerns the present. It argues that "at the present time, we should (or should not) place this value on that entity." Some sample propositions of value:

Japan (no longer) builds better cars than America.

Capital punishment should (not) be considered anti-Christian.

We overpay our professional athletes.

We should (not) condemn strikes by firefighters or policemen as sinful.

Money spent on outer space represents money well-spent.

Photography should (not) come under the classification of "true art."

The speech to convince on a proposition of value ordinarily would not use the PSA plan, since its own stock issues do not fit that plan. For the value speech you would argue two other basic stock issues that we find inherent in any issue of value:

1. We define the *criteria* for ——— as ———.

2. XXXX meets (doesn't meet) the criteria for ———, which indicates that we should (not) consider XXXX as ———.

Put more concretely:

1. A panel of international experts agree that the criteria for classifying something as "an art" are X, Y, and Z.

2. We can (or cannot) consider photography an art since it certainly does (does not) fit the definition according to criteria X, Y, and Z.

Your chances of getting into a seemingly unending and thankless argument increase when an issue becomes one of value. The reason? Little attention gets paid to defining and agreeing on the criteria by which to judge. Few people can readily agree on a definition of *overpaid, sin, right, wrong, Christian, moral, best, or better.* But once people can agree on criteria and a definition, disputes of value resolve themselves with remarkable ease. Most true issues of value divide people deeply because they lack common definitions. In this respect the ongoing abortion debate has many features of an issue of value. One side defines *life* as the beginning of conception, whereas the other defines *life* as "capable of independent existence outside the womb," or some such. One side calls abortion murder; the other side calls it self-management of one's own body. One side declares itself as "pro-choice" (as they define it); the other side proclaims itself "pro-life," whatever that means to them. (And who would really wish to claim an "anti-choice" or a "non-pro-life" stance?). Women who patronize abortion clinics admit only to "exercising their legal rights of choice," whereas the Operation Rescue people who trespass on abortion clinics and defy court orders by physically blocking the entrances to these clinics claim that they follow a "higher law." Should we wonder if these groups will ever come to any kind of agreement on this emotional, semantically tangled issue?

QUESTIONS OF FACT   The third kind of speech to convince argues a question of *fact*—whether a certain cause-effect relationship exists, whether some event happened (or happened in a certain way), or whether such-and-such exists (or exists in a certain form).

Of course, we would not argue most issues of fact, although we often find ourselves embroiled in such an argument before we know it. But why argue over an issue such as "Who was named MVP in the 1989 World Series?" A simple check of the record books can save a lot of time, effort, and breath. However, many issues of fact cannot be resolved in the library. Most issues settled by criminal and civil court cases, for instance, constitute controversial matters of fact. Do we find the defendant guilty of murder (robbery, burglary, arson, embezzlement)? Other issues of fact we might argue:

Do UFO's represent visits from interplanetary neighbors?

Does no-fault insurance do what it's supposed to do?

Did Lee Harvey Oswald assassinate JFK all by himself? Or at all?

Have more ships and planes disappeared in the so-called Bermuda Triangle than in any other comparable area of ocean?

Does air pollution actually shorten human life?

Do viruses cause cancer?

Do large doses of vitamin C aid in warding off colds?

Does AIDS pose a major health threat to middle-class America?

Issues of fact present a unique problem for the speech designed to convince. Unlike the issues of policy and value, the issue of fact does not automatically generate a set of stock issues that demand answers. The speaker must look to the content of the topic to discover the particular propositions that he or she must prove to establish a thesis.

Some issues of fact do lend themselves to a stock issues analysis, of course. To prove, say, that John Doe murdered his business partner in the first degree, legal doctrine decrees that a number of propositions must be proven in court:

1. John Doe had a motive for killing his partner.

2. John Doe had the opportunity to kill his partner.

3. John Doe had the ability to kill his partner.

4. John Doe's murder of his partner was premeditated; he planned it for some time, and did not kill the partner in a sudden fit of rage.

For other, less formalized issues of fact, one must study the content of the issue to find the propositions one needs to argue or prove. For instance, take the question "Does cigarette smoking cause lung cancer?" Antismoking advocates say "Yes"; the tobacco industry says "No," citing the fact that "only correlational" evidence exists, which does not prove causation. To prove an answer to the question one way or the other, you would have to look at all the evidence and, from this body of information, find the propositions (arguments) to defend.

Recently the Consortium for Mathematics produced a series of educational videotapes on statistics, called "Against All Odds." One of these tapes, titled "The Question of Causation," used the smoking controversy to illustrate how scientific studies, combined with statistical analysis, determine causation. The tape shows how a medical commission reached the conclusion that cigarette smoking causes cancer:

I. Retrogressive studies show a strong correlation between smoking and cancer (people with lung cancer were checked for past smoking habits).

II. *Progressive* studies, done later, also show a strong correlation between smoking and cancer (people who smoked or didn't smoke were followed for a number of years to see who did and did not develop lung cancer).

III. Other progressive studies ruled out the effect of confounding variables by matching smokers and nonsmokers on nineteen variables that might influence both smoking or nonsmoking and cancer or no cancer, with the same results as other studies.

IV. Animal studies show that tobacco contains carcinogens, which cause cancer.
  A. Tobacco tar caused cancer on the skin of mice.
  B. The more smoke hamsters inhaled, the more often they contracted lung cancer.

ETHICS OF THE COMPLETE ARGUMENT   I believe that every person who elects to take on the responsibility of convincing others should take *full* responsibility by delving into and, as much as possible, presenting *the complete argument*. By this I do not mean that you must present all the points in your favor and then turn around and present all the points against you. I mean that you must think your subject through, research it thoroughly, and then present the complete case for your side so far as possible. Let me illustrate.

All too many people, both inside and outside speech classrooms, give one-issue speeches that really constitute one-third (or less) of a complete discussion. They probably do this because they find it easy. I constantly hear speeches arguing theses such as: "Our country needs a new energy policy"; "Federal health insurance for all will greatly benefit the needy"; or "We should license each U.S. citizen, at birth, to reproduce himself or herself once and only once, thus solving the problem of the population explosion."

Consider the speech on our country needing a new energy policy. No person of ordinary intelligence would have difficulty citing problems with how we use, waste, and store energy in this country. This represents only the "problem" step in the entire issue of policy (and most people would already agree on the problem anyway); the speaker does not take on the responsibility of showing how we can improve our policy, that such changes would be beneficial and practicable, and so on—the speaker does not take on the really difficult task. The speaker takes a cheap shot. Why stir up people without showing that we can have something better?

Or take the issue of federal health insurance and how it will benefit the needy. Certainly, if our government passed a bill to provide national health insurance for all, the poorest people would benefit. No real need to prove this point. But this one-point shot doesn't go on to consider whether all people need a one-plan-fits-all health care system. The thesis of the speech also seems to disregard the arguments of practicality, such as how the plan would be funded. Again, one would find it very easy to show that *any* costly program will have *some* benefits to *some* people or groups.

Finally, let's consider the idea of controlling population by licensing citizens to reproduce themselves only once. A speaker could easily show that our growing population causes problems, and logic (and mathematics) tells us that if each citizen reproduced himself or herself only once, we would have zero population growth. But what about the legality, constitutionality, or even simple general practicability of this policy? For instance, what if a couple had triplets? What about sanctions? And how do we enforce such a law?

> *Strive to present complete arguments in your speeches. If you argue for a new policy, for instance, cover all the stock issues.*

Under some conditions, we could perhaps consider these incomplete arguments as ethically justifiable. For instance, we could accept both the energy policy and the federal health insurance policy speeches, if considered parts of overall campaigns, in which the missing issues would receive attention at other times. Even the speech proposing reproductive licensing might have useful social results if the speaker actually intended the speech as a satire that would shake up the audience and cause them to think about the population explosion problem and other, more reasonable solutions.

But in class you will probably not give individual speeches as part of any campaign. So strive to present complete arguments in your speeches. Avoid the whiny "We gotta do something about . . ." type of speech. If you argue for a new policy, for instance, cover all the stock issues. And try to avoid what legislatures too often do: they adopt policies without careful thought about possible unintended results. One state recently cracked down on DUI (driving under the influence) penalties in order to reduce drunk driving. One unintended result: an increase in hit-and-run offenses. Drivers easily figured out that they could receive a lesser sentence for leaving the scene of an accident and later turning themselves in (giving them time to sober up) than to fail the breathalyzer test at the scene and thus get the stiffer DUI penalty.

Speeches to Actuate

The speech to actuate tries to motivate the audience to *do* something in particular. The audience may not even consider the suggested action controversial; they may already agree they should do what the speaker wants. So why do they not already do it? They lack motivation. The speaker must supply this motivation.

Just about everyone would agree that we ought to read more good literature and watch less junk on TV; that we should get more exercise and eat a more balanced diet; that we should give more to charity; that we should donate our time to worthy causes and our blood to the Red Cross; that we should buy more life insurance and eat less snack food. But we go along our lazy way and watch TV, eat junk food, avoid buying life insurance so we can spend money on more fun things, and so on. We choose these alternatives because of our motivations; only changed motivations will change our behavior.

The speaker must find and communicate the personal benefits of choosing the better alternatives. The PSA plan provides the ideal organizational and psychological tool for accomplishing this aim. Here are some possible thesis topics for the speech to actuate:

Take up sewing.	Bake your own bread.
Vote in the next election.	Take up jogging (or ———).
Do not swim in the ocean.	Conserve water (or ———).
Subscribe to ———.	Begin Christmas shopping *now*.
Spay or neuter your pet.	Get an emergency CB radio for your car.
Recycle.	
Take a course in ———.	Get flu shots this fall.
Read a weekly news magazine.	Join Triple A (or ———).
Get a physical exam yearly.	Attend the college play.
Open a Christmas club account.	Join a book club.

Attend a concert.

Write or wire your congressional representative about ———.

Read a prize-winning novel.

Take up skydiving (or ———).

Speeches to Stimulate

Most people find the speech to stimulate more difficult to carry off than any other, because this type of speech urges an audience to do or believe something that they *already* do or believe. The speech, to achieve success, must further heighten existing emotional commitment—must excite people to behave or believe more fervently and with more devotion than they already do. Coaches, sales managers, and ministers probably use this form of speech most often.

> *The speech to stimulate must excite people to behave or believe more fervently and with more devotion than they already do.*

Coaches must somehow inspire their players to more fervently wish to win (they already want to)—to psych them up so they will throw their minds and bodies into the contest with more and more spirit and abandon (they already believe that they play hard). The sales manager, by the same token, must harangue his already-trying sales representatives to see more clients, spend more time and energy, renew their enthusiasm for their products, and so on. The minister must face the same flock each week (sometimes more than once a week) and motivate them to commit themselves both emotionally and monetarily to the already-accepted tenets of their church. All of these speakers must face, by and large, the same audience each time they attempt to persuade. And all must have a fresh approach or fresh material for each encounter with their audience. Perhaps we can now understand why people in these professions change jobs so much—they go in search of fresh audiences. (Professors have no such problem: they get fresh audiences every term, so they can use the same material nearly indefinitely!)

If you must give a speech to stimulate, you will have the most success with the PSA plan, with especially heavy emphasis on the arousal step. By its nature, the speech to stimulate must rely on emotional proof; this makes the speech difficult, for you must also stimulate yourself in order to stimulate others. The successful stimulator comes close to our definition of the haranguer. And success as a haranguer seems to come from the genes one inherits, rather than what one can learn from textbooks. If you are not a natural haranguer, you can borrow well-written, emotional material to stimulate both yourself and others. Again I recommend the various collections of quotations; also, you may find inspiring stories and anecdotes in magazines, newspapers, and books.

On Proof

Before concluding this chapter, we must briefly consider *proof*, although you may think I already covered that in Chapter 4.

The Greeks of Aristotle's time divided all oratorical proof into three categories, which we still find useful now as we approach the twenty-first century: *logos*, *pathos*, and *ethos*.

We define *logos* as logical proof, supporting material, or evidence,

> *The Greeks of Aristotle's time divided all oratorical proof into three categories:* logos, pathos, *and* ethos.

the types of which I did cover in Chapter 4. That chapter tells you what kinds of evidence you need to find, how to find it, and how to use it. You may want to review that chapter briefly at this point. The Greeks correctly pointed out that *logos* "resides in the speech itself." You find the evidence and put it into your speech.

The Greeks saw *pathos* as residing in the audience. Because humans already tend to habitually respond to their own emotional needs and wants, the speaker who appeals to those emotions taps the proof already within the audience members' psyches. If I "prove" that you should do or believe by appealing to your pride, your greed, your patriotism, your sex drive, or whatever, I have utilized your own nervous systems as proof.

Ethos, or ethical proof, resides within the speaker—within you. Modern writers, eschewing the perfectly sound old term ethos, now prefer the more sophisticated term *source credibility*. We can compare ethos to the concept of personality. Everyone possesses both ethos and a personality, and either can impress others on a scale ranging from very bad to very good. If an audience tends to believe something (or refuses to believe something) for the sole or main reason of who said it, we say that the speaker's ethos produced the belief (or lack of it).

Aristotle wrote of two types of ethos: prior and developed. *Prior ethos* we can also call reputation. Your reputation, or what we know of your credibility before you ever begin to speak, might influence how we respond to your words. The speaker acquires (or fails to acquire) *developed ethos* during the speech. If what a speaker says and the way she says it strike you favorably, your regard for her credibility rises (and vice versa). Good speakers tend to develop favorable ethos; poor speakers tend not to.

Aristotle contended that one should never rely on one's own prior ethos, or reputation. He insisted that one should speak in such a way as to acquire ethos with each speech, rather like the one-time motto of a U.S. airline: "We have to earn our wings every day." I concur with Aristotle's advice: Do not depend on reputation (as a beginner you have little anyway); earn your credibility with every speech you give.

And how does one earn credibility? Research shows that three specific factors create ethos:

1. *Content:* Speakers with low to moderate prior ethos who use solid, fresh evidence acquire ethos.

2. *Delivery:* Speakers who demonstrate poise, communicate enthusiasm, and appear sincere acquire ethos.

3. *Impartiality:* Speakers perceived as not benefiting from the success of their persuasion acquire ethos; speakers perceived as arguing for their own special interests do not acquire ethos. Of course, few people can appear completely impartial when arguing fervently for a strongly held conviction; in such a situation, research shows, an audience will settle for fairness in the absence of real impartiality.

It seems we can conclude here that, to acquire the credibility you need, you ought to follow most of the directions contained in this book and give well-prepared, solid, well-delivered speeches on topics that you know thoroughly and believe in fervently. In fact, I can offer documented proof that students who concentrate on and succeed at producing textbook-quality speeches will not only succeed at persuasion but will also probably excel at getting high grades on speeches.[2]

Let's consider another useful analysis of ethos. Modern factor

[2]Charles R. Gruner, Marsha W. Gruner, and Donald O. Olson, "Is Classroom Evaluation Related to Actual Effectiveness of Classroom Speeches?" *Southern Speech Journal*, 24 (Fall 1968), 36–46.

analysis tells us that it contains two major components: authoritativeness, *or expertness* (does the speaker seem to know the subject matter?) and character (whether the audience trusts or likes the speaker). A speaker may strike an audience as strong on one factor and weak on the other. One striking example: a U.S. president who had to resign from office. He was not forced from office because he lacked expertise or authoritativeness; we believed he knew his stuff. But the country came to see flaws in his character; we lost our trust in him. And by the way, research tells us that the speaker who uses a modicum of relevant, apt humor in speaking will likely receive higher ratings on character, if not on authoritativeness. It seems that people respond more positively to a speaker who uses humor. In short, how you speak and what you say will determine how credible you appear to your audience.

I believe that this chapter gives you sound advice on how to develop any kind of persuasive speech. I strongly urge that you review it before beginning work on any such speech. And as usual, I also admonish you to review Chapter 2, the basic "blocking and tackling" chapter, before beginning serious work on any speech, whether persuasive or not.

10

SPEAKING TO ENTERTAIN

Accounding to a recent book by Russell Joyner, Americans receive more entertainment from radio, TV, magazines, movies, and other media than anyone else in the world. But despite the ubiquity of media entertainment in our culture, Americans also get a lot of entertainment from individual persons speaking. For many occasions few options for entertainment exist other than "the evening's (or afternoon's) speaker." Organizations that meet on a regular basis, particularly, have an ongoing need for speakers to provide programs. Because of my profession, I usually notice such items in the local newspaper as

The local chapter of the Audubon Society will hold its monthly meeting Tuesday at the Ramada Inn.. Local ornithologist Max Williams will speak on "Latest Moves to Reintroduce the Peregrine Falcon to Georgia."

or

Dr. Gene Stotlar will speak on "New Research on Preventing Cardiac Arrest" at next Monday's meeting of the Rotary Club.

Now, you might think that speeches on the peregrine falcon or the prevention of heart attacks don't sound like "speeches to entertain"— they sound more like speeches to inform. You probably harbor such thoughts because you immediately equate "speech to entertain" with "funny speech." But, as we shall see, "after-dinner speech" does not automatically mean "funny speech." Granted, much after-dinner speaking seems to devote itself to light, airy, frivolous, even ludicrous *humor*, but even more after-dinner speaking does not.

Just what do you consider entertaining? Must everything you call "entertainment" make you laugh or smile? Of course not.

Do you go to the movies? Sure you do. Only to comedies? Certainly not. And on TV, do you watch only standup comics, sitcoms, or Jay Leno on *The Tonight Show*? How about your reading? Do you confine that to *MAD* magazine, joke books, the comics pages, Dave Barry's columns, or cartoons in *The New Yorker?*

Actually, we find all kinds of entertainment in our mass media and elsewhere that we can't, by any stretch of the imagination, call funny. In fact, anything that holds our interest qualifies as entertaining.

Holding Audience Interest

So, we can call the primary goal of the speech to entertain that of *holding the audience's interest*. The speech to entertain might also persuade, it might inform, it might amaze, or scare, or even baffle an audience (as do stage magicians). But to entertain, it must, first and last, hold the audience's interest.

This requirement of interest involves some specific corollaries that we might consider here:

1. A group that invites a particular person to speak on a particular topic usually does so because they have a prior interest in that speaker or topic. Audubon Society members would have a keen interest in reintroducing the peregrine to their area; Rotarians would want to learn about precautions for avoiding heart attacks.

2. The "entertaining speaker" should feel an obligation *to emphasize* the interest component of his or her speech over any other. If the host group pays a fee to the speaker, this obligation looms even larger.

3. Selection of a specific topic or thesis and how to handle it become acutely important in the case of a more heterogeneous audience. You can expect bird lovers to have an interest in falcons and Rotarians' to have concern over cardiovascular health; but what topic would interest a mixed group of people assembled to celebrate a birthday, an anniversary, or a retirement?

4. If you must entertain through holding interest, then you should use the factors of interest. first discussed in Chapter 8. As students, you often sit through informative (maybe even persuasive) lectures in class; you would probably agree that these lectures usually emphasize factors other than those of interest.

In Chapter 8 we considered the various factors of interest and attention in light of the speech to inform. Let us now consider them as elements of the speech to entertain.

Animation

Animation can refer to "lively delivery," which certainly can help hold the audience's interest, but it also means that, in a speech to entertain, things must move right along. You cannot allow dead spots to lull your audience into daydreaming. We attend to the fast-paced, the moving target, the constantly changing scene.

Do this sometime: pay close attention to the many quick changes in a movie or television show. Notice how often the camera angle switches, how many times the camera-to-subject distance jumps from long to short to medium-close, how briefly the camera plays on one face before replacing it with another, how the characters (and their vehicles) seldom remain stationary. Even the most juvenile and junky commercial television fare will hold the attention of nearly any human through little more than sheer animation. Book reviewers often call the most fascinating murder mysteries real page-turners. So your speech should skip the often dilatory asides and do what we used to call "pull a Hank" ("Keep movin' on . . ." from Hank Snow's famous country-western song).

> *Even the most juvenile and junky commercial television fare will hold the attention of nearly any human through little more than sheer animation.*

Vitalness

Vitalness refers to whether the audience members perceive a direct, specific impact on their own welfare. If they perceive *no* direct correlation between your topic and their wishes, they can hardly feel entertained by what you have to say. So, as with the speech to inform or to persuade, if you know that the audience does not already have a keen and vital interest in your topic (the way bird lovers are interested in falcons, Rotarians in healthy hearts, and so on), it behooves you to provide the material that will link your topic to your audience's vital concerns. One usually does so in the speech's introduction, but sometimes this motivational section can go near the end of your speech. For example, I make a speech to entertain and inform on the topic of a lot of false things that most Americans "know" and believe. I point out that poor reporting, sloppy research, wishful thinking, deliberate lies, and thoughtless repetition have instilled in unsuspecting people many beliefs that have no foundation in fact. My exposing of these myths carries its own inherent dose of interest (see the sections on familiarity, novelty and conflict that follow). For instance:

Edison did not invent the electric light.

Bell did not invent the first workable telephone.

Abner Doubleday did not invent baseball.

Galileo did not drop two dissimilar weights from the Leaning Tower of Pisa to demonstrate his theory of gravity.

The Bermuda Triangle contains no more mysterious wrecks of ships and planes than any comparable area of ocean.

In the Civil War, the *Monitor* did not do battle with the *Merrimac*.

There is no evidence that Betsy Ross created, or was commissioned by the Continental Congress to create, our first flag ("Old Glory").

After explaining a number of myths like these, I have held the audience's attention quite well. Then I add vitalness to the point of why knowing about these untruths can affect us: I add two stories that show how incompetent investigation and reporting have produced mischievous results.

The first example involves Charles Drew, a black physician who invented a new blood procedure that has saved thousands of lives, both black and white. Ironically, he died without having been admitted to a whites-only hospital in South Carolina, after a car wreck. This "news" became widely disseminated as proof of Southern bigotry. Actually, three white physicians at the hospital did their utmost to save Drew's life in that hospital emergency room, but the accident had mortally damaged his heart. No one denied that the staff never formally *admitted* Dr. Drew to the hospital, but they had bypassed that form-filling ritual in order to rush him directly to the emergency room.

The other example I use involves a newspaper report that a middle-aged New Yorker had died as the victim of street violence after intervening in a dispute among teenagers to rescue a thirteen-year-old from harm. An autopsy later revealed that the Good Samaritan had suffered a heart attack, had injured his head while falling to the pavement, and then had his ribs broken in the ambulance as a hefty attendant tried to revive him with CPR.

The point: hold cherished beliefs only tentatively, and don't swallow whole everything you read.

Familiarity

We like to hear and read about places we have visited or lived in; we enjoy references to events we have experienced; we listen again and again to our favorite music; we love to get back home, even after a stimulating but relaxing vacation. And any mention in a speech of entities familiar to the audience will create and intensify interest (of course, if *everything* in the speech comes across as too familiar, the speech will bore).

In my "myths" speech I refer to stories virtually everyone in America has heard of: the stories of Alexander Graham Bell and his telephone, Thomas Edison and his incandescent light bulb, Abner Doubleday and baseball, Betsy Ross and "Old Glory." Refuting of these familiar myths by explaining their sources and by providing information directly counter to their truthfulness makes for a particularly strong piquing of interest in these once-cherished "lies."

Novelty

As I pointed out in Chapter 8, advertisements use the word *new* probably more than any other as an attention-getter. In entertainment, the newer, the more surprising, and the more unusual frequently translate as the more interesting and entertaining, too. In my "myths" speech, the listener gets banged on the head with new information that totally contradicts old beliefs.

The correct information: Frenchman Jean Foucalt made an arc light that could light up the Place de la Concorde in Paris three years before Tom Edison's *birth;* both a German and an Englishman had produced workable "telephones" fifteen years before Bell's; a committee of politicians and sports figures (not historians) in 1908 arbitrarily chose Abner Doubleday as baseball's inventor so as to make baseball seem an all-American game, unsullied by European influence; the Tower of Pisa story of Galileo originated years after the great man's death; researchers cannot find any national registration for many of the Bermuda Triangle "victim" ships and planes, and one ship claimed as sunk in the triangle actually went down in the Pacific Ocean, and one "victim" airplane actually crashed in the North Atlantic on its way to Newfoundland. Most people do not know that the Confederate ship that the *Monitor* fought to a stand-off near Hampton Roads, Virginia, actually bore the name of *Virginia.* Yankees scuttled the wooden Northern warship named *Merrimac* in its harbor at the beginning of the war; The Confederates raised and rebuilt the *Merrimac* as an ironclad and renamed it the *Virginia*. The demythologizing of the Betsy Ross legend perhaps hits the hardest; few Americans realize that no contemporary evidence exists for her making the flag, and the first story of this deed did not surface until 1870, nearly a century after its supposed occurrence.

So you see that in this speech *familiarity* contrasts strongly with *novelty*, producing, in turn, our next factor of interest.

Conflict

Why do we see so much violence on television, even in kiddy cartoons? Because producers of our TV fare easily recognize violence as the simplest and cheapest form of conflict to produce, and this conflict captures and holds our interest. Why does *Reader's Digest* feature a "True-Life Adventure" each month? Because the editors know that we delight in stories of real people risking their lives by climbing mountains, surviving attacks from grizzly bears, challenging wild rivers, and escaping from blazing infernos. Their knowledge of our delight in conflict also leads to a certain style for almost all their articles, in which real people grapple with some adversity at first greater than they are but that they either eventually overcome or else optimistically conclude that forces presently at work will soon eliminate or greatly alleviate it.

> *Producers of our TV fare easily recognize violence as the simplest and cheapest form of conflict to produce, and this conflict captures and holds our interest.*

I use what I consider an interesting case for the fact that we need conflict as entertainment in human life. In his 1932 novel *Brave New World*, Aldous Huxley created a fictional world whose leaders, through lifelong conditioning, eliminated all aggressiveness and competition (conflict) among humans. All humankind, at the great price of individual freedom, lived peacefully with one another, without either war or crime. But when these futurists went to the movies (in the book they were called feelies) for entertainment, what could they watch? Murder mysteries? No, people did not kill people. Slapstick humor, a la Laurel and Hardy? No, people did not slap or hit other people. War movies? Of course not. Horror movies, a la *Frankenstein* or *Friday the Thirteenth XXV*? Not at all. Cowboys versus Indians, or settlers versus cattle ranchers? Certainly not. The *Brave New World* folks saw *no* films pitting one human against another. No film even pitted one man against another for the hand of the heroine. But the feelies would totally lack interest without *some* kind of conflict, so they portrayed only two kinds: humans against nature (hurricanes, earthquakes, beasts, etc.) or a situation in which people "lost" their "dehumanizing programming." Solving the latter conflict involved only reprogramming, not prison.

Our discussion of factors of interest has now brought us to humor. Let's save discussion of that factor until we get to the humorous speech to entertain. For now, let's consider the various kinds of nonhumorous speeches to entertain.

Nonhumorous Speeches to Entertain

Nonhumorous speeches to entertain include those that relate true-life adventures, nonuseful information, travel stories, and anecdotes.

The True-Life Adventure

Most people derive vicarious pleasure from the danger, suspense, action, conflict, and movement of other people's adventures. Popular magazines try to satisfy the desire for these second-hand thrills with such articles as "The Marines Who Beat the Odds," "Volcano Hell in the Philippines," "Trapped in a Flooding Cave," "Lone Trek Across Antarctica," or "Face to Face with Hurricane Hugo." So if you have had an adventure that illustrates some revered human quality, such as faith, courage, inventiveness, or the like, and can relate it with proper sequencing and climax, you will find audiences ready to listen to you tell it. But perhaps you have not had such excitement in your life; then, by reading you can find others' adventures , and can use them to entertain and enlighten your listeners.

But don't fall into the trap of thinking of yourself as a mere storyteller; instead, make a speech. By this we mean you don't just tell a story and sit down. You develop an introduction that will create audience interest in your topic, indicate that you have a thesis or point to make, tell the story (or stories) as the body of the speech, then conclude with (maybe) a summary and (definitely) a restatement of your thesis.

A speech of this kind should emphasize the unusual—that which the audience would probably not already know. The speech should deal with specifics of the adventure, not the general foundation knowledge that the audience already has. For example, any halfway educated person would know that Antarctica has very cold weather. But to say, "The spittle that shot from his mouth froze and crackled before it hit the ground" vividly impresses on the listener's mind a graphic picture of nearly unbelievable frigidity.

Fred Birchmore, a native of Athens, Georgia, hiked the more than two thousand miles of the Appalachian Trail, from Georgia to Maine, at the age of sixty—and he and his son, a medical student at the time, did it in one hundred days. Birchmore gives a speech and slide show about the trip. Everyone knows that the trail follows the spine of the Appalachian Mountains, that there are lots of trees and plants along the way, that people consider hiking as hard work, that bad weather may cause trouble, and so on. Birchmore does not make much of this common knowledge in his presentations. Instead he points out such interesting details as the facts that he and his son wore tennis shoes instead of hiking boots (they wore out three pairs apiece); that they shunned the pest-ridden wooden shelters along the trail in favor of sleeping in their two-dollar tube tent; that they found and collected Indian relics. They noticed a vast contrast among the many bridges they crossed (from a magnificent steel-and-concrete span to a simple flattened log). They ate "strange" quick-fix food five or six times a day, then binged on "regular food" as they passed through a civilized spot. Birchmore's presentation holds his audiences entranced for over an hour each time he makes it.

> *The true-life adventure speech should deal with specifics of the adventure, not the general foundation knowledge that the audience already has.*

Nonuseful Information

A speech that provides information that, at least at first glance, shows no promise for making a useful contribution to the audience's physical or psychological well-being entertains more than informs. People just seem naturally interested in unusual information, no matter how personally helpful or useless they consider it. How else can you explain the long popularity of the Ripley's *Believe It or Not* feature? Whence the demand for such books as *The Guinness Book of World Records*, now published annually, or the many and varied trivia books, such as *Imponderables, Why Do Clocks Run Clockwise?, When Do Fish Sleep?,* and *Why Do Dogs Have Wet Noses?*—all by David Feldman; *Big Secrets* and *Bigger Secrets* by William Poundstone; *Why Things Are* by Joel Achenbach; and the several editions of *The Book of Lists* by Wallace, Wallechinsky, and Wallace? Bertrand Russell may have correctly judged the human condition when he said, "There is much pleasure to be gained from useless knowledge."

In the dull days of our gray existences, we seek any material, from scientific or cultural breakthroughs to the most trivial gossip or useless detail, to satisfy our inborn curiosity.

Why do people demand a steady stream of gossipy information about movie and rock stars, sports heroes, TV entertainers, and the like? Why could *Time* magazine find success by expanding its "People" column into a full-blown monthly magazine? Our citizenry certainly must take great delight in consuming this kind of information, regardless of whether it will make them richer, healthier, or better educated. To emphasize this fact, Desmond Morris devoted an entire chapter ("Exploration") of his best-seller *The Naked Ape* to show that humans, of all the animals on the earth, possess the greatest natural curiosity. In the dull days of our gray existences, we seek any material, from scientific or cultural breakthroughs to the most trivial gossip or useless detail, to satisfy our inborn curiosity.

In the Appendix of this book you will find a speech to inform by Jack H. Kirkman ("With Speed in the Dark"), which he presented in my honors speech class. I present it in this book as a model speech, but not just as one to inform. The speech also has the qualities of a first-rate speech to entertain: in association with animated delivery, the speech about blockade runners during the Civil War moves along quickly from point to point; it relates blockade runners to our familiar image of Rhett Butler of *Gone with the Wind*; it provides novel information about how low-slung ships had to speed past blockaders in the dark of night, and what rich profits the blockade runners earned; it also conveys the conflict and suspense of this dangerous wartime activity.

Now, you might argue that Jack's information hardly seems nonuseful; after all, he speaks on American history, and this information might come in handy for a quiz some day. And who could find fault with such an argument? But actually, one might never get a chance to use this information for anything more than cocktail party conversation. But then, who can tell *what* information will turn out as useful, and when?

In college I pushed myself through the required course in art appreciation, often wondering why a university would require students to study such a subject. A few years later I found myself (an aviation cadet applicant) in an interview with a panel of five U.S. Air Force officers; they tried to ascertain whether I fit the qualifications of "an officer and a gentleman." The one question asked of me by the one female officer (a captain): "Who painted the *Mona Lisa*? I immediately blurted out, "Michelangelo!" Then, "No, no. Not Michelangelo. He wasn't even a *painter*. It was da Vinci." The startled officer made a face at me: "What do you mean, Michelangelo wasn't a painter? Who do you think did the Sistine Chapel?"

"Oh, he painted that ceiling, all right, but he was sort of forced into trying that," I replied. "Michelangelo considered himself first and foremost a sculptor, not a painter." Then I proceeded to tell the story, remembered somehow from that long-ago class in art appreciation, of how the sculptor's envious rivals talked the pope into requiring Michelangelo to decorate the ceiling of the Sistine Chapel. These enemies of the great artist delighted in their conviction that he would certainly fail and lose face. My somehow-remembered bit of "useless" trivia amazed and impressed the panel of officers. I passed with high marks.

So you will commit no crime if your "nonuseful" information in speech to entertain turns out to have some use for your audience. And even a speech directly intended to usefully inform could greatly benefit from proper attention to making it entertaining, too. In fact, the best speeches to inform or to persuade that I have heard held my rapt and undivided attention—the main requirement of a speech to entertain.

The Travelogue

Travelers have probably bored their reluctant listeners with tales and pictures (maybe drawn in the dirt) of their various journeys since long before travel became a major form of vacation. It seems that people can't consider a trip worthwhile until they have returned and told someone else about it.

Of course, we cannot deny that the tedious vacation travelogue imposed on us by friends, neighbors, or relatives, perhaps accompanied by pictures, slides, home movies, or videotape, has become the popular and common butt of many jokes and cartoons. And many of these creations can bore us to stupefaction. But this type of presentation does not bore people simply because of its genre: most dull travelogues suffer from poor selection of material or lackluster presentation. Travelogue presentations can succeed as both education and entertainment; just consider the many fine professional offerings that public (and, occasionally, even commercial) TV offers.

In your own travelogue speech to entertain, you must follow the specific tactic of concentrating on what the audience members would most want to see and hear about if they could have had your same experiences. I suspect that most bores who weary their audiences to sleep with slideshows of their vacations spend too many words on their own reactions and feelings and not enough on what the audience might find interesting. Suppose I were making a speech on my tour of the state-preserved home of Alexander H. Stephens, vice president of the Confederacy, former congressman, and one-time governor of Georgia, and said:

Here you see a slide of the outbuilding that produced the gas for lighting the main house. That's my wife, Marsha, standing in front of the building. She didn't want me to take this picture, since she hadn't been to her hairdresser for a week. And she's wearing those faded shorts for a very interesting reason. When we were doing laundry the week before our trip . . .

Dullsville. Who cares? But suppose I said:

Here you see a slide of the outbuilding where they produced the gas for lighting the main house. Stephens' house was one of the first in the South to be lighted by gas, but not by the *natural* gas we have today; they had to *manufacture* it. Stephens's old records show that he bought fifty-gallon barrels of *gasoline*; this gasoline was mixed with straw in a tank, evaporated into gaseous form, and was pumped from here to the main house. Such an operation entailed the danger of fire or explosion, so they had to place the "gashouse" some distance from the main residence!

More interesting, eh what?

A speech professor friend of mine toured Europe during a sabbatical. He decided to specialize in visiting the two things Europe has in abundance that the United States does not: great cathedrals and works of art. In preparation for his trip he spent a year reading about and studying the great cathedrals and art treasures of Europe; he also bought a fine 35mm camera and trained himself to use it well. During his tour he took over two thousand color slides. He also gathered a great deal of reading material on his subject. After returning home he had his slides developed and organized them into logical sequences in carousel trays, properly identified with title slides; he also devoured the further reading material he had secured while touring Europe. As a result of this endeavor he can now sit in his living room holding the remote control for his projector and keep any audience absolutely fascinated for hours, showing slides of and talking about the great cathedrals and art treasures of Europe.

Perhaps you could base your short speech to entertain on a trip or vacation you took. But if you do, analyze your audience to determine what and what not to show and tell. We have all seen pictures of London's Big Ben, France's Eiffel Tower, and Hawaii's Diamond Head. You should feature places and events we don't see regularly on TV.

> *If you base your short speech to entertain on a trip or vacation you took, analyze your audience to determine what and what not to show and tell. You should feature places and events we don't see regularly on TV.*

The One-Point Anecdotal Speech

Next we turn to the kind of speech in which the speaker has a single point to make and supports it with a number of (often personal) anecdotes or stories. These anecdotes need not make us laugh; if they did, they would come under the classification of humorous speeches to entertain. The anecdotes must only come across as *interesting* to the audience. Many after-dinner speeches made at sports banquets by invited athletes or coaches fall into this category. Typically, the speaker begins by saying nice things about the local sports program, then tells a number of personal experience anecdotes he or she has experienced, and concludes with the thesis, such as "And these kinds of experiences really make coaching (or, playing ———) such a (fun, exciting, enjoyable, exasperating) job."

I occasionally speak on "coincidences." Whenever I experience an unusual coincidence, I write it down and file it. I have quite enough now for an entertaining speech with the thesis, "The law of large numbers ensures that two or more events will eventually occur coincidentally." One of the least spooky of my coincidences: I once decided I needed to contact a former student whom I had not seen for over two years. I decided to write her at her old address from her class card in the hopes that the postal service could forward my letter to her. As I was addressing the envelope, she walked through my office door "to just drop by and chat," since she had just come by my building on another errand.

I probably have not covered all the various types and subtypes of nonhumorous speeches to entertain. But these major types should get you started. The main thing to remember: Your speech might inform or it might persuade; but to entertain, it must interest, interest, interest.

Humorous Speeches to Entertain

The humorous speech to entertain (typical after-dinner speech) finds its home mostly at events when like-minded people gather for some pleasant activity such as a party, an anniversary, a celebration, or a commemoration. The audience members revel in a mood of joviality and comradeship, willing participants in a basically recreational setting. When the after-dinner speaker rises, the audience expects relaxation and fun, not a serious treatise on earth's deteriorating ozone layer or the international chaos produced by the fragmentation of the USSR.

You must clothe your ideas in the raiment of the light and digestible; recreation, even fun, should dominate your mood.

As I cautioned in the previous section, your speech to entertain must not entirely exclude any educational or enlightening thesis; you might even implant in your audience some seeds of thought that may eventually bear the fruits of changed attitudes or behavior. But you must remember your primary aim: to entertain. And to do so, you must clothe your ideas in the raiment of the light and digestible; recreation, even fun, should dominate your mood.

But again, remember: the speech to entertain must remain a *speech*. You should give a speech, not try to do a standup comedy routine. This means that you have an introduction, in which you state or imply your main point, or thesis; that you logically organize the meat of your speech in the body; and that you round out the speech at the end with an apt conclusion, including, at the very least, a restatement of your thesis. Your speech should have a point; a standup comedy performance need not do so.

As a professional student and researcher of humor, I have concerned myself mostly with the why's of humor: What makes humor funny? Why do we laugh? I became a charter member of the International Society for Humor Studies; have written a book (*Understanding Laughter: The Workings of Wit and Humor*, Nelson-Hall, 1978) and a number of articles and professional papers on my research on humor; and have attended several international conferences on the topic. At one of these conferences, a group of well-paid Hollywood comedy writers confessed that they do not know much about *why* comedy works, but they know how to *make* it work. In the spirit of their attitude, I will limit my discussion of humorous speaking to how to make it work rather than delve into the psychology of why it works.

We might categorize humorous speeches in several ways. In fact, a major series of programs at the 1991 International Conference on Humour held in St. Catherines, Ontario, concerned itself (rather unsuccessfully) with a major effort to devise a workable taxonomy of humor. I choose to classify humorous speeches into four categories: the one-point speech, mild satire, reversal of values, and parody.

The One-Point Speech

The one-point speech strongly resembles the one-point anecdotal speech discussed earlier; it differs only in that the jokes and funny stories substitute for the nonhumorous anecdotes.

For instance, my daughter, Val, developed a speech whose one point was that "Sick humor has a long history." She began with some up-to-date models of sick humor, of the "dead baby" variety. Then she went back to the 1950s for some "Bloody Mary's," such as "Aside from that, Mrs. Lincoln, how did you enjoy the play?" and several vampire jokes, such as:

"Mommy, what's this in my cup?"
"Shut up and drink it before it clots!"
"Daddy, I don't want to be a vampire!"
"Shut up and drink your blood!"

Next, Val went back to the 1930–1940s to show that some of the little moron jokes of the time were pretty sick:

Did you hear about the little moron who . . .
    cut off his fingers so he could learn shorthand?

jumped off the Empire State Building because he wanted to become
 a smash hit on Broadway?
chopped off his arms so he could wear sleeveless sweaters?

Turning further back, to 1899, she quoted some of the "Ruthless Rhymes for Heartless Homes" from a popular book by Englishman Harry Graham:

Billy, in one of his nice new sashes
Fell in the fire and was burned to ashes.
Now, although the room grows chilly,
I haven't the heart to poke up Billy.

She then quoted several "Little Willie" quatrains that Graham's book had inspired, such as:

Willie found some dynamite,
Couldn't understand it quite.
Curiosity never pays.
It rained Willie seven days.
Willie fell down the elevator,
Wasn't found til six days later.
Then the neighbors sniffed, "Gee whiz,
What a spoiled child Willie is."

Finally, Val's speech went back to the world's first joke book, now referred to as *Joe Miller's Jestbook* (1739), from which she recounted three jokes of the sick or gallows variety, including one about two brothers whom the authorities publicly hanged. After the first brother got strung up, his brother spoke up, saying that his brother hanging there made "quite a spectacle," and that in a few moments, he, too, would get hanged, and then folks could look upon "a pair of spectacles." (OK, an old and not very good joke—but that's why they call them "Joe Millers.")

I include in my lecture on visual aids a little minispeech (to inform and to entertain) expounding the thesis that "Students should check with the instructor before using any possibly destructive or dangerous visual aids." I support the thesis with examples, some quite hilarious. I tell about the ROTC cadet who demonstrated the M-1 bipod-mounted, shoulder-fired .30 caliber machine gun; he ended his brief speech by loading and *cocking* the weapon. He then asked if there were any questions. Questions? No one even *breathed*, much less asked questions! I also mention the man who spoke about the gasoline-powered chainsaw, who concluded by starting up the machine, revving it to an ear-shattering crescendo, and then sawing through an old wooden chair, blowing wood chips and choking fumes throughout the closed room, while audience members dove for cover, gasping for air.

The one-point speech can have more than one main idea as part of the central thesis. For instance, our home economics school hired me to present a speech at the concluding banquet of a weekend educational retreat for students, faculty, and alumni. The retreat took as its topic and main theme "Coping with Stress in the Modern World." I therefore chose as my thesis "We must have and use our sense of humor to cope with stress in modern America." I argued that people need to exercise their ability to laugh at themselves. One main point: that physicians need to appreciate jokes that make fun of doctors. Several doctor jokes followed. Another main point: "College administrators should have the capacity to laugh at themselves." Some dean jokes followed ("What do you call an associate dean? A mouse, studying to become a rat!"). A point that teachers need a sense of humor, too, allowed for several teacher jokes, and so on.

> *The one-point speech can have more than one main idea as part of the central thesis.*

Satire

Many after-dinner speeches make fun of or kid a person, institution, or idea through mild satire, usually using the technique of irony or exaggeration. Ironic statements seem to say one thing but really mean the opposite. For instance, when Art Buchwald complains that everyone should remain free to buy any kind of handgun since "what better way to end a family argument than with a six-shooter?" he only *appears* opposed to gun-control laws.

Buchwald uses irony as his regular stock-in-trade. He once ridiculed the time-consuming delays in our transportation system by suggesting that we turn the system into a university. Then commuters could use the delays for study and test taking; motorists could listen to radio lectures during traffic jams; toll collectors could accept motorists' homework, grade it, and return it on tomorrow's commute, and so on.

Faced with the need for a satiric speech as my doctoral dissertation, I wrote the following, then tried it out on college freshmen to see whether it came across as persuasive as well as entertaining. I intended to show the ridiculous position that government finds itself in when it attempts to censor entertainment and literature since, once we've begun, we can find no logical place to stop.

A DEMURE PROPOSAL

Ladies and Gentlemen:

As professor Harold Hill, the Music Man, has said (or rather, sung), "We got trouble . . . we got a whole lot of trouble" these days, and I mean trouble with the growing problem of juvenile delinquency. It seems that the entire younger generation has lost any respect for authority it ever had. And, if you will just pay some serious attention to our mass media—our movies, television, magazines, and paperback novels—I think you will find it not too difficult to see *why* our young people are what they are. The violence, obscenity, and leftist propaganda in our entertainment media these days are enough to corrupt good upbringing in any youngster.

Some well-meaning citizens would fight the problem with strict government censorship of movies, television, and printed material. This is undoubtedly a good idea, but I am convinced that such censorship, needed as it is, is inadequate. It does not go far enough to be completely effective. For our children are brought up in an atmosphere *saturated* with fictional violence and depravity from a very early age. And they receive this corrupting influence not from Hollywood or New York, but at their mothers' knees! I am speaking, ladies and gentlemen, of that insidious literature we innocently call *nursery rhymes*.

A preposterous charge, you say? You think that nursery rhymes can have nothing in common with say, *The Untouchables?* Look at some examples with me.

Take, for instance, "Rock-a-Bye, Baby." What happens to the innocent babe of this horror story? You know how it ends: down comes the baby, cradle and all, crashing to the ground from the treetops! Now, isn't that a lovely little ditty to croon to your preschool child! Isn't that a pretty image with which to send him off to beddy-bye!

Look at another example: "Humpty Dumpty." He stupidly falls from a high wall to a death gory enough to turn the stomach. But what then? Do they sweep the carcass into a rubber sack for decent Christian burial? No! These men and horses try to paste the sticky mess back together again! Now, I ask you: just how revolting can you get? After enough of this kind of horror, should we be surprised when six-year-olds occasionally dissect a playmate?

These two cases are not isolated examples, either. Nursery rhymes abound in violence, sadism, and deviant behavior. There's "Georgie Porgie," who kissed the girls against their wishes, making them cry (sound like a future sex offender?). But this Georgie is so cowardly that he runs when the other boys come out to play. There's "Tom, Tom the Piper's Son," who stole a pig and away he run. There is the brutal story of the attempt to *bake alive* four-and-twenty blackbirds, one of whom retaliates upon the person of an honest maid by biting off her nose in the garden. In the story of the brutal bow-and-arrow slaying of Cock Robin, the fish freely admits to catching the murder victim's blood in a dish! Again I ask: How long can we allow our children's minds to be poisoned by this trash?

What must little children think when they hear of the farmer's wife sadistically cutting off the tails of three defenseless, blind mice? How will they feel toward Little Johnny Green, who threw pussy in the well down there in "Ding Dong Dell"? Will they condone the crime of Peter, the pumpkin eater, who apparently killed his wife and stuffed her corpse in a pumpkin shell simply because he could not afford to keep her?

Perhaps you have been wondering why youngsters today seem to be so lazy, shiftless, and irresponsible. They're probably emulating another nursery rhyme hero, Little Boy Blue, who slept under a haystack while the cows and the sheep he was supposed to be tending ate away at his father's corn and meadow.

I haven't time now to discuss with you the murky Freudian implications underlying the story of Jack and Jill. You remember that they went *up* a hill supposedly in search of water, when anyone knows that water is found in *low* places. But I would ask you to ponder the sorts of ideals being suggested to our kids by that mysterious woman who lives in the house shaped like a shoe. She apparently lives off relief and the Aid to Dependent Children handout—but you will notice that there is not one mention of a husband!

Do you begin to see *now* the extent to which our children are exposed to objectionable material? Is it not shocking to realize that all this garbage is taught them by their mothers and nursemaids?

By now you are probably wondering what can be done about this menace.

The protection of our young people demands that we rid our nurseries of the despicable influence of so-called nursery rhymes. Nothing less than a nationwide ban on their printing, with penalties of fines and jail terms for their publication, would be adequate. In addition, mothers, nursemaids, and others having intimate contact with our toddlers must be educated, then *warned* against the repetition of such trash. After a suitable time, punishment for recitation of nursery rhymes would be imposed. A motto of the John Birch Society says, "If Mommy is a Commie, you gotta turn her in"; for mommies who tell nursery rhymes to children, our motto might well be "If Mother goes and Mother Gooses, she'll pay in one of our calabooses."

After we successfully stamp out nursery rhymes, we can forge on to the wide and fertile field of children's literature. Mrs. Thomas J. White of Indiana has shown the way for us here. Mrs. White was part of a state committee to investigate school library books. As far as I know, she is the first to decry the communistic undertones of that famous children's classic *Robin Hood*. The concept of robbing the rich to give to the poor is a technique for creating a classless society right out of Marx and Engels!

And while we're about it, let us take note of how far Robin Hood lives outside of his cultural norms. He lives, you remember, not in a house but in the woods. Not only does he scorn the solid responsibilities of home ownership, but he is a bachelor, as are all his band. And do they work? Of course not. They make a living breaking the fish and game laws!

One of Robin's top henchmen is Friar Tuck. Although he is a church cleric, you would not want your son or daughter to take him as a model of religious piety. For he would much rather bash in heads with his trusty stave than read from the Good Book. And you *know* whom he most enjoys bashing—the sheriff!

One could go on and on with the objectionable episodes and nuances of Robin Hood and like stories; for instance, there's the unseemly number of times the unchaperoned Maid Marian manages to slip off to see Robin Hood—*in the woods*—but I'm sure you see my point now.

Ladies and gentlemen, the time to move against these pernicious forces in our society is now. We must launch a new crusade—a crusade of the spirit. Even as we sit here, some innocent child is being twisted and warped by the horrors of Mother Goose; his older brother is learning utter rebellion from Robin Hood; and Daddy sits entranced watching the carnage of *The Gangster Chronicles*.

The battle must begin. And we will not find it easy, for censorship has enemies everywhere. Those of low taste and vicious character will fight us every step. It will be an uphill battle all the way. But this is a battle we must fight; and it is a battle we must win. For, even though the corrupt are strong, their vice cannot stand against the might of our righteousness; we must blast the enemy from their entrenchments; we must engage them on the open barren ramparts; we must strike them down as they run for cover; we must *kick* and *beat* and *grind* and *stomp* them until they are defeated utterly. For only then can we sweep into oblivion the befouling influence of nursery rhymes.

Exaggeration

In the above speech, exaggeration combines with irony to enhance its effect. Humorists and joke writers consider exaggeration one of their major tools. Several years ago Art Buchwald ridiculed, through exaggeration, our visionless policy of not recognizing Red China (which we now call Mainland China, or just China). Buchwald reported what happened when a group of officials in the U.S. State Department discovered down in their basement some maps showing a huge, unexplored land mass just across the sea from Japan. They tried to figure out what this supposed land mass represented but had great difficulty. One Far East expert said he heard that some people called the area "China," but the old heads there disagreed; they knew where China belonged on the map—right there where it says "Formosa." In another piece Buchwald ridiculed union work rules by applying them to the military. In this piece he has a naval officer tell a navy chaplain that it goes against the union's contract for him to pass ammunition to the gunners during a terrible battle. The chaplain then decides he will sing "Praise the Lord and Pass the Ammunition." The officer calls this illegal and disallows it unless the chaplain hires a full orchestra and pays them time-and-a-half since they would have to perform beyond midnight. The ship begins to sink, but the officer warns the padre that he may not don his own life jacket; that job contractually belongs to a member of the Deckhand Dresser's Guild.

Another satirist, Erma Bombeck, laces her columns with zanily exaggerated people and situations, sometimes reflected in her titles, such as "Can You Open Your Closet Without Hurting Yourself?"

The Reversal of Values Speech

If you treat an important subject in a quite trivial manner or treat a trivial subject as overly important, you use the reversal of values approach.

> *If you treat an important subject in a quite trivial manner or treat a trivial subject as overly important, you use the reversal of values approach.*

I make the speech to entertain an optional choice for the final speech in my class, but few students rise to the challenge; they almost universally prefer to tackle the job of producing a straight persuasive speech. I suspect that the straightforward speech to persuade seems more achievable than reproducing the high level of interest demanded of the speech to entertain (perhaps people feel they cannot compete with the ubiquitous TV?). As a result, I hear few speeches to entertain in class.

One such speech I remember well. A young man gave a mock-serious speech to inform on how to use the common wooden toothpick. He analyzed in great detail the problem of selecting just the right toothpick: that one should consider balance, grain, shape, length, thickness, texture, color, and taste. He described and demonstrated the various grips one might use: the "thumb-index finger with curved pinkie" grip, the "overhand antislip" grip, and the "two-handed, all-or-nothing" grip. He discussed the various strokes, such as the "twixt-gum-and-molar pluck," the "inter-incisor stab," and the "bicuspid bend." One main point detailed the various aspects of toothpick etiquette, such as in what kinds of mixed company and at what times of the day experts allowed for public toothpicking, and, once a bit of food had been dislodged from the choppers, whether experts considered it more polite to spit it out or to swallow it. He also considered the special problems with dentures, plates, and dental bridges. The class laughed in uproarious appreciation.

A young woman in one class had obviously analyzed her fellow class members well, especially from what they had talked about in their speeches. Her final speech, to entertain, predicted the future of each classmate based on the speeches each had given during the course. She predicted that, after graduation, "Tom," a religious young man, might disappear from our sight into the foreign mission-ary field. But, she predicted, if "Tom" dies before us, we'll find him standing at the right hand of St. Peter at the Pearly Gates, checking our credentials for entering. She guessed that "Harry," an ROTC cadet, would become the first infantry platoon leader in army history to get tarred and feathered by his own enlisted men. "Harriet," a preveterinary major (who, of course, loved animals), she predicted, would fall in love with and marry a Russian wolfhound. The class loved it.

Parody

Parody imitates the particular style of an author, speaker, composer, or composition, but with different content, in order to amuse. It uses the interest value of familiarity; if the audience doesn't already know the style that the speaker imitates, the trick of parody fails. As I write this (fall 1991), an ad for Wendy's grilled chicken sandwich parodies the spooky voice from heaven in the Kevin Kostner film *Field of Dreams:* Wendy's dad hears "Create the sandwich, and they will come."

In making fun of the modernized prose of the New English Bible ("The Lord is my shepherd, I shall want nothing. He makes me lie down in green pastures and leads me beside the waters of peace . . ."), Art Buchwald rewrote Hamlet's soliloquy in a similar vein:

Should I or shouldn't I? That is the question
I don't know whether it would be better for me to
Take
A lot of guff and that sort of thing
Or to fight back against all this trouble I've been
Having.

One student in my honors class parodied the entire PSA arrangement for persuasive speeches detailed in Chapter 9. Troy Schmidt gave a mock-persuasive speech to convince the audience to attend the movies shown on campus by the student union.

Troy's introduction reminded the class of the great times we can all have here at Georgia on home football weekends. Crowds, excitement, parties, and pep rallies all add up to a festive mood to prepare us for the exciting game on Saturday afternoon.

But in his problem step, he described how dismal some students find the weekends without a home football game. He greatly exaggerated the deep pits of loneliness into which some could fall; the campus is semideserted, and friends have either gone home for the weekend or followed the football team out of town. In desperation a student might wind up blowing twenty bucks on pinball or videogames in the local arcade. Troy's hyperbole painted a gloomy picture resembling solitary confinement on bread and water.

> *Troy's hyperbole painted a gloomy picture resembling solitary confinement on bread and water.*

But cheer up, he urged in his solution step. Each night on the weekend, the student union shows movies. Troy rhapsodized over the cinematic pleasures that await there; he expounded on the high class of people one could meet at the filmings; he glorified the good fun the audience has cheering and jeering back at the flickering silver screen.

In the arousal stage, Schmidt's hyperbole ran amok. He told the stories of two college friends, John and Bob. John felt lonely, with nothing to do on an away-game Saturday night. He went to the student union film. There he met four like-minded fellows who eventually became his best friends; one actually became the best man at his wedding, and another some years later used his influence to get John a fulfilling and lucrative position with his company. That same night at the movies he met Sue, and they fell in love at first sight. They married immediately after graduation (and innumerable student union movies), settled down in a four-bedroom house in a fashionable Atlanta suburb, and shared marital bliss forever after. They had two children, both beautiful and talented, who got accepted to the best and most politically correct schools. And all of this happiness stemmed from attending the union movies.

Bob, on the other hand, felt the same loneliness on an away-game weekend. But instead of going to the movie, he drove to a local saloon, there to drown his misery. At the bar he fell in with some unsavory characters. They all got roaring drunk, smoked marijuana, and snorted cocaine. Crazed by the alcohol and dope, the gang went tearing off into the night in a car. One member suggested breaking into a vacant house for kicks, to which they all agreed. They broke into a darkened home and began an orgy of burglary and vandalism, but the family who owned the house came home in the middle of their spree. To eliminate witnesses, the culprits slaughtered the entire family, including their little dog, Sparky. Making their escape at high speed, they ran three red lights and crashed into a brick building at the end of a cul-de-sac, badly injuring Bob and killing his three ill-bred cohorts. Bob, after much pain and many operations, survived, but now sits in federal prison, convicted of burglary, murder, DUI, reckless driving, and driving with an expired license. He has a lifetime of prison in which to brood over his mistake of not going to the student union movie that fateful night.

One thing that makes humor so interesting comes from the fact that it almost defies clear classification.

In his conclusion, Troy directly urged his audience to begin attending student union movies on weekends, to improve their station in life and avoid a wasted life of crime and prison. He ended with a quotation from an ancient sage, "Troyus Schmidtius."

You can probably think of other types of humorous speeches to entertain, but they will use many of the techniques of the forms described here. Of course, we find much overlapping; for instance, Troy's speech on student union movies certainly exaggerates, greatly inflates the possible values of film attendance, and, in a way, satirizes the persuasion process. One thing that makes humor so interesting comes from the fact that it almost defies clear classification. This fact makes it difficult for humor researchers to devise any sort of workable taxonomy of humor.

The Humorous Speaker

You often hear the remark, "Some people can tell jokes and others just can't." This cliché refers to the fact that some people *because of their basic nature* can or cannot evoke laughter from their fellows. But most people don't know that they can learn to *become* funnier if they wish. What does it take?

Most important, the humorous speaker must have a genuine sense of humor. And most people have a better one than they might think.

A sense of humor doesn't mean only that you laugh a lot or laugh at a lot of different things. It involves the ability to see even the most important aspects of life in a slightly silly or ridiculous light. It means the ability to keep a sane perspective on the blooming, buzzing, illogical, and random chaos of modern life. It means not taking oneself too seriously, which means accepting oneself even while recognizing the weaknesses and shortcomings that make one human. As the late, great speech teacher William Norwood Brigance once said about the sense of humor, "It includes not only the readily perceived absurdity of characters, situations, and consequences, but also the not readily perceived pathos. . . . Humor is not the opposite of seriousness, but is rather the opposite of solemnity. . . . Fanatics . . . are lacking humor because they lack perspective . . . unable to laugh or smile, and unable to see their subject in a human light."[1] And Clive James concluded, neatly, that "Common sense and a sense of humor are the same thing, moving at different speeds. A sense of humor is just common sense, dancing."[2]

In addition to a healthy sense of humor, budding humorous speakers need lots of exposure to humorous material. They should regularly read all the newspaper comic pages (and even the cartoons in the editorial section); humor publications such as *MAD* and *Spy;* humorous newspaper columns such as those by Art Buchwald, Dave Barry, Erma Bombeck, and Lewis Grizzard; humorous stories and books, including books of jokes; and jokes and cartoons in magazines. Such a speaker should watch comedy shows and standup comedians on TV; go to (and rent on video) comedy movies; listen to recorded comedy routines; and play tapes of the old radio comedy shows (many of which have become widely available). One point on which all the members of the comedy writers' panel at the 1979 humor conference agreed: funny people must absorb a lot of funny material.

In addition, the humorous speaker should try to see the funny side

[1]William Norwood Brigance, *Speech: Its Techniques and Disciplines in a Free Society* (New York: Appleton-Century-Crofts, 1961), p. 81.
[2]Comment from *The Observer* of London, as reprinted in *Reader's Digest,* September 1980, p. 194.

of each new encounter, experience, accident, or even tragedy. You need to "think funny." Then articulate that humor, practice it. Sprinkle your conversation with apt, appropriate stories and gags; you can practice your timing and accentuation doing this. The more often you tell a story, the better you will get at it—especially if you pay attention and adapt to any feedback you get from your fellows.

To succeed at entertaining humorously, you must come across to your audience as a person of immense goodwill toward them. You must exude the sense that you have come to share with them some happy time. This means that you will not use any jokes, anecdotes, personal experiences, or other real-life stories that will insult or offend. You will avoid the off-color, ethnic, racial, or otherwise tasteless quip. Not that you cannot kid some, or even all, of the audience members, but they must clearly perceive that you do so in the high good spirits of fun, and within the overall framework of goodwill. Your entire demeanor must suggest the playful nature of your remarks. Once, while speaking to a banquet audience that included my university president and most of his vice presidents and college deans, I commented, "As we all know, those who can, do; those who can't, *teach*; those who can't teach, teach others to teach; and those who can't teach others to teach become college administrators." I said this with a smile, looking directly at my boss. He and his fellow administrators laughed the loudest of all.

> *To succeed at entertaining humorously, you must come across to your audience as a person of immense goodwill toward them.*

You should establish your goodwill toward the audience and your playful attitude early in the speech, preferably in the introduction. A little self-deprecating humor here may help (this point even has research results to back it up).

A psychologist, speaking on his chosen field, could begin with some comical definitions of his profession, such as:

My topic tonight is psychology. You all know the definition of a psychologist, don't you? He's a guy who pulls *habits* out of *rats*. Another definition I like: a psychologist is a guy who fathers a set of twins, then has one of them baptized and keeps the other one for a control.

An economist might introduce a speech on his field like this:

I suppose you have heard that, if all the economists in the world were laid end to end—they would still each point in a different direction? Some people, you know, try to escape reality by using dope and alcohol; others study economics.

As a humorous speaker you must come across as immensely confident and poised, the master of your subject, and completely in control of the speaker-audience situation. If the audience perceives you as timid, halting, nervous, or downright afraid, they will pick up on your misery through the process of empathy, and no one will enjoy anything. This means that you must know your material backward and forward, that you must rehearse so often and so well that you know your material as well as your own name.

The humorous speech to entertain virtually precludes the use of a manuscript. Notes will not detract, but you must use them surreptitiously. They must not get between you and your audience. If planning to use several stories or jokes, abbreviate each one with just a word or two on your notecards; have them in chronological order; tell one story, then, as the audience responds (you hope), you can glance down at the key word for the next.

Don't laugh at one of your own stories in advance; wait for audience response, then maybe chuckle a bit, or smile. Certainly, do not laugh as heartily as your audience (after all, you *have* heard this story before!). Then pause before the next story; don't begin until the audience becomes almost completely quiet again. If your story evokes no laughter, pause and smile. Give them a moment. It may take a second or two for them to get it. If still no laughter comes, just go on to the next story—unless, of course, the story has a second punch line, as do many of the double-barreled jokes used by many comedians, such as:

I come from a very poor hometown. Very poor. If they made *Gone with the Wind* there, Tara would have to be a mobile home. (Pause, smile) . . . A 1939 model mobile home. . . . Rhett Butler would have made his fortune making moonshine whiskey. (Pause, smile) . . . And Scarlett O'Hara would hold the title of Miss Turnip Festival of Carter County.

The attitude that you take to the dais will greatly determine your effectiveness. You must get into the proper spirit of the occasion. Approach the speaking job with the strongly positive belief, "I'm going to have fun doing this!" After all, if you really do have a good sense of humor, and if you really do bear feelings of goodwill toward the audience, and if you really like your humorous material (and enjoy relating it), this positive approach should come to you as naturally as a float does to a parade. Nervousness? Sure, you will have some, because you will feel anxious to succeed. But remember, your attitude toward the situation is more important than the actual situation. Don't tell yourself, "I feel scared"; instead, say to yourself, "This gig has me so pumped up that I will surely just *wow* this audience!"

You don't need the attack attitude of the typical standup comedian (who wishes to *slay* the audience), but the kind of positive attitude I outline here will certainly help you lay 'em in the aisles.

Resources for the Humorous Speaker

As I have noted, the successful humorous speaker will absorb much humorous material on a regular basis, through newspapers, books, magazines, radio, TV, and movies. That speaker also needs to keep track of what goes on in the world, nation, state, and local area. Humorous events or good jokes you learn should go into your repertoire, so you ought to record and file them somehow (more on that in a moment).

In addition to staying well-read and knowledgeable, humorous speakers should have at their disposal an assortment of materials to use in speech preparation. Any speaker or writer should own a good dictionary, a thesaurus, a current almanac of facts, and an encyclopedia. In addition, humorous speakers should expand their libraries to include humorous material. Joke books abound, and speakers should own several, including books of cartoons. You probably won't find more than one usable gag in a hundred of these jokes, but by reviewing several hundred you can come up with several jokes or stories for your speech that *will* work. I would include here the many jokes and funny stories in back issues of magazines, such as *Reader's Digest*. Even though millions of people read those jokes, my experience tells me that people rapidly forget them, so you can always find "fresh" material in back issues. Many libraries have collections of these magazines.

Because people find entertainment in trivial information, I also recommend that you have a collection of trivia books like the ones I mentioned earlier in this chapter.

Melvin Helitzer has published two books that you might find especially helpful: *Comedy Techniques for Writers and Performers* (Lawhead Press, Athens, Ohio, 1984) and *Comedy Writing Secrets* (Writer's Digest Books, Cincinnati, Ohio, 1987). Helitzer teaches a highly popular course on comedy writing at Ohio University and frequently attends and contributes to our international conference on humor.

A resource I learned of at the 1991 Ontario conference has begun to occupy my spare time. I refer to the Humor Processor, a software package that comes from Responsive Software, 1901 Tunnel Road, Berkeley, CA 94705 (about $50). It comes on one 3 1/2" or two 5 1/4" disks plus a book of instructions. The package has two parts.

The Humor Processor provides you with a brainstorming facility to help you create your own jokes.

The first part of the Humor Processor consists of a database of jokes (an electronic joke book). The jokes come numbered, as well as classified by type (sports, travel, etc.) and by the type of event for which you might use them (after dinner, awards luncheon, etc.). You may also retrieve jokes by key word. Or you may simply call up the database and browse through it. After you create (more on this later), hear, remember, or find a joke you think you might use in the future, you can add it to the database; when you do so, you can also tell your computer under what type and event you want the joke classified, so that you can find it easily. Also, you tell the computer the key words you might wish to use to find the joke for future reference. For instance, I recently filed away a golf joke. I had the computer classify it as a "golf" joke, for use primarily in "after dinner" situations, with the key words *golf, slice, tee off*, and *19th hole*, which I can use to call up that joke or any other in the database with those key words. I find this an excellent way to file jokes for easy future access, and I plan to use it extensively.

Now, how about "creating jokes," as I mentioned above? Well, the second part of the Humor Processor provides you with a brainstorming facility to help you create your own jokes (eleven different types). You decide what type of joke you want to create, then type onto the screen a setup you want to start with, such as Rodney Dangerfield's "I don't get no respect . . ." or "My boss is so mean that . . ." Then you see a left and a right window; each can accommodate a preprogrammed list of "images" from several categories. For instance, you might place a list of images from an office setting (desk, boss, water cooler, coffee break, typewriter, Xerox machine, and so on) in the left window. Into the right window you might place a list of images from the school category (teacher, student, recess, lecture, pencils, cleaning the erasers, and so on). After filling your windows, you can scroll up or down through one list of images to find a particular image that you think holds promise. Then you can scroll through the other window's images until you find one that might combine with the first image, plus your setup, to produce a joke or at least suggest a possible joke.

For instance, on the first day I tried out this program, in order to learn how to use it I typed in the Rodney Dangerfield setup of "I don't get no respect." For my left window I arbitrarily chose the list of office images; then, for my right window, I chose the list of school images. I scrolled the left window until I came to "Xerox machine," where I stopped. Then I scrolled the right window until I came to "cleaning erasers." I reasoned that Xerox machines don't erase; they do the opposite by copying. After a little thought and a realization that the reversal formula could work here, I wrote the joke: "I just don't get no respect. Even our office machines hate me. Whenever I try to use the Xerox machine, it erases my original." (This joke might not get me onto the *Tonight Show,* but it does represent my very first attempt at this process.)

The book that comes with the Humor Processor includes a bibliography of joke and humor books and a list of humor newsletters and organizations. So if you have access to a computer, a yen to catalog and create your own jokes, and $50 to part with, I think you will find this package quite useful.

If you get really serious about using humor in public speaking, you can subscribe to "Current Comedy" (700 Orange Street, Wilmington, Delaware 19801). This newsletter provides public-speaking-oriented humor based on current events, such as: "Light travels faster than sound. That's why some folks appear bright until they start to speak," or "Right now people on the other side of the earth are waking up and leaving home to go to work while our civil servants in Washington are just waking up and going home from work." This service was begun by comedy writer Robert Orben, who has semiretired. You will find it a bit expensive (last I heard: $55 for twelve issues), but a special introductory offer includes extras.

When I first taught public speaking as a graduate teaching assistant at Southern Illinois University, a kindly professor gave me a list of "Some Suggested Subjects for Speeches to Entertain." Some of my students have found it useful; perhaps you will, too. Here's the list:

Why horses don't bet on people

Mules, their care

A case of mistaken identity

Glories of spinsterhood

Life in a small town

Stamp collectors

Types of dates

Deep-sea living

Party-crashing adventures

Snoring

A puppy who adopted me

A class prophecy

My luck with a French menu

Blind dates

Proposing made easy

Thoughts of a slow driver

Gownless evening straps

The poet's concept of women

The bluff that failed

What to do with razor blades

Women's hats

The radio (TV) bedtime story

Men's fancied superiority

Mystery dramas

An unforgettable boner

Golf

Slips of speech

Sir Walter Raleigh and modern chivalry

Thrills in stunt flying

Experiences in mountain climbing

Deceiving figures

Adventures of a firefighter

Do you remember when . . .

Stories by Woolcott

Male plumage

Folktales of the Southwest

What TV does to people

Deep-sea fishing

Washing the dishes

Why men should not shave

Flying saucers

Join the navy—see the world

Davy Crockett

Unusual patents

How to avoid work

Idiosyncrasies of names

A practical joker

A pie and its consequences

Among the "hillbillies"

Foolish questions

Why worry?

Our speech class

Personal development according to the ads

Our professors

Barber shops

This smoking world

Slang

If babies could talk

What's in a name?

Blasting famous traditions

Modernizing Mother Nature

Jigsaw puzzles

Experiences of a reporter

Been hypnotized?

How to live to 100—but why?

New Year's resolutions

A husband's gifts to his wife

The wit of Calvin Coolidge

Coon hunting

If I were president

How to become an orator	American life in the movies
What college did to me	American life in TV sitcoms

Your teacher may or may not assign a speech to entertain, and you may or may not choose to try this particular genre. But you would find such a speech both work and fun. If you try it, I wish you luck. As we say in the theater, "Break a leg."

11

SOLVING PROBLEMS IN GROUPS

C ourses in beginning public speaking commonly include a unit on group discussion (or group problem solving). Those who become able public speakers often find themselves on decision-making boards, committees, or "task forces" for various civic, educational, business, and charitable organizations. The basic thinking and talking done by these groups underlies the decisions by which Americans govern themselves; in a democracy we govern ourselves with *talk*.

You might not often think of the fact that talk governs our decisions (as opposed to the other method, force). But it does, and therefore talk should proceed as sensibly and logically as we can make it in order to make the best possible decisions. As I have emphasized throughout this book, particularly in Chapter 9, most of the time we humans tend to think and act as we wish—in other words, more emotionally than rationally. But when we have an important problem to solve, we generally form a committee and put several heads to work on it, employing all the logic, evidence, and common sense we can muster.

Characteristics of a Discussion Group

Just what do we mean by "group discussion"? Speech texts define it as serious talk by a small group working at solving a mutual problem. These texts further define it as a process that requires careful planning, relative informality, wide participation from its members, a common goal by all concerned, and some leadership. Let us look at each of these criteria in more detail.

Planning

Any problem-solving situation will benefit from careful and thoughtful planning. The group should judiciously lay out the steps they will follow in an agenda of some sort. They can divide any research tasks among themselves, to avoid duplication of effort. They should decide when and where to meet. They should ensure that each has the address and telephone number of the others, so they can communicate before and after meetings. If the group contains a large number of members, perhaps subgroups should be formed. Careful planning at the beginning of a group's work can prevent wasted time and energy later.

Informality

Discussion should take place in a group small enough for members to converse easily and to exchange and evaluate ideas and information face-to-face. The group need not follow parliamentary procedure; for instance, the chair should feel free to participate in the discussion, offering and critiquing ideas and information and even proposing motions or other actions for the group (larger groups, governed by Robert's Rules of Order, must conduct business much more formally, and presiding officers may not offer or even debate motions, in order to maintain the chair's appearance of impartiality).

Participation

Wide participation by members enhances problem solving. The reason for having a group, rather than one or two individuals, consider a problem stems from the idea that several viewpoints and information sources results in better decisions. If everyone contributes, such variety occurs, and the group's work benefits.

Common Purpose

The members of the group must share a common purpose toward which all will work. Otherwise the group will spin its wheels in factionalism, rivalry, face-saving, and friction, rather than in cooperative inquiry, investigation, and consensus. A wise group spends some time in its initial session to try to determine whether they share unanimity of purpose. Without such unanimity, the group may as well disband.

Leadership

Much time, effort, and research money has been spent on trying to define *leadership* and how to detect potential leaders, how to train people for leadership roles, what traits correlate with leadership skills, and the like. The military would love to know how to find, train, and make the best use of leaders.

Leaders generally fall into three general types: laissez-faire (a leader in name only who performs no leadership functions); autocratic (a leader who makes all decisions and gives all the orders—the term "iron-fisted" comes to mind); and democratic (a leader who participates, assists, uses many questions to draw out information and opinion, strives to achieve genuine consensus among participants, and so on).

Researchers have studied which type of leadership produces the best results. For instance, some of the early research showed that laissez-faire leadership produced nearly nothing; autocratic leadership produced the most results, but only in the leader's presence ("When the cat's away . . ."); and democratic leadership produced the next-best results—the groups made sound decisions and continued to do good work even in the leader's absence.

In the "real world" the leader of a group occupies that position because of his or her job or because of appointment by some higher-up person or parent organization. At other times a group will elect its own chair. With no designated, appointed, or elected leader, a group sometimes proceeds with its work and waits for a leader to emerge as the group pursues its normal course. We call this emergent leadership.

By whatever means a group member becomes a leader, we do know that groups benefit from certain leadership behaviors no matter who in the group provides them. These leadership behaviors, or functions, include the following:

1. Building a permissive climate, so that members will feel free to contribute and evaluate information and ideas.

2. Making sure that the group follows the plan, or agenda.

3. Occasionally giving accurate summaries or obtaining them from others. This summarizing helps to confirm that the group remains together in their work thus far.

4. Giving or getting clarification of any vague, ambiguous statement that, if left hanging, might lead to confusion or inaction.

5. Promoting evaluations of generalizations, especially broad ones: "OK, Jim, you claim last year's program completely flopped. Maybe it did. Do you think so, Mary? Sam? How about you, Susan?"

6. Protecting minority opinion, when voiced (otherwise a minority of one might remain clammed up): "All right, I think we all kinda agree on this, except for Mitch. Mitch, why don't you tell us what you think, and explain your position as

clearly as you can. And we'll all give you our full attention and try to give your thoughts a fair hearing. OK?"

7. Minimizing extrinsic conflicts. Conflict over substantive issues often serves to bring out information and ideas necessary for the solution of the problem. But conflict over extraneous matters (such as who has been doing the most work, who has the purest motives, and so on) can only prove counterproductive.

8. Performing only *necessary* functions. If the leader limits himself or herself to only needed activities, the other members will do more and thus become more committed to the work and solutions reached by the group.

The Discussion Process

Discussion should normally proceed through a six-step process, beginning with a question (inquiry) and ending with a solution. (Debate, on the contrary, begins with a solution and argues for its acceptance.) I cannot emphasize enough the need for members to come to the discussion process in an attitude of true inquiry, meaning with an open mind, from which the process will benefit. A member who comes to the task with one or more preconceived notions of what solution the group should adopt (especially if that solution proves self-serving) will constantly promote his or her own hidden agenda, and the group's progress will suffer accordingly.

The problem-solving group should follow the seven steps of reflective thinkings: (1) recognize the problem, (2) word the problem as a question, (3) explore the problem, (4) develop criteria for evaluating solutions, (5) consider possible solutions, (6) choose the best solution, and (7) implement the solution.

Recognize the Problem

Some might not include recognizing the problem as a step, but usually a problem-solving group never even forms unless someone perceives that a problem *exists*.

Word the Problem as a Question

The importance of this second step stems from the fact that the wording of a question will usually determine the wording of the answer (and may determine how to go about looking for the answer). Follow these rules:

1. Make sure that each word in the question fits a definition on which all can agree. As in science, operational definitions would serve best for this purpose. This rule means that, for instance, you should avoid all vague abstractions like *government, big business, labor,* and almost any word ending in -*ism.*

2. Make sure that the question, as worded, has an answer that you can discover. Unanswerable questions can lead to frustration and demoralization; most such questions begin with *why* or *should.* ("Why do we have this particular problem?" or "Should we really take the responsibility for those people?")

3. Word the question fairly, leaving out any loaded words ("What can we do to control the *vicious* behavior of . . . ?")

4. State the question so as not to evoke a "Yes" or "No" answer initially. Starting out with "Should we raise our dues?" might evoke immediate, albeit silent, answers from each member of the group Thus, minds close and prepare to argue. Such immediate answers even more strongly close the mind of the member who states a position publicly. A better question would promote thoughtful inquiry, such as "What can our group do to increase our income?"

Explore the Problem

Usually the members will have researched the problem just as they would research a topic for a speech (see Chapter 4). During this step—probably the longest your group will engage in—you and your group members will share and evaluate information gathered about the problem, through the give-and-take of conversation. You will discuss the basic nature of the problem: Should we consider it an economic or ethical problem? A political, social, or moral problem? What about its history? Has the problem existed for some time, or has it only recently surfaced? What about solutions that have been tried in the past? What can we find out about the extent or seriousness of the problem? Does it affect many or few people, and how and to what degree does the harm occur? And so on.

Develop Criteria for Evaluating Solutions

Only after thoroughly familiarizing yourselves with the problem should you turn to the fourth step: developing criteria for evaluating possible solutions. Why do this before discussing the possible solutions? Because discussing solutions without first agreeing on the criteria by which you will evaluate them can again allow members to close their minds by voicing support for one or another possible solution. But although people might readily begin disagreeing over solutions, they usually agree on criteria quite easily. For instance, people find most general criteria quite undebatable. Just about any solution that you decide to adopt would have to satisfy you on several factors: cost, legality, morality, and constitutionality. Failure to meet any of these criteria should doom any proposal. In addition, unenforceable solutions will not work, and neither will solutions that will cause more problems than they will solve. Finally, solutions do not work unless large numbers of those affected *accept* them (remember Prohibition?). With all solutions otherwise "equal," people generally opt for the *simplest* solution.

> *Although people might readily begin disagreeing over solutions, they usually agree on criteria quite easily.*

Consider Possible Solutions

After compiling your list of criteria, you will find yourselves ready to begin considering possible solutions to which you will apply these criteria. Here you will probably benefit from *brainstorming*, a procedure in which members blurt out possible ideas for solutions, regardless of how far out, illogical, wacky, nonsensical, or visionary they might seem at first blush. One particular feature of brainstorming enhances this process: during this idea-generating phase, no one may criticize in any way the ideas offered. The resulting lack of inhibition can produce a large number of ideas in a short time. And although one member's wild idea may not produce a viable solution, it might inspire even better, more practical ideas. Brainstorming has a good track record for producing ideas that generate further discussion.

Choose the Best Solution

After your free-wheeling brainstorming, you replace your critical thinking caps and begin applying your already-agreed-upon criteria to the list of solutions you have generated. If you selected clear, comprehensive, and sensible criteria, you should find it relatively easy to use them to select the best solution from your list. Unfortunately, this stage of the process often brings out previously hidden agendas, which can throw a monkey wrench into the works. The group will have to deal with these problems in a calm and rational manner, referring back as much as possible to the agreed upon criteria.

Implement the Solution

What happens after you have followed this tried-and-true six-step process and come up with a solution on which you all agree?

Ordinarily, you will take some action to implement your solution. You leave inquiry behind and embark on advocacy. A group of concerned citizens might want to contact their senator, congressperson, state representative, or county commissioner to urge adoption of their plan. A committee of a parent organization would (through its chair) report back to the larger group, probably orally (see "Oral Reports" in Chapter 8), concluding with, "And therefore our committee moves that we take the following action: . . ." The solution now becomes a proposition, out on the floor of the real world, ready for debate. Discussion, which began with inquiry and ended in a solution, lies behind you; ahead lies advocacy for the solution's acceptance and implementation.

Selected Research Findings

Experimental research supports certain generalizations about the discussion process. Some of the most important of those generalizations can help us understand the group problem-solving process.

This chapter has already emphasized the importance of common goals for all members of a group. But another feature, *cohesiveness*, also affects results. If group members get to know one another, understand the power relationships among them, learn their own roles in the group, and learn to get along with each other, cohesiveness, or closeness, emerges—and the group becomes productive. If cohesiveness fails to develop, the group will accomplish little.

This "getting along" emerges (or doesn't emerge) through what we call group maintenance functions, such as joking to release tension and making supporting statements, such as "I agree with you" or "That idea strikes me as excellent." In other words, you maintain group morale with tact and good manners. And whenever someone tells me, "I just can't behave tactfully and show good manners easily," I generally reply, "You have no difficulty with tact when you deal with your boss, do you?" After the person agrees, I then just recommend that he or she pretend that the other group members pay his or her salary.

Decisions reached after discussion generally prove superior to those made by individuals working alone. This generalization holds no matter whether the question involves what kind of new grievance plan a company should adopt or how many white beans a three-ounce spice jar will hold.

Decisions reached after discussion generally prove superior to those made by individuals working alone.

One personal attribute seems related to success as a problem-solving discussant: reflective thinking ability, as measured by the Johnson Test of Reflective Thinking Ability. An inspection of the Johnson test and its purpose indicates that the trait mainly represents a willingness to withhold judgment until more information becomes available. People who jump to conclusions based on less information tend to score low on the test. Practically speaking, willingness to suspend judgment until satisfactory information becomes available seems like a pretty sound trait to exercise in problem-solving discussion.

An apparent majority position can cause members holding a minority opinion to acquiesce and agree to go along with the majority. Researchers have found the "minority of one" especially susceptible to group influence; however, if only one other person sides with the deviant (making a minority of at least two), resolve against the majority opinion stiffens. But research also shows that a stubborn minority of one will attract stronger and stronger counterarguments from the others in the group; if the deviant remains obdurate, the group will usually wind up rejecting him or her.

In direct contradiction to this point, however, research also shows that a minority skilled in persuasion can often turn around an initial majority position. For example, when one jury retired to the jury room after hearing a will-breaking case, a majority voted in favor of the plaintiffs' urging revocation of the will. The minority argued that the jury should concentrate on the will's legality, not on whether they

189

considered the deceased a mean, spiteful man or whether they sympathized with the poor, deprived plaintiffs. In this case, strong argument and legality won out.

Reaching sound decisions to solve important problems constitutes the very basis of democratic decision making. I hope that you will heed the advice of this chapter in practicing self-governance and that it will help you achieve that biblical dictum, "Come, let us reason together."

APPENDIX
SAMPLE SPEECHES AND OULINES

*T*he playwright writes a *script*, not a *play*. The script may exist as a play in the playwright's mind, since he or she can imagine the actors, stage, historical setting, action, costumes, and so on. But for the rest of us, the script becomes a play only when the actors, director, stage manager, prop crew, lighting operator, and scenic designer breath life into it on a real stage before a live audience.

By the same token, I cannot give you "real" sample speeches in this appendix. I can present only the words—the scripts of speeches made in the past by living, breathing speakers, who interacted with live human audiences. These manuscripts lack the cadence of the speaker's rhythm and personality, the vocal stress and emphasis, the pregnant pauses, and the subtle (and sometimes not-so-subtle) interplay of speaker and audience.

Even though the vital speech *events* do not appear here, you can learn something of the organization, language, content, and phrasing of successful short speeches by reading, studying, and emulating the manuscripts in this appendix.

Speech 1: A Speech to Inform

Mark B. Perry gave the following speech to inform at the University of Georgia. I have edited for print.

YOU DON'T HAVE TO KEEP TAKING IT

Have you ever watched a mother feeding her baby split-pea mush—and the baby eats until it has had enough and decides to spew the green mush back all over Mommy? Well, maybe sometimes you have felt like spewing back the split-pea mush poked at you by a radio or television station. Maybe something you have heard or seen on the media really ticked you off, and you wanted to complain about it. I know that happens to me regularly. But most people never put in their complaint; they may not know just how to go about it, or they may think, "Oh, what the heck. What good would it do anyway?"

Well, I want to tell you today that you have the right and the power and the opportunity to complain and *get results* from the electronic media. And I would like to explain how to do this effectively. First, I would like to explain how the FCC—the Federal Communications Commission—operates to regulate broadcasting and how you can use the FCC to put pressure on local broadcasters *and* networks. And then I want to explain how to get specific results in certain cases involving local stations or networks, whether you want to ask a question or make a specific complaint.

First of all, let's suppose your complaint is a real biggie: some station or network is obviously violating its commitment to serve in the "public interest."

You want to stop them. You will want to contact the Federal Communications Commission; that's the governmental agency that has sole regulatory power for granting and renewing broadcast licenses. Just as you need a license to drive a car, a broadcast station needs a license to use the airways, which belong to the public. Just as you can lose your driver's license by breaking the law, so can a station lose its broadcast license for violating regulations.

Broadcast licenses are usually routinely renewed every three years, unless there is evidence that the station is not operating in the public interest. And the station is required to ascertain the needs of the community and to program to meet those needs. That's why you hear so many editorials and public service announcements on radio and TV; these are clearly "in the public interest." You can have an active role in this license renewal process.

Suppose a station in your area has too little music or too little news; maybe they have too many commercials or show obvious discriminatory practices in their hiring procedures or refuse to carry certain stories in the news because of favoritism. You can submit a petition to the FCC asking that they deny the renewal of the station's license.

What you do is gather some signatures and evidence of misconduct and send them to the FCC in Washington. They will have hearings and, in the process, consider this petition in the renewal process. If they find justification in your complaint, they will issue a cease-and-desist order; that is a temporary probation for the station warning them to clean up their act. If, during the probationary period, the station fails to correct the situation, the FCC can lift its license and award the frequency to some other individual or company. It has been done before, many times.

But maybe you don't want to go so far as to get a license suspended because a station broadcasts a lot of garbage riddled with sexual stereotyping and senseless violence. But you still would like to complain, maybe put a stop to what you feel is offensive. Well, you can still make your complaint known to the local station.

It's really a little ironic. Local stations *want* your critical letters. If you write in and complain, and the station can do something about the complaint—say, correct it completely—they will keep your letter and show it to the FCC at renewal time, along with an explanation of how they responded. It makes them look great!

So don't hesitate to write. Get those loads off your chest, and become a mover and shaker.

Now, the key to getting your letter read by the right person is to address it to the proper individual at the station. For instance, if your complaint or question concerns overall station policy, find out the name of the general manager or the owner of the station (a simple phone call will get it) and send it to that person, in care of the station. If you are bothered by the news, send your complaint to the specific producer of the news. The point is, mail your letter to the specific individual; and above all, write "Confidential" on the envelope. That will ensure that it gets to the person's office and into the person's hands to be read.

I was once troubled by a program on CBS radio. So I wrote the show's director, Mr. Andrew Rooney; I got satisfaction in a letter from Mr. Rooney almost by return mail.

Of course, now we're talking about network complaints. Here you have to remember that *you* are the lifeblood of the networks. Without an audience, ABC, NBC, CBS, PBS, and HBO have no reason to exist. So, tell 'em what you like and don't like.

Before I go into how to write your letter to the network, let me talk for a minute on how the networks handle the huge quantities of mail that come into their shops. First, it all comes into the mailroom. Here it is sorted out according to the addressee. If mail is addressed to an individual, then it's sent right to that individual's office, where it will be read either by the addressee or by his or her secretary; from here, it may go to the agency in the network best qualified to answer the question or reply to the complaint. Most letters come in addressed either to a show or just to the network itself. These go to an office known as the Audience Information Office. This office answers some of the letters; others they refer to another agency, just the way the individuals do.

Another important point to remember about the Audience Information Office is that it occasionally reports to the network's top brass on how the mail is going. For instance, they may keep score of how the mail is running for and against a particular program or issue (like TV violence); they tally up the scores and send them up to the bosses, such as the president of CBS, who can then review them and see what the public is thinking. So if you think that your one letter is not going to have an impact, just remember that there are probably thousands of people out there writing in on the same matter. The only way you can get your vote in is to write, yourself.

Again, the key to success is to direct your letter to the particular program, agency, or individual who can take action in your letter. If you need to learn the name of the particular individual you want to write to, you can often find it in *Standard and Poor's* directory of U.S. businesses and corporations.

So remember, limit your complaint or query to one particular point, so that your letter can go directly to the agency that can handle it. And wherever possible, address your letter to a particular person.

Here are a few more points that might prove helpful.

State your credentials. Yes, even if you are a college student, they will listen if you tell them that. After all, the college market is a very lucrative one for the media. Also, send a copy of the letter to the sponsors of the program. They are the folks putting up the money for the program, and they don't want to offend potential customers of their products. And sponsors want to know what people think about the programming they support. You ought to send a copy of the letter, also, to the local station carrying the material, for the same reasons.

Above all, check to make sure your facts are correct; your letter should seem to be the work of an incisive, calm, knowledgeable critic or inquirer who seems to know what is really going on—you don't want your letter to go in the ashcan as the work of a kook.

You, the viewer or listener, are the key to broadcasting. You can control what is being flushed into your home on the cathode-ray tube. So the next time the media irk you, take action. Write that letter. You can complain or ask questions on the local level or the network level, or in extreme cases, you can even petition to deny the license of the broadcast station. After all, if the media are required to program in the public interest, then the public has to be interested enough to let the broadcasters know just what *is* the public interest.

Speech 2: A Speech to Inform

Louise C. Hoke gave this speech to inform in my honors course at the University of Georgia. I provide both her outline and her speech.

Outline for "How to Remember What's-Her-Name"

Purpose: To teach the audience how to use the principles behind one method of remembering names.

Introduction
  I. Here at school we all meet lots of people whose names we can't remember, right?
  II. Well, remembering those names is not so difficult if you will remember and use a simple four-step process I would like to explain.

Body
  I. The first step in becoming a name expert is getting the name right the first time.
     A. Do not let a name slip past you in an introduction.
     B. Block out everything but the name that is being stated.
     C. If you did not understand it the first time, ask for a repetition of the name.
     D. If necessary, ask for a spelling of the name.

Transition: Making sure you heard the name right the first time is fine, but there is more to do.

  II. The second step is to hammer the name into your memory through repetition.
     A. Use the name as much as possible during the course of the conversation.

       1. Begin the conversation by addressing the new acquaintance by name.

       2. Precede as many sentences as possible with the new acquaintance's name.

       3. In parting, be sure to use the name in any farewell remarks.

  B. As soon as possible, write the name down for future reference.

Transition: And there's something else to do while you are repeating the name so often.

III. Fasten in your mind an image of the new acquaintance's face.

  A. During an introduction be observant of any distinguishing characteristics the person might have.

       1. Look for anything unusual at first, such as scars, warts, wrinkles, or moles.

       2. Study other things, too, like ears, nose, eyes, hair, weight, and height.

  B. Do this often enough, and you will learn to be observant almost as a habit.

Transition: But there is one more thing you can do also.

IV. Finally, anchor the name through *association.*

  A. Think of anyone else you know with the same name.

  B. Concentrate on any facts you learn during a conversation that you can associate with this person.

  C. Try to connect the name with a slogan, an allusion, or a familiar quotation.

  D. Try to make a rhyme out of the name ("Here's Mr. Hummock, with a large stomach") so that the person's appearance will suggest the name.

Conclusion

  I. So remember to get the name right at first, to repeat it as often as possible during your conversation, to remember the face that goes with the name, and to anchor the name by association.

  II. Do these four things regularly, and enjoy the most important part of college life: meeting people!

HOW TO REMEMBER WHAT'S-HER-NAME

Going to college is one great experience after another, isn't it? There are new classes, new rooms, clubs, activities, and social customs. But most important of all is new friends. And with each new friend comes one new face and one new name that make that person unique.

I know that you've each met a lot of people since coming to the university. And I'm equally sure that you have forgotten many of their names already. Am I right? The faces still are familiar, maybe, but the names just won't come to mind. Well, making new friends takes time, and one way to turn acquaintances into those new friends faster is to use names. Remembering names and faces doesn't have to be hard. It just has to be more systematic. Today I would like to explain a simple four-step process that will help you put names and faces together. First, you have to get the name right in the first place. Second, you hammer the name in by repetition. Third, you fasten the image of the face in your mind. And fourth, you anchor the name through association.

The first step is to get the name straight off the bat. This is probably the easiest of all the four steps. In an introduction, don't let a name just slip past you. Very often the person making the introductions knows both names so well that the name will be zipped hurriedly through or badly slurred, and you won't quite catch it. So if you don't hear the name well, be sure to speak up. Say, "I'm sorry—I didn't hear the name. Could you repeat it?" Usually, when you do this, the person you just met will be flattered because you are interested enough to inquire about his or her name. You are *interested* in this person. Of course, often the other person will respond with, "Well, I didn't catch yours, either." And so mutual respect is established.

Another important thing to remember at this point is to mentally block out everything but the name you are hearing. Concentrate! Often you will be so wrapped up in the sight of the person you are meeting that you'll forget to listen for the name—you'll just not be paying any attention. So be sure to wait until that name has sunk into your head before you begin to notice what the person is wearing or looks like or anything else. And don't be distracted by listening to see if your name has been pronounced correctly. That can be cleared up later, if necessary. Listen for the other's name. Don't just hang back, expecting to catch it later in the conversation, because it may never happen. Speak up if you don't hear it well; getting that name right to begin with is absolutely essential, and it's the easiest step of all.

OK, now, after hearing that name correctly in the first place, move on to the second step, which is to hammer the name in by repetition. This means simply thinking about the name as much as possible, saying it as much as you can in conversation, and listening every time the name is used. An easy way to do this is to use the person's name in the first statement you make after being introduced. Say, "Hello, George" or "Hello, Sarah," along with "It's so nice to meet you." Use that name. From then on, use it as much as you can, in every sentence. People *love* to hear their own names in someone else's discourse!

Now, if you are with a big bunch of people this might be hard to do. But you need to use the name at the ends of sentences, in the middle, and wherever else you can. Don't make it too obvious, but still use it often, so that the name sinks into your brain. And if you *are* in a large group and don't have a lot of time to talk and say that new name, just repeat it to yourself silently three or four times. This helps a lot.

Finally, when you are getting ready to leave, think about all the times you have left someone and he or she has said, "Well, sure nice to meetcha" without your name. They've forgotten it. Then you say this: "Well, it was certainly nice to meet you, Harold (or whatever), and I hope to see you again soon." Do this and Harold will be flattered—and truly interested in seeing you again soon, too.

Another trick used by many is to write the name down, especially if it is an unusual name or has an unusual spelling. And it's a good idea to have someone spell his or her name during the introductions if the name is unusual. I read once about a businessman who ran into an old customer on the commuter train but could not for the life of him remember the customer's name. During the conversation, the customer said that the businessman should call him soon for a new order. The businessman became desperate over the customer's name. Finally, he said, "I need to write down your name, but I want to be sure it is spelled correctly. Could you spell out your name for me?" The *former* customer replied icily, "Sure. It's B-O-B Bob. S-M-I-T-H." So be careful about the spelling bit. You have been warned.

But writing the name down works. It's a technique that Napoleon III used. When he first got into power, he needed the support of all his subjects. He figured a good way to get it would be to learn as many names as possible. So whenever he met someone, he would write the name on a little piece of paper as soon as he could, and he would then sit and look at it for a few minutes. And it worked for him like a fine watch.

Salespeople use this technique also. People successful in sales write down and file away the names not only of their clients but of their secretaries and other employees. They know that remembering the receptionist's name is a real plus in getting in quickly to see the boss, and that knowing and using the names of the store's sales force will make them enthusiastic in pushing the sales representative's particular brand of merchandise.

Well, now, steps one and two help you learn and remember names. Step three helps you put the names with the faces; it helps by fastening the faces in your mind. So after that name has been heard correctly, and as you are using it as much as you can in conversation, start becoming observant of the person you just met. Remembering faces is not a matter of eyesight but of careful observation.

An important element of careful observation is *calm*. Be calm. I know it's difficult sometimes, in the flush and excitement of meeting a new potential friend, but you have to practice. Look at the face. Are there any unusual features, like scars, moles, or warts? Any wrinkles, red hair, or anything else that stands out? After the unusual things, start taking in the more common things, like hair color, weight, age, voice, stance, the way of walking or talking—the arrangement of facial features, like eyes, ears, nose, mouth—anything like that.

Now, being observant is a useful but not an easy-to-acquire trait. If you are not a really observant person, you need to train yourself and to make being observant more or less a habit. Most police officers become unusually observant through training and motivation, as do the president's Secret Service men. You can practice being observant of people anywhere: walking down the street, riding a bus, just about anywhere. Glance at a face, then close your eyes (or look away) and try to reconstruct a picture of that face in your mind. Then check the face with another glance.

At a movie, try to learn as many names of the actors and actresses as possible, and not only their names but the names of the characters they played also. This is excellent practice. And practice is what you need in order to develop the habit of observation. And once you have this habit of observation, you will be surprised at how many things you notice about people that you never noticed before.

The fourth and final step is to anchor the name by association. You need to try to link that name to as many related impressions and facts as you can, so that later on it will just pop right back into your head.

Now there are several methods you can use to do this. First of all, say to yourself, "Do I know anyone else by that name?" It doesn't have to be a close friend or a relative. It can be a politician, or a movie star, or some famous person in history. Just associate that new name with the other person, and it will help loads—especially if the two persons share some likenesses.

Also, associate something about the person's name with something you know or learn about him or her. For instance, you meet a Mr. Parr, then you find out he's a golfer. Parr, par. This should be easy. Or you meet a Mrs. Cobb. Think of her as eating corn on the *cob.* You meet an older man, say a Mr. Sands. You can associate his name with the sands of time. Associate a name with something that rhymes. You meet a Mr. Hughes, who is chewing gum. "Mr. Hughes chews," you say to yourself. Just the fact that you have taken the extra mental effort to make some association of this kind will cement the name more firmly in your skull.

Of course, associations can trip you up sometimes, too. A man met a rather portly woman named Mrs. Hummock. He thought he could remember her name easily by associating her name with her round, protruding abdomen. "Hummock, stomach," he thought. Weeks later, however, he met her in the supermarket. "Good afternoon, Mrs. Kelly," he smiled.

You also need to realize that you can help others remember *your* name by using similar techniques. Ralph, here, could tell people he meets, "My name is Ralph. You know how the dog barks in the old Pogo strip: 'Ralph, Ralph!'" Mr. Gruner told me about a retired dentist he met down at Jekyll Island who said, "Name's Quiggle. Rhymes with wiggle." And I imagine a lot of his patients *did* wiggle!

So there you have it. There are four basic steps to remembering names and faces. Get the name straight the first time. Hammer that name in by repetition. Fasten the face in your mind. Then anchor the name by association. Practicing these four steps can make your boring life exciting. So put them to work for you, and enjoy one of the most important aspects of college life: meeting people.

Speech 3: A Speech to Inform

Jack H. Kirkman, a freshman at the University of Georgia, presented this speech to inform in my honors class. I reproduce it here, edited for print.

WITH SPEED IN THE DARK

All of you have seen *Gone with the Wind*, right? Well, in *Gone with the Wind* you get the picture of Clark Gable, blockade runner, as he walks through the big dance, with his white suit, white Panama hat, and Havana cigar. He's making loads of money by profiteering off the fall of the South. Unfortunately, this is the only view that most people have of the Confederate blockade running, and just as unfortunately, this view is totally false. So today I am going to give you a little background on Civil War blockade running. I recently did a term paper on the subject, and I found it fascinating. I hope you do, too.

On April 19, 1861, which is five days after the fall of Fort Sumter, Abraham Lincoln issued a proclamation saying that the North would blockade all Southern ports. Now there were two important aspects of this proclamation: number one was that a nation only blockades the ports of an *enemy nation;* therefore, the North had in effect recognized the South as a belligerent. And as a belligerent, the South's side received certain rights under international law. And the second important point was the use of the word *blockade* itself. According to the Treaty of Paris, which the United States had signed, the blockade was not to be taken seriously unless it was effective. In other words, it was legal for ships of other nations to run the blockade as long as they weren't caught.

Now this legality allowed Great Britain to perform a major role in the blockade running. As a matter of fact, the British did about 70 to 75 percent of it. There were very few actual Confederate blockade runners. This can't be underestimated—the role that Great Britain played. Her textile mills needed the South's cotton, and her factories could supply the South with most of its arms, equipment, and other hard goods. In fact, when the blockade running was finally shut down, when the last port was effectively closed, the war was over within four months. There was just nothing left for the South the fight with.

When Lincoln issued his proclamation, there were only *four* federal ships in any position to enforce the blockade, and there were four thousand miles of coastline to blockade, both the Atlantic and Gulf coasts. So from the beginning, the blockade was, in fact, a farce. By 1862, however, the federals had recalled their ships from foreign waters and had raised the level of the blockade from a farce to that of a rough joke. Then, by 1863, they began to put some real teeth into the blockade. It became no longer profitable or possible for the blockade runners to use their large, heavy, deep-draft steamers direct from Great Britain to ply the blockaded Southern ports. What they needed were small, light, fast ships.

Smaller ships meant they would have to transship the materials. And to facilitate this transshipment, they used the British colonies of Nassau and Bermuda. They'd used Nassau for running in to Savannah and Charleston, and Bermuda for running in to Wilmington, because these islands were close to the respective Confederate ports. They used Wilmington more than any other because it was easy to slip into and had a much larger outlet, and the waters were trickier for the federals to navigate with their big men-of-war. So a typical blockade runner would form a cycle: From Bermuda to Wilmington with the war materiels, and then from Wilmington back to Bermuda with a load of cotton.

At this time cotton could be purchased in the South at around six cents a pound, whereas it could be resold in Great Britain for around fifty to sixty cents a pound, creating an enormous profit. So blockade runners would put as much cotton as they could on the ships. They would totally fill up the hold and then actually stack it too high on the deck. The bales of cotton had already been compressed to half their normal size by steam presses on the Southern coast. So they would actually work the ship from an artificial deck made up of bales of cotton. Now, in this way, depending on the size of the steamer, they could get between six hundred and twelve hundred bales of cotton on board. Therefore, an average ship could make a profit of maybe $420,000 off the cotton run out alone. Once in Bermuda, they would unload the cotton, take on coal, water, and provisions, and load up the ship with war materiels. Now came the trickiest part of it, and that was running the material back past the blockade warships.

The three keys to running safely into the Southern ports were (1) invisibility, (2) speed, and (3) knowledge of the coast.

First, let's consider invisibility. For their size, these ships were extremely long, about 180 feet long, and only about 20 feet wide in the beam. And they were built very close to the water. They decks rose only about 8 feet above the water. There were hardly any masts or smokestacks to speak of; these were kept very short. The result was a long, small, low ship that had a very small wheelhouse atop it. The blockade runners didn't want to be spotted easily at all, under sea conditions. They painted the ships gray, the exact shade being obtained by experience with the sea in that area. The crew wore gray, also. Their clothes were specifically woven and dyed for this purpose on the islands of Bermuda and Nassau. And, of course, no lights were allowed on deck. A properly camouflaged blockade runner was not visible from a range of seventy-five yards on a dark night. And, indeed, it was quite common for the runners to pass the federal blockade squadrons within a hundreds yards of their ships.

OK, so these runners were practically invisible; now let's consider their speed.

These slim, low ships *were* speedy. They would run between fourteen and twenty-two knots an hour, which was a fantastic rate for those times and isn't bad even today. And the federals had no ships that could go that fast. The runners would just scoot right past the big battlewagons.

So invisibility and speed were vital to the blockade runners. But so was their knowledge of the coast. This was extremely important because they ran in on pitch-black nights. They would choose a night of no moon, preferably even a foggy or stormy night. The Carolina coast in this section is extremely flat, with no rocks and no landmarks. The pilot had to know the area like the back of his hand.

The method was to run in north of the inlet, turn parallel to the shore, and hug the shore all the way into port—and I mean *hug* the shore! Even though these ships ran six hundred to eight hundred tons, their draft was only four to eleven feet. They would actually run inside the first line of breakers, because the coast drops off rather steeply there. They would steam along just about seventy yards or so from shore, and they would run on into the port around the end of the federal blockade squadron.

With these three elements mastered—invisibility, speed, and knowledge of the coast—the blockade runners were very rarely caught. And on their first voyage they could realize a profit of about 125 percent on their investment, even including the cost of building the blockade-running ship. And from then on the amount of money they could make became much higher, of course, with each successful return trip. So you can see from the actual numbers what a big business it really was. In the port of Wilmington they did about $150 million worth of goods on that one end alone. And that was on the gold standard, not the Confederate money standard. To illustrate what that means in terms of what the Confederacy could buy, in one month, from one island (Nassau) to one port (Wilmington), they ran in over 130,000 rifles alone, not to mention all the other war materiels and hard goods.

So blockade running, mostly by British ships, was extremely profitable and overwhelmingly successful as long as those three important factors were mastered: invisibility, speed, and knowledge of the coast. It was not until the blockade became nearly 100 percent effective that the supply of materials to the South was choked off, bringing to an end the Confederacy's ability to fight on.

Speech 4: A Speech to Convince

The university's summer banking school, operated through the Continuing Education Center, met for two weeks during each of three years. Bank personnel honed their knowledge and skills in banking and finance; they also studied public speaking as a skill necessary for career advancement. Sandra G. Smith, of the Bank of Dade in Trenton, Georgia, presented the following speech to convince. As usual, I have edited it for print.

YOU'VE COME A LONG WAY, BABY, BUT . . .

Thanks to the Virginia Slims ads we're all familiar with the phrase, "You've come a long way, baby." And that's a very true statement. Women *have* come a long way. But that coming has been a long, drawn-out process, and frankly, women haven't fully arrived yet, either. For years women have tried to convince the world that they are more than just "stay-at-home, do-nothing-all-day squaws." Of course, even when we stay home, we don't exactly do "just nothing." Back in 1897 a piece appeared in a magazine called *The Garden and Farm Journal* that directly relates to this issue. This short article, titled "The Industrious Woman," presented some statistics on how the average Michigan woman used up her time at home: "A Michigan woman made 191 pies, 140 cakes, 84 loaves of bread, 729 biscuits, 156 fried cakes, and 1,026 cookies in her statistical year, which ended September 1." And this was in addition to caring for her children and doing her regular housework. This information may aid those men who wonder whatever it is that a woman does with all her time back in the little cottage.

Well, I don't know how convincing this article was to the male population back in 1897, but I'm glad that a woman's success today isn't dependent on the amount of baking she does in a year. Today women are able to compete much more fairly in work situations with men, and they are proving themselves to be both capable and efficient. This opportunity, never thought possible before, is the result of such things as federal legislation decrees, equal pay and equal credit, and a rapid increase in the number of women in the work force. Last, but not least, is the women's liberation movement.

Now, don't get me wrong. I do *not* count myself as a hard-line women's libber. I appreciate very much the traditional and biological differences between men and women. In fact, I like to repeat a little couplet I ran across in *Reader's Digest* not long ago. It goes:

Women, it now appears are very much like men.
Except, of course, for here and there, and sometimes now and then.

In other words, I don't think *equality* need get confused with any sense of *superiority*. The point of the women's movement that I *do* support is equal opportunity for equally qualified people, whether male or female. This is something that is becoming more and more accepted, especially in the business world. According to the most recent figures available from the Bureau of Labor Statistics, 27.3 percent of the nation's banking officials and financial managers are now women. That's not bad, and another proof that we *have* come a long way.

The most fascinating thing about the whole subject, though, is that women are gaining this right to prove themselves not because men are giving it to them, but because they are giving it to themselves. By this I mean that women's support of other women has become the catalyst for the movement. We don't see this yet as much in our geographical area as in other parts of the country, because although it might kind of hurt our pride to admit it, the South tends to lag a little behind some other areas in accepting some trends. Patricia Scott, management consultant for the National Association of Bank Women, Incorporated, says that in her dealings with women bankers she is finding that more and more they are beginning to support each other. It can be in just little ways—as simple as not being overly critical of each other. I am sure that right now possibly many of you sitting there think that the women that I know and work with certainly haven't learned to stop being so critical of one another. I would have to agree with you, too, and that is what I mean when I say we tend to lag behind some other parts of the country.

It is a bitter dose of medicine for us gals to swallow, but the fact is, we women are often our own worst enemies. Maybe you men here have been accused of male chauvinism. And maybe those charges are a little justified? If so, you deserve anything you get, for my money. But even if we women don't have to cope with male chauvinists in our place of work, even if we get solid support from the men working around and with us, we still have serious problems without the support of other women.

Quite frankly, I think that both sexes will benefit when women learn this lesson in "self-support." Can you ladies here imagine being told that you are getting a promotion, and taking that news *without* a sudden, funny little feeling deep down in the pit of your stomach that there are going to be other women in the bank that are going to get mad at you for getting the promotion? In such a situation, I think, some men might also be envious and jealous of the woman's promotion, but they cover up these feelings much better than women. Not that men just have a different emotional makeup than us women; I think it's just that women are relative newcomers to the business world and, as tyros, we have not had as much time as men have had to learn the ropes, to absorb and follow the ethics of the business place.

I saw something on the local Chattanooga television news a few weeks ago that shows that that area, which is my home stomping grounds, has quite a way to go as far as support among women is concerned. This was during National Secretaries Week, and the reporter was interviewing a woman who had worked for one of the area's leading industries. She very emphatically stated that she would rather work for a man than for a woman! According to her, it "just doesn't seem right" to work for a woman. Now, if she had been a true supporter of other females, she would never have admitted this, even if she believed it. Can you imagine a man going on TV and saying that he would prefer a woman boss over a man? If so, I would like to speak to you after this speech session about a little bridge I have for sale—in Brooklyn.

Even in my own bank, I know of a situation that shows lack of woman-to-woman support. We have two senior officers, and they are of equal rank as far as the corporate structure chart goes. One officer is male, the other female. But if you ask the women in our bank to rank our officers, every one will rank the male higher than the female. Now, this is not the guy's fault; it's just the trend of thinking among women in this area of the country. Obviously, our bank is not what Miss Scott was talking about.

I said earlier that women have come a long way but still have a way to go. Sally Buck, president of the Women's Bank of Richmond, Virginia, has expressed the same belief. She says: "There's no going back. Women are going to play a larger and larger role. It's going to be quite a while, though, before we are complete equals with men." In order to get there from here, it's the women as well as the men who are going to have to have their ways of thinking completely overhauled. Until women learn to accept and support other women, we are asking too much of the men when we expect *them* to do so. Now, we aren't going to let you guys off the hook completely, but we women with open minds realize that women themselves are responsible for part of our dilemma. So we women will accept *half* the blame for our equality problem. If women *want* to have equality, they are going to have to start to *think* equality, *believe* equality, and *behave* equality. After all, equality is what it's all about. As Ashley Montagu once wrote, "It is the mark of the cultured man that he is aware of the fact that equality is an ethical and not a biological principle."

Speech 5: A Speech to Convince

Marsha Gruner wrote this speech as part of the work for her master's thesis. It was presented by another student. The speech, to convince, argues against a current policy.

SAY "NO" TO CAPITAL PUNISHMENT

The body leaps as if to break the strong leather straps that hold it. There is a thin wisp of smoke and the faint odor of burning flesh. The hands turn red, then white, and the cords of the neck stand out like steel bands. After what seems an age, but is really only two minutes, the body sags and relaxes, a mere mass of clay. Not a very pretty picture, is it? This is what happens when we civilized Americans execute a man in the electric chair. But perhaps the hiss of the poison gas pellets seems more humane. Nonetheless, the end result would be the same. A life is taken. Today, I would like to discuss with you the subject of capital punishment. It is my hope that this discussion will lead you to believe, along with me, that capital punishment should be abolished. It should be abolished because first, it is no deterrent to crime, and second, it is morally wrong.

Let's investigate the first point: capital punishment is not a deterrent to crime. When we look at the uniform crime reports submitted to the FBI by all law enforcement agencies, we find that homicide rates per one hundred thousand population vary from state to state. But the rate is essentially the same for states in the same region. Let's look at some examples. During the period from 1931 to 1951 Rhode Island, which does *not* have the death penalty, saw its homicide rate drop from 1.2 to 1.0, while Connecticut, right next door, *with* the death penalty, had a homicide rate drop from 2.4 to 1.9. Michigan, in another region, *not* having the death penalty, had a homicide rate drop from 5.0 to 3.4, while in the same period Indiana, in the same region, w*ith* the death penalty, saw a rate drop from 6.2 to 3.2. This same trend appeared in all regions. There is *no significant variation* to homicide rates with states having the death penalty and states not having the death penalty within the same region. So much for statistics. Let's look at the psychological aspect of homicide and punishment for it.

Homicide is probably the most complex of crimes, usually occurring in the heat of passion and under great emotional stress. Most authorities agree that the possibility of the death penalty does not enter the criminal's mind. The story is told about the three pickpockets working the crowd attending—of all things—the hanging of a pickpocket.

Warden Lewis E. Lawes, for many years the warden of Sing Sing, stated that "almost every one of the 151 persons I have escorted to the death chamber has told me that never once in the events leading up to their conviction did the fact that the death penalty existed enter into their thoughts or affect their actions."

Our very method of execution repudiates the claim that we even *think* the death penalty deters crime. If it is so successful as a deterrent, why aren't executions *public* so that the full effect of the punishment could be felt by a larger number of people? But they are *not* public; instead we hold our executions in the middle of the night under top security measures with only a handful of people to witness the act, as if we were totally ashamed of our act of murder.

Therefore, we can see that the effect of the death penalty in preventing crime is essentially zero. So let's turn to the second point: Capital punishment is morally wrong.

From the beginning of Christian society we have been taught "Thou shalt not kill." The old Judaic code of an eye for an eye and a tooth for a tooth was supposedly outdated by Christ, who taught that mercy is the greatest of human virtues. And yet many of our states look the other way when it comes to legalized murder in the form of capital punishment. For regardless of what language we use in the name of justice, and regardless of our mistaken notion that it deters crime, capital punishment is the taking of one human being's life by another human being. And—it is deliberate. In fact, as pointed out by attorney Herbert B. Ehrmann, we have actual prejudicial jury selection in that people who don't believe in the death penalty are usually barred from serving on juries in states with the death penalty. Capital punishment is the most barbaric effect of society's desire for revenge.

Also, the death penalty arbitrarily discriminates against a segment of our population. According to the American Academy of Political and Social Sciences, women are almost never executed. Blacks are executed more readily than white men. The poor, and not the wealthy, are executed. Warden Lawes has said, "All the people I escorted to the death chamber had one thing in common. All were poor and friendless. Wealthy or influential people are almost never executed."

The most horrifying fact about capital punishment is that innocent people may be executed. Lafayette recognized this when he said, "I shall ask for the abolition of the penalty of death until I have the infallibility of human judgment demonstrated to me." There are documented cases where innocent people have been executed. The most notable case in the United States is Tommy Bambrick, who died in the chair at Sing Sing while Warden Thomas R. Osborne was trying to reach the governor of New York with news of last-minute evidence that had just come to light. We also have a lengthy history of convicting innocent people, as Edwin R. Borchard demonstrates in his book *Convicting the Innocent*. Any one of the sixty-five convictions he discusses could conceivably have resulted in the execution of a man for a crime he did not commit.

Since the available evidence shows that the death penalty does not deter crime, and that it is morally wrong, I sincerely hope that we can all agree with what Robespierre said when he spoke before the French National Assembly:

Listen to the voice of justice and reason. It tells us and tells us that human judgments are never so certain as to permit society to kill a man being judged by other human beings. Why deprive yourselves of any chance to redeem such errors? Why condemn yourselves to helplessness when faced with persecuted innocence?

Therefore, I believe we must all agree that the death penalty serves no purpose in modern society and should be abolished.

INDEX

A

abstract ideas, 114
abstract language, 112
Achenbach, Joel, 158
actuate, speeches to, 144–145
after-dinner speeches, 162
"Against All Odds," 141
agenda, 182
alarm reaction, 20
Albany, New York, 5
alertness, in delivery, 97–98, 110
Alexander, Shana, 85
allegory, 82–83
alliteration, 83
analogy, 83
anecdotal speeches, 161
animation, in delivery, 31, 109–110,
    151–152
antithesis, 81, 83
appearance, 98–99
Aristotle, 147
argument, complete, 142–143
arousal, of audience, 124, 130–132
arrangement, of main ideas, 67–68
artifactual communication, 99
attention-getting devices, 109–113,
    125–126
attitudes
    of audience, 120–123, 136
    toward speaking, 4–5, 28
Auburn, Alabama, 5
audience
    analysis of, 10, 105, 108–109, 123
    as followers, 99–100
    motivation of, 120–123, 144–145
authoritativeness, 148
autocratic leaders, 183, 184
autonomic nervous system, 21, 23,
    30
Ayscough, John, 52

B

Barry, Dave, 150, 173
Baruch, Bernard, 43
Behan, Brendan, 84
beliefs, 121
Bell, Alexander Graham, 143, 154
Bermuda Triangle, 153, 154
Berne, Rosalyn Wiggins, 44
Best Quotations for All Occasions,
    51
Birchmore, Fred, 147
body, of speech, 64–65, 126–132
Bombeck, Erma, 169, 173
brainstorming, 187
Braun, Wilma, 116
Brave New World (Huxley), 155–
    156
breathing, deep, 31
Brigance, William Norwood, 173
Buchwald, Art, 165, 168, 169, 170,
    173
Bunker, Edward, 42

C

campaigns, persuasive, 134–136
card catalog, library, 39
Castro, Fidel, 4
causal arrangement, 67
chronological arrangement, 67,
    113–114
Churchill, Sir Winston, 81, 94
cohesiveness, group, 188
coincidence, 161–162
Collins, Mary, 49–50
Colton, Charles Cobb, 51
communication apprehension, 3
comparison, 48, 49
computerized indexes, 38
conclusion, 65–66, 100-101
    of persuasive speeches, 132–134
    "Thank you" as, 34, 66, 1101
concrete language, 112
conflict, 112, 155–156
contrast, 48–49
controversial topics, 63–64, 136
conversation, enlarged, 89
convince, speeches to, 136–144,
    202–207

Corbin, Kingsley, 78
countering physiological reactions, 30–31
credibility, 146–148
    humor and, 54–55, 148
criteria, for evaluating solutions, 186–187
Croce, Jim, 84
Crown Treasury of Relevant Quotations, 51
"Current Comedy," 178

D

death, fear of, 20
defenestration, 74
definition
    disagreements on, 140
    as support, 52–53
delivery, 92
    don'ts of, 102
    leadership in, 99–101
    lively, 151–152
    visual, 96–99
    vocal, 93–96
democratic leaders, 183, 184
description, as support, 53–54
diction, 94
discoveries, speeches on, 114
discussion, group, 185–188
Disraeli, Benjamin, 44
distractions, 17
Donovan, John B., 64
Doubleday, Abner, 154
dress and appearance, 98–99
Drew, Charles, 153
dullness in speeches, reasons for, 2–4

E

E-Prime, 88–89
Edison, Thomas, 153, 154
Education Index, 38
effort, need for, 2
egocentricity, 2
emotion
    arousal of, 130–132
    versus emotion, 33

emotion-laden words, 17
emotional versus intellectual activity, 31–32
empathy, 16, 86, 96–97, 110
    negative, 97, 175
entertain, speeches to. *See* speeches to entertain
entertainment, 150
epigrams, 84
epithets, 84
ESP, 121
"essay on its hind legs," 14, 76
ethics, of incomplete argument, 142–144
ethos, 146–148
euphemism, 17, 86–87
Evans, Chris, 70
exaggeration, speeches of, 168–169
examples, as support, 44–48
experts, as speakers, 2, 9, 13, 36, 148
expression, facial, 98
extemporaneous delivery, 76, 175
eye contact, 97

F

facial expression, 98
fact, questions of, 140–142
factors of interest, 108–113, 150–156
facts, as support, 42–44
familiarity, 110–111, 154
fear, symptoms of, 20–23
    see also stage fright
Feldman, David, 158
fight-or-flight reaction, 22–23, 30
figures, as support, 43–44
figures of speech, 81–88
Ford, Gerald, 86
Foucalt, Jean, 154
Freberg, Stan, 134
Furnas, J. W., 53

G

Galileo, 153, 154
Gentry, Dave Tyson, 50
gesture, 98
Gilovich, Thomas, 121

goal, of speech, 10–11
government publications, 41
Graham, Harry, 164
Great Quotations, The, 50
Greenwald, Harold, 90
Grizzard, Lewis, 173
group discussion/problem solving, 182–190
Gruner, Charles, 54, 163, 166
Gruner, Marsha, 205
Gruner, Val, 163

H

handouts, 59, 107
hands, placement of, 97–98
haranguers, 4, 145–146
Hardwicke, Sir Cedric, 26
Harris, Sydney J., 111
Hearst, Patty, 85
Heine, Heinrich, 84
Helitzer, Melvin, 176–177
Henry, Lewis C., 51
Hoke, Louise C., 195
Holm, James, M., 131
Howe, Ed, 51
humor
    as ethos enhancing, 148
    for interest, 113
    sense of, 173
    sick, 163–164
    as support, 54–55
Humor Processor, 177–178
humorous speeches to entertain, 162–172
    delivery of, 174–176
    material for, 173–174, 176–178
Huxley, Aldous, 155–156
hyperbole, 84–85
hypothetical illustrations, 45–46

I

ideas, speeches about, 114
impartiality, 147
informality, in group discussion, 183
informative speeches. *See* speeches to inform
intellectual versus emotional activity, 31–32
interest, maintaining, 108–113, 150–156
introduction, 62–64, 100
    for oral reports, 117
    for persuasive speeches, 125–126

using quotations for, 32
unforgettable, 31–32
irony, 88, 165

J

James, Clive, 173
James-Lange theory, 101
jargon, 104
Jastrow, Joseph, 110
Joe Miller's Jestbook, 164
Johnson Test of Reflective Thinking
    Ability, 189
jokes. *See* humor
Jones, Jenkin Lloyd, 4, 45, 97
journals, professional, 41
Joyner, Russell, 150

K

Kennedy, John F., 81
King, Martin Luther, Jr., 52, 81
Kirkman, Jack H., 158, 200

L

laissez-faire leaders, 183, 184
language
    concrete, 112
    E-Prime, 88–89
    plain, 89–90
    technical, 104
    written versus spoken, 74–77
Lardner, Ring, 84
leadership
    in group discussion, 183–185
    in speaking, 99–102
learning by doing, 5
library research, 12–13, 36–42
Lincoln, Abraham, 83, 95
listening, effective, 16–18
logos, 146
Long, Huey, 4
loudness, 93–94, 95
Lynd, Robert, 83

M

MacArthur, Douglas, 84
main points, 11–12, 64–65
    arrangement of, 67–68
    listening for, 16–17
    number of, 106
manuscript speech, 76–77
Martin, Janet, 49
mass media, 150
Merrimac, 155
metaphor, 85–86
metonymy, 86–87
Michelangelo, 159
Milne, A. A., 84
mind-appeal speaker, 4
mnemonics, 32, 109
Monitor, 154–155
monotone, 95
Moore, Mary Tyler, 53
Morris, Desmond, 158
motivation, 120–123
Murphy, Edward F., 51
myths, American, 152–153, 154

N

Naked Ape, The (Morris), 158
Nasser, Gamal Abdel, 4
negative egocentricity, 3
New York Times, 40
New York Times Index, 40–41
nonuseful-information speech, 157–159
nonverbal communication, 96–99
novelty, 111, 154–155

O

objections, responding to, 129–130
Odell, Joseph H., 53
one-point speeches, 115
    anecdotal, 161–162
    humorous, 163–165
onomatopoeia, 88
oral reports, 115–117
oral versus written style, 74–77
oratory, 77–78
Orben, Robert, 178

organization of speeches, 62–72, 109
    see also PSA plan
outlining, 13, 68–72
    examples of, 70–72, 195–196
Overstreet, Bonaro, 28
Oxford English Dictionary, 40
oxymorons, 87

P

parallel structure, 81
parody speeches, 171–172
participation, in group discussion, 183
partitioning pattern, 62–67
pathos, 146
Pavarotti, Luciano, 20
people, speeches about, 115
periodic sentences, 112
Perry, Mark B., 192
Personal Report on Confidence as a
    Speaker (PRCS), 24
personification, 88
persuasive speeches. *See* speeches to
    persuade
Peter's Quotations, 50
Peter, Laurence J., 46, 50, 51
phonemes, 94
physiology of fear response, 20–23
pitch, of voice, 95
planning a speech, 8–15
policy speeches, 137–138
positive egocentricity, 2–3
posture, 97–98
Poundstone, William, 158
preparation, importance of, 29, 60
problem solving, group, 182–190
problem-solution order, 67-68, 114
problem/solution/arousal plan. *See*
    PSA plan
process speeches, 113–114
product speeches, 114
projection step, 131–132
projectors, 59
proof, oratorical, 146–148
    see also supporting materials
proposition of fact, 140–142
proposition of policy, 137–138
proposition of value, 139–140
PSA plan, 68, 79, 124–134
    example of, 79–81

purpose
    of group discussion, 183
    of speech, 10–11, 63

Q

quality, vocal, 94–95
questions, rhetorical, 87–88
quotations, using, 50–51, 133

R

rate, of delivery, 93
Reader's Guide to Periodical Literature, 37–38
reading speeches, 3–4, 76–77
realism, in rehearsal, 15
Reasoner, Harry, 85, 86
recommendations, in oral reports, 117
red-flag words, 17
reference works, 37–41, 176–177
reflective thinking, 189
rehearsing, 14–15, 17–18, 59
reinforcement, 16
religious beliefs, 121
repetition and restatement, 16, 51–52, 64–65
reports, oral, 115–117
reputation, speaker's, 147
research, 12–13, 36–42
reversal-of-values speech, 169
rhetorical questions, 87–88
Roosevelt, Eleanor, 51, 101
Roosevelt, Franklin D., 81, 101
Ross, Betsy, 153, 154
Russell, Bertrand, 158

S

sacred cows, 123
sarcasm, 54
satire, 54
satirical speeches, 165–168
Schmidt, Troy, 171
Seldes, George, 51
self-image, stage fright and, 24–27, 28
seven steps to speech building, 8–15

sex roles, 24
simile, 85–86
size, arrangement by, 67
sleep, speaking and, 30
Smith, Sandra G., 203
Socrates, 51
source credibility, 146
spatial order, 67
speaking rate, 93
speech defects, 94
speeches
    basic plan for, 8–15
    content of, 36
    delivery of, 92–102
    extemporaneous versus read, 76–77, 175
    gathering material for, 36–42
    giving versus *having* to give, 4, 33–34
    language in, 77–78
    leadership in giving, 100
    organizing, 62–72
    rehearsing, 14–15, 17–18, 59
speeches to entertain
    humorous, 162–172
    maintaining interest in, 150–156
    topics for, 178–180
    types of, 156–172
speeches to inform
    examples of, 192–202
    failure of, 104–108
    maintaining interest in, 108–113
    organization of, 67, 106, 113–114
    types of, 113–118
speeches to persuade
    in campaigns, 134–136
    examples of, 202–207
    proof in, 146–148
    PSA plan for, 124–134, 138
    types of, 136–146
spoken versus written language, 74–77
stage fright, 3
    origins of, 21–23
    remedies for, 27–34
    self-image and, 24–27
    symptoms of, 20–21
Stan Freberg Ltd., But Not Very, 134
Standard & Poor's, 39
statistics, 43–44

Stephens, Alexander H., 160
stimulate, speeches to, 145–146
stock issues arrangement, 138
summaries, internal, 76
Sunday, Billy, 85
"Sunday driver" speaker, 11
supporting material, 12–13
    finding, 36–42
    types of, 42–60
suspense, for interest, 112

T

tact, 188–189
tape-recording, for rehearsal, 14
telephone directories, 39–40
testimony, 49–50
thesaurus, 78
Tieman, Norbert, 135
topic, choosing, 9–10, 28–29, 104–
    105
topical order, 68, 114
transitions, 65
travelogue speeches, 159–161
true-life adventure speeches, 156–
    157

U

*Understanding Fear in Ourselves
    and Others* (Overstreet), 28
Understanding Laughter (Gruner),
    54, 163

understatement, 87
unique selling proposition, 52

V

value, questions of, 139–140
variety, vocal, 95
Vaughan, Bill, 52
visual aids, 55–60
visual delivery, 96–99
vitalness, 110, 152–153
vividness, in language, 81–88
vocabulary, 78–81
vocal delivery, 93–96
vocal quality, 94–95
vocal variety, 95
volume, of delivery, 93–94, 95
Volvo, 133–134

W

Winter, William L., 43
wit, 54–55
    see also humor
words
    appropriate, 77–78
    "red flag," 17
    see also language
*World Bibliography of Bibliogra-
    phies,* 38
written versus spoken language, 74–
    77